Functional Job Analysis

A Foundation for Human Resources Management

SERIES IN APPLIED PSYCHOLOGY
Edwin A. Fleishman, George Mason University
Series Editor

Teamwork and the Bottom Line: Groups Make a Difference
Ned Rosen

Patterns of Life History: The Ecology of Human Individuality
Michael D. Mumford, Garnett Stokes, and William A. Owens

Work Motivation
Uwe E. Kleinbeck, Hans-Henning Quast, Henk Thierry, and Hartmut Häcker

Psychology in Organizations: Integrating Science and Practice
Kevin R. Murphy and Frank E. Saal

Human Error: Cause, Prediction, and Reduction
John W. Senders and Neville P. Moray

Contemporary Career Development Issues
Robert F. Morrison and Jerome Adams

Justice in the Workplace: Approaching Fairness in Human Resource Management
Russell Cropanzano

Personnel Selection and Assessment: Individual and Organizational Perspectives
Heinz Schuler, James L. Farr, and Mike Smith

Organizational Behavior: The State of the Science
Jerald Greenberg

Police Psychology into the 21st Century
Martin I. Kurke and Ellen M. Scrivner

Benchmark Tasks for Job Analysis: A Guide for Functional Job Analysis (FJA) Scales
Sidney A. Fine and Maury Getkate

Stress and Human Performance
James E. Driskell and Eduardo Salas

Improving Training Effectiveness in Work Organizations
J. Kevin Ford, Steve W. J. Kozlowski, Kurt Kraiger, Eduardo Salas, and Mark S. Teachout

Team Performance Assessment and Measurement: Theory, Research, and Applications
Michael T. Brannick, Eduardo Salas, and Carolyn Prince

Job Feedback: Giving, Seeking, and Using Feedback for Performance Improvement
Manuel London

The Russian Theory of Activity: Current Applications to Design and Learning
Gregory Bedny and David Meister

Functional Job Analysis: A Foundation for Human Resources Management
Sidney A. Fine and Steven F. Cronshaw

Functional Job Analysis

A Foundation for Human Resources Management

Sidney A. Fine
Sidney A. Fine Associates

Steven F. Cronshaw
University of Guelph, Canada

LAWRENCE ERLBAUM ASSOCIATES, PUBLISHERS
1999   Mahwah, New Jersey   London

Lawrence Erlbaum Associates, Inc., Publishers
10 Industrial Avenue
Mahwah, NJ 07430

Cover design by Kathryn Houghtaling Lacey

Library of Congress Cataloging-in-Publication Data

Fine, Sidney A., 1915–
Functional job analysis : a foundation for human resources
management / Sidney A. Fine, Steven F. Cronshaw.
    p. cm.
Includes bibliographical references and index.
ISBN 0-8058-1274-1 (cloth)
1. Job analysis. I. Cronshaw, Steven F. II. Title.
HF5549.5.J6F563 1999
    658.3'06—dc21   99-20566
                                                              CIP

Books published by Lawrence Erlbaum Associates are printed on
acid-free paper, and their bindings are chosen for strength and du-
rability.

Printed in the United States of America
10 9 8 7 6 5 4 3 2 1

In fond memory of Dr. Maury Getkate

Contents

Series Foreword   ix
Edwin A. Fleishman

Preface   xiii

1   Introduction   1

Part I: Learning and Understanding the FJA Model

2   The Work-Doing System   13

3   The Work Organization   24

4   The Worker   34

5   The Work   45

6   Reducing Friction in the Work-Doing System   55

Part II: Generating the FJA Data

7   Generating Task Data With Workers: The FJA Focus Group   71

8   Consulting With Management to Introduce FJA Into the Work-Doing System   84

9   The Use of FJA in TQM   90

Part III. Using FJA in HRM Applications

10 Recruitment—Attracting a Workforce 101

11 Selection—Testing Applicants 115

12 Selection—Interviewing Applicants 128

13 Training—Improving Worker Skill 139

14 Performance Appraisal—Acknowledging Worker Contributions 156

15 Career Development and Coaching—Encouraging Worker Growth 177

16 Pay—Rewarding Worker Performance and Growth 190

17 Job Design—Building Better Work 207

18 FJA and the Law—Meeting the Legal Test 220

Appendix A: FJA Scales 240

Appendix B: Selecting Functional Job Analysts 255

Appendix C: Training and Accrediting Functional Job Analysts 258

Appendix D: FJA Task Bank Editing Manual 270

References 299

Author Index 303

Subject Index 305

Series Foreword

Edwin A. Fleishman
Series Editor

There is a compelling need for innovative approaches to the solution of many pressing problems involving human relationships in today's society. Such approaches are more likely to be successful when they are based on sound research and applications. This *Series in Applied Psychology* offers publications that emphasize state-of-the-art research and its application to important issues of human behavior in a variety of societal settings. The objective is to bridge both academic and applied interests.

In an earlier book, *Taxonomies of Human Performance: The Description of Human Tasks* (with Marilyn Quaintance), I tried to show the centrality of human tasks to our understanding of human behavior and the need for generalizable constructs in this domain of study. In our book we compared alternative ways of describing human tasks and stressed how the purpose of the task analysis shapes the kinds of constructs and descriptions that are most appropriate. Prominent among the job analysis systems discussed in our book was the Functional Job Analysis (FJA) system developed by Sidney Fine.

For more than 40 years, Sidney Fine has been a major contributor to theory, research, and practice in the fields of job analysis and occupational classification. In 1940, he, along with Ernest Primoff, joined Carroll Shartle, then Director of the Occupational Research Section of the United States Employment Service. Fine remained with the Section for 20 years, where he formed the Functional Occupational Research Project. FJA developed from the theoretical formulations and empirical findings that grew out of this project. Since those years, Fine and others have extended and refined the concepts and methods of FJA, and have applied them to many critical human resource functions. Although Dr. Fine has published a number of his ideas and findings and his work is widely cited, this book is the most comprehensive treatment of the topic. It represents the capstone of a career that has become increasingly humanistic in its orientation. We are fortunate to have his insights on the applications of these concepts to so many aspects of human resource management. In this book, Fine and Cronshaw show how a comprehensive description of work tasks can satisfy the needs of the organization for effective staffing, training, compensation, career planning, and job design.

They bring into focus ideas that Fine first generated shortly after World War II. His elaboration of these ideas in the 1950s and 1960s served as the basis for the fourth edition of the *Dictionary of Occupational Titles* of the U.S. Department of Labor. The major development of these ideas for human resource management took place while Fine was working as a research scientist at the W. E. Upjohn Institute for Employment Research, later at the Advanced Research Resources Organization, and in his own consulting work for a wide variety of companies, government agencies, unions, and institutions.

Fine conceptualized the structure and dynamics of work, study, and leisure activity as a blend of three components of human skills: Functional, Specific Content, and Adaptive. Each component has a different origin and serves a different objective. Functional Skill originates in the physical, mental, and interpersonal capacities of the individual and manifests in how individuals grapple with the Things, Data, and People in their environment. Although few in number, these are "enabling skills" essential in processing an infinite number of specific content areas in the world of work. Specific Content Skills originate primarily in an activity situation (work, study, or leisure) and are the competencies necessary to master the requirements and standards of particular crafts and/or areas of knowledge. Adaptive Skills have their origin in an individual's experience in growing and adjusting, and like Functional Skills, enable an individual to deal effectively with the physical, social, and interpersonal environment in which activities are practiced.

It might help to understand the significance of this seminal concept by recognizing that years before the computer revolution, Fine, in effect, had distinguished the basic operating system (functional and adaptive skills) from the multitude of software programs (specific content skills) run by the operating system. The distinction is of considerable practical importance in such human resource operations as personnel selection, training, and performance appraisal, delineated in particular chapters in this book.

Another central idea is that work is a holistic experience. Workers bring all of themselves to the workplace. Each individual worker has a unique pattern of needs and capabilities with regard to physical, mental, and interpersonal involvement. Depending on the opportunities, facilities, and challenges available in the job–worker situation, each worker juggles these needs and capabilities to achieve balance, satisfaction, and wholeness.

A third basic idea is Fine's conception of the work-doing system, consisting of three major subsystems—Work, Worker, and Work Organization—interacting to achieve productivity and worker growth. According to Fine, this fundamental notion of pairing worker growth and productivity serves as the basis for validating MacGregor's Theory Y approach to human resource management. A great deal of today's commentary and research in management and industrial/organizational psychology points to the importance of establishing trust—a quality relationship— between management and workers. Perhaps this is a reaction to the vastly increased instability and reduced tenure of workers in their jobs. On the other hand, perhaps it is a recognition that the productivity and quality required to compete in today's global marketplace is not likely to be attained and sustained without workers who trust management to recognize and meet their needs. Many studies show that management knows this and is struggling to achieve compatibility between this recognition and the demands of the bottom line. Fine and Cronshaw make a distinctive contribution to this process, especially as it relates to respecting and acknowledging the premises of MacGregor's Theory Y.

It is interesting to note that these ideas were promulgated long before the current trend to achieve trust and humanistic goals in industry. As often stated in annual reports, management views workers as its most valuable asset. Fine and Cronshaw present ways management can make the most of this asset, beginning with an open and wholesome interaction in an FJA focus group. However, as amply demonstrated in this book, a focus group is seen only as the starting point for building a trusting relationship between manager and worker. For FJA to take full effect, an organization must channel the energy provided by the focus group into the widest possible range of HRM applications. In describing these applications, Fine and Cronshaw go well beyond the conventional description of HR techniques. They capture the excitement and vitality—the spirit—of FJA and JR activities as diverse as recruitment, job design, career development, and individual accommodations for disabled workers. Fine and Cronshaw feel deeply that this spirit, which reflects the wholeness of the individual in trusting and healthy organizations, represents a better future for Americans at work. Their hope is that FJA will have a role to play in bringing about that better future.

This book will be of special interest to industrial and organizational psychologists, human resource management practitioners, counselors, and to researchers and teachers in these areas. Along with its companion book (*Benchmark Tasks for Job Analysis: A Guide for Functional Job Analysis Scales*) in this Series, it provides a comprehensive understanding of an important approach to the analysis and understanding of work behavior and performance.

Preface

Sometimes people have the experience of discovering a jewel without having looked for it. They go about their everyday business and suddenly they become aware of it and a gleam of light illuminates their life. Some people discover the love of their life this way. Others become aware of a remarkable talent previously unknown to the public. Still others have an insight that changes the course of their work. It is a wonderful experience that has the power to change lives, to give life its direction and motivation.

This happened to me in the late 1960s. While working at the W. E. Upjohn Institute for Employment Research, I was asked to do a job analysis of social workers for the Rehabilitation Services of the U.S. Department of Health, Education, and Welfare (now the Department of Health and Human Services). The need for social services personnel to staff the welfare agencies was great throughout the country. There were not enough professional social service personnel available. The question was: Would an analysis of the work being done by the social workers indicate shorter routes to train the personnel needed?

With more than 20 years of job analysis experience, I was dissatisfied with the existing procedures. At that time, a variant of a checklist was in use—essentially an impersonal instrument that presumed to know what job information was important. The checklist was constructed by interviewing a sample of incumbents and formulating items from the information obtained. Although dissatisfied with the checklist, I knew its appeal was in its apparent economy. Once constructed, the checklist could be administered to very large samples of incumbents to provide massive amounts of data that could then be evaluated statistically.

My dissatisfaction with the checklist derived from intensive research in occupational classification. During this research, I found that most of the data gathered with checklists had to do with the work that was completed and described very little of what workers did to get it done. It was as though the worker was simply an adjunct to the technology involved. Yet what workers "did" is the key to the various human resource management (HRM) operations. I was determined, therefore, to be innovative in my study of social workers. I wanted to learn not only what got done, which I had a pretty good idea about anyway, but how social workers went about doing it, task by task.

I arranged to interview six social workers of journeyman status, all more or less doing the same work. I built the interview around the need to learn what got done, the knowledges required to get it done, the skills and abilities involved in applying the knowledges, and the performance standards to which the work needed to be done. These, of course, were traditional categories of information. In addition, I asked whatever questions were necessary to determine how, task by task, the incumbents functioned, using as a guideline the functional categories relating to Things, Data, and People (TDP) that had been developed as part of my earlier classification research. This line of inquiry, I hoped, would lead to better items for a checklist if that turned out to be the way to go. This exploratory interview, which extended over several days, was the place and time where I discovered my jewel. The jewel, the brilliant light, was that I did not need to construct a checklist. I could use the focused group interview to serve the same purpose with much more powerful effect. Here is why.

- The group, which came to be called a focus group, had far more to say about the work they did than could ever be learned from a checklist. For example, in describing the standards according to which a particular task needed to be performed, the participants would describe the problems they faced in achieving those standards and the adaptations they needed to make. At the same time they suggested things that management could do to make it easier to achieve those standards.

- Management had a very superficial idea of what people actually did in their assignments to get work done. Even in highly structured situations, workers were innovative. They extended themselves beyond the standing operating procedures (SOP).

- When the analyst functioned as a facilitator, asked open-ended questions, and in no way presumed to know the work of the participants—relinquishing control of the job analysis to the participants—they were very open about their work, willing to share, and not prone to exaggerate.

- The resulting task bank, in effect an inventory of tasks, could be validated with other incumbents having more or less the same assignments.

Inadvertently, I had stumbled on a fact I had been aware of subliminally from my research in classification: Workers were whole persons and when challenged and given support, function as though there were no boundaries on their productivity. I had an insight into a central truth of participatory management, a truth that would color my reflections on every aspect of HRM.

This insight is central to what follows in this book. In it Steven Cronshaw and I join other writers and HRM researchers, for example, Drucker and Argyris, Bennis and MacGregor, in understanding work as a collaborative effort between workers and management, producing its greatest fruits—high productivity, high return on investment, and high satisfaction—when spurning the traditional, adversarial, negative relationship.

Functional Job Analysis (FJA) is intended to provide a map to the world of work. This book contains the knowledge needed to read that map and begin the journey through the world of work. In learning to read and use the FJA map you can put shape and coherence to the indistinct and jumbled landscape that is our everyday understanding of work. As Polanyi and Prosch (1975) said in their book *Meaning*:

> To use a map to find our way, we must be able to do three things. First we must identify our actual position in the landscape with a point on the map, then we must find on the map an itinerary toward our destination, and finally, we must identify this itinerary by various landmarks in the landscape around us. Thus map-reading depends on the tacit knowledge and skill of the person using the map. Successful identification of actual locations with points on a map depends on the good judgement of a skilled map reader. No map can read itself. Neither can the most explicit possible treatise on map-reading read a map. (p. 30)

This book introduces you to a rich language of job description and provides basic navigational terms and a coordinate system in terms of TDP. You provide the itinerary, picking out landmarks (some familiar, some newly apprehended) from the panorama that is the world of work—perhaps using your own job as the starting point—and walking about in the real world where the work gets done. Hopefully, after you have digested the contents of this book, your judgment, your skill, and your tacit knowledge in reading and interpreting the FJA map will improve with experience. You must walk the work terrain yourself and visit the varied people and places along your chosen route. Although any journey requires an investment in time and energy, we believe you will find the effort expended on studying FJA more than worthwhile.

—Sidney A. Fine

ACKNOWLEDGMENTS

We would like to express our gratitude to Edwin A. Fleishman, Series Editor, and to the people at Lawrence Erlbaum Associates (especially Anne Duffy and Lane Akers), for their work in putting this book into print. Their encouragement and patience is greatly appreciated and has been instrumental to the completion of this work. Sidney Fine would like to acknowledge Freda Bernotavicz and Wretha Wiley for their contributions early in the conception of the FJA focus group technique. Marilyn Gordon-Ross (wife of Sidney Fine) devoted endless hours to questioning and editing the material and to achieving the clarity and lucidity it has. If murky sections remain, the reader can attribute them to the original writing that somehow missed her editorial acumen. I am forever indebted to her. Steven Cronshaw would like to fondly thank his family, Kayla, Kristjan, and Kenton for sacrificing family weekends and evenings as he worked on this book. Dr. David Jackson pointed out Mihaly Csikszentmihalyi's work, which helped in expanding and enriching the Applications section. Dr. John Munn steered the research toward Edward Shapiro and A. Wesley Carr's concept of the shared interpretation of experience, which is picked up as an important theme in this book. Steven Cronshaw also thanks the Department of Psychology at the University of Guelph for providing the supportive environment needed for a lengthy project of this type.

—*Sidney A. Fine*
—*Steven F. Cronshaw*

Chapter 1

Introduction

DOES HRM HAVE A FUTURE?

It has become a cliché that we live in a time of tumultuous and rapid change. And although the winds of change can be exhilarating, many of us feel the need for an anchor to keep from capsizing. Departments of HRM are faced with such a possibility and such a need. Stewart (1996) stated in a *Fortune* article:

> Nearly every function of this department (human resources) can be performed more expertly for less by others. Chances are its leaders are unable to describe their contribution to value added except in trendy, unquantifiable, and wannabe terms. . . . Why not blow the sucker up? (p. 105)

He reported on a study by the Corporate Leadership Council of Washington, DC, that concluded that four big dollops of human resource (HR) work have "significant potential to outsource fully: benefits design and administration; information systems and record keeping; employer services such as retirement counseling, outplacement, and relocation; and health and safety (workers compensation, wellness programs, drug testing, and OSHA compliance)." He continued:

> Why stop there? A slew of other traditional HR functions can also be outsourced or devolved from HR to the line. Take recruiting. Everywhere I've worked where I had to hire people, the rule of thumb among managers was to involve HR as little as possible in the process. When HR professionals are themselves looking for work, two thirds of the time they find it by networking or using search firms (a form of outsourcing) according to a survey of the HR job market by Manchester Partners International, a Philadelpia based coalition of outplacement and executive coaching consultants. (pp. 105–106)

Stewart quoted Vikesh Mahendroo, vice president of William M. Mercer, the HR consulting firm, as saying, "Human capital management has become important enough that it is an acceptable career path for an up-and-comer. However, many people doing the work now can't cut it in the HR of the future" (pp. 105–106).

Although Stewart may be caught up in the drive of the past 10 years for downsizing and reengineering, we are inclined to take him seriously. What he has to say is not very encouraging for the existing HR bureaucracy. We know from the downsizing already taking place that Stewart's observations are not academic or mere wishful thinking. The confrontational ideas he expresses are already being implemented. Nucor, the steel giant with 6,000 employees, runs HR with a headquarters staff of three people, a secretary and two other employees reporting to plant general managers, not to corporate managers. HR is, in short, a line function.

THE HR DISCIPLINE NOT THE HR DEPARTMENT IS THE ISSUE

Is this the harbinger of the future—HR administrative detail outsourced, and staffing, training, performance monitoring, and design of job and team functions shifted to line activity?

Possibly. However, the continuance of the HR department is not the issue. The issue is whether the discipline of HR, its principles and practices, has a role to play in achieving profitable productivity, effective organizations, and growing, satisfied workforces.

This issue looms large in these turbulent times, cliché or not. These days few organizations remain unaffected by globalization and international competition for markets and resources. Private enterprises operating within the confines of a single country must deal with offshore competitors that take advantage of relaxed tariff rules. Companies seeking markets in other countries must adapt to local conditions and face competition from firms based in the home countries. Even governments and nonprofit agencies providing services without any direct competitors in the boundaries of a single country have felt the need to restructure in response to the trend in the private sector for flatter organization structures and greater accountability for customer-oriented delivery of goods and services.

The global marketplace has placed a special premium on organizations to have skilled and adaptable workforces in order to survive and compete successfully. Organizations must be especially sharp in their recruitment and training of employees who work willingly with management in achieving goals that are often mutually set. How will this be done? Who will do this?

In response to these developments, the management of private sector companies has adopted various means to deal successfully with the uncertain environments brought about by global competition, including the following:

- a retreat from hierarchical, bureaucratic organization structures toward flatter organization structures to increase response flexibility.
- increased worker participation and autonomy, particularly on the shop floor, thereby drawing more heavily on worker know-how.
- computerization of information flow, eliminating bottlenecks frequently on middle management levels.
- computerization of design and production to meet the need for greater precision and adaptability in production processes.
- increased mergers and acquisitions among companies both within countries and across national lines to consolidate operations, reduce overhead by eliminating large portions of their workforce, and increase profitability.
- intensification of responsive customer-oriented systems requiring a high degree of adaptability to changing market conditions.
- intensification of the demand by industry that governments do more to upgrade their educational and training resources and equip workers with the skills required by an increasingly competitive world economy.

Can it be Stewart is unaware of the significant role played by practitioners of the HR discipline in promoting flatter organization structures, increased worker participation and autonomy, and a more flexible approach to the use of worker skills (e.g., as stated by Petersen and Hillkirk in *A better idea*)? When HR personnel have the opportunity to implement progressive notions that have emerged from their research and practice, they add significant value to the productivity and profitability of their organizations.

HRM has a wealth of resources to draw on in the thinking and writing of MacGregor and Argyris, Drucker and Peters, Bennis and Maslow, among others, to meet the challenges of globalization. These thinkers set forth a central theme: The worker needs to be viewed as a whole person and not as an adjunct to a machine. Only with this approach can the full potential and adaptability of the workers be tapped.

FJA, in development during the last 40 years, picks up on this theme. Its methods systematically and consistently distinguish between what gets done and what workers do to get it done task by task. FJA casts a clear light on tasks that contribute to productivity and those that are superfluous. It does so by documenting the knowledges, skills, and abilities (KSA) required to perform the tasks and how the tasks mesh with one another to achieve the outputs. FJA thus adds value to informed decision making and communication wherever a job's content and context figure prominently into personnel operations.

FJA

The conceptual ideas that are referred to as FJA were developed during the years from 1950 to 1960 at the U.S. Employment Service and served as the guiding hypotheses for research on a new occupational classification system for the *Dictionary of occupational titles 1965.* It is still in effect today, more than 30 years later.

During the 1960s, the concepts were further refined and developed into a job analysis tool. This tool has been used to analyze hundreds of jobs at every level of skill in government, nonprofit organizations, and private industry. The following core propositions of the FJA approach give the reader an initial sense of why the information provided by FJA can serve as a foundation for HRM in the 21st century. These core propositions are:

- *People Are Whole Persons*—People involved in any activity (learning, playing, working) are always functioning as whole persons, instrumentally (actively performing a task) and latently (adapting to the situation in which the task occurs). Content and contextual variables are always involved simultaneously. In order to get a true picture of what is going on, it is imperative to describe performance holistically. (Perhaps the reader is inclined to say, "So what else is new?" Too often the inclination of professionals has been to use tests that fractionate performance and individual qualifications.)

- *Tasks Rather Than Jobs Are Basic Units of Work*—FJA starts with the task rather than the job as the center of attention. A task can and needs to connect *what a worker does* (behavior) and *what gets done* (result). A task is more stable than a job, which is made up of several to many tasks— all variable as to scope, difficulty, and content. Job titles are especially misleading.

- *The Objects of Work Are TDP*—TDP make up the universe of objects of work. *Things* are all tangible materials. *Data* are information and ideas. *People* includes persons and live animals with which workers interact.

- *Functional Skills Denote Work Behaviors in Relation to TDP, Persons Function in Relation to Things Physically, to Data Mentally, and to People Interpersonally*—The names of these functional relationships are unique to each category. The functional relationships are defined as functional skills and occur in behavioral hierarchies from simple to complex.

- *Specific Content Skills Denote KSA Acquired in Particular Job–Worker Situations*—Workers, when applying functional skills to TDP objects in job–worker situations, acquire specific knowledges to efficiently and effectively attain specified performance standards. These specific knowledges (and associated know-how) constitute a worker's specific content skills.

• *Tasks Are Basic Modules of a Work-Doing System*—The linkage of *behaviors* (functions), *objects* (TDP), and *results* produces tasks that are basic modules of the internal technology of a work-doing system. The system has three interacting components: Work Organization, Worker, and Work. A systems approach is applied to evaluate the linkages among tasks, their overall contribution to output, and the value they add to the productivity of a work organization.

• *A Systems Approach Involves Both Content and Context*—A systems approach is not only sensitive to the workings of the internal technology of a work-doing system but also to the variables in the environment that can impact on its functioning. The functional and specific content skills comprehend a worker's instrumental behavior focused on producing the organization's outputs. They do not include the latent skills required to deal with the work organization's context. These latent skills are the *adaptive skills*—those competencies that individuals need to manage themselves in relation to conformity and change in their environment. They are largely invisible willingnesses that activate functional and specific content skills, contribute to *whole-person functioning,* and play a central role in the quality of performance.

• *A Major Adaptive Skill Is How a Person Relates to the Instructional Mix of Prescription and Discretion*—Implicit in every task, in every connection between a behavior and a result, is an instruction involving some combination of prescription and discretion. Prescription and discretion are two inversely related continua. The more complex the behavior, the more discretion it involves in relation to prescription; the simpler the behavior, the more prescription it involves in relation to discretion.

• *Whole-Person Functioning Involves the Three Kinds of Skills Simultaneously*—All three kinds of skills—functional, specific content, and adaptive—come into play simultaneously in the performance of any job–worker situation. This conceptual framework comprehends the totality of human work performance.

These core propositions describe information that is not likely to be forthcoming from job analysis checklists containing predigested snippets of job data. In no way can checklists indicate how workers engage the problems they face in their work and improvise and innovate to go beyond their training and specified procedures to get work done. This kind of information needs to be obtained directly from the workers.

The purpose of this book is to describe and demonstrate how FJA implements these core propositions, gathers the information in structured focus groups, and applies the information in personnel operations.

THE ORGANIZATION OF THE BOOK

In this book, we describe both the theory and application of FJA. To accomplish this, the book is organized into three major parts. In Part I, which spans chapters 2 to 6, the theory and concepts underlying FJA are discussed in detail. Particular emphasis is given to the holistic, unifying nature of FJA. In Part II, consisting of chapters 7 to 9, the FJA process is described in detail including the generation of the task bank by the worker focus group and the subsequent reception of that information by management. Special attention is given to the use of FJA in total quality management (TQM). In Part III, comprised of chapters 10 to 18, 30 years of FJA applications are described. These applications cover a wide range of interventions familiar to HR managers, including personnel selection, training curriculum design, job design, and career development. All of these applications flow naturally from the FJA theory explained in Part I and the methodology described in Part II. To more fully detail the content of this book, a synopses of the chapters follows.

In chapter 2, the systems concept for understanding work is explained. In FJA, the work-doing system is comprised of three subsystems (Work, Worker, and Work Organization) focused on a common purpose: productivity, efficiency/effectiveness, and worker growth. The discussion in chapter 2 shows how the HR manager can assist the organization to achieve the respective purposes of the three subsystems. When these are in balance in an organization, it can be maximally competitive.

In chapter 3, we examine the Work Organization subsystem. A full understanding of the Work Organization is essential to an informed application of FJA. We discuss the start-up of work-doing systems by *progenitors* —sometimes called *entrepreneurs* or *charismatic leaders*—and how they transform a perceived need in society and their personal values to fulfil a purpose. We show how, in order to achieve the purpose, the progenitor must break the purpose down into goals (intermediate term) and objectives (short term). Finally, we discuss the inherent rivalry of the two simultaneous goals of the work organization—to fulfil its mission and to maintain itself—and the impact this rivalry has on HRM.

In chapter 4, we examine the second component of the work system, the Worker. The HR manager must recognize and acknowledge workers' capacities, education, training, experience, interests, and cultural background so they can be most effectively integrated with organizational and technological needs to achieve the organization's competitive position in the global marketplace. We note that the merger of Worker with Work Organization is most successful when there is a recognition of mutual interest. This becomes evident when a special emphasis is given to the development of worker skills and the need to draw on workers' multiskill potential to give the organization a competitive edge.

In chapter 5, we discuss the third component of the work system—Work. An understanding of Work, its structure and dynamics, is essential to the efficient and effective use of both technological and human resources. We show that work content across all organizations can be analyzed in terms of the TDP outputs that Work is designed to produce and the functions workers perform to produce these outputs. The functions performed in relation to Things are unique to Things and correspond to a worker's physical capacities; similarly, the functions performed in relation to Data are unique to Data and correspond to a worker's mental capacities; and finally, the functions performed in relation to People are unique to People and correspond to a worker's interpersonal capacities. In each instance the functions are hierarchical and form ordinal scales that help quantify the work content of any job in relation to TDP.

In chapter 6, we discuss the central role of trust in reducing friction in the work-doing system. If trust is present, the work-doing system has the capacity for great accomplishment, but without it self-destructiveness can overwhelm the system (acrimonious labor stoppages and lockouts, industrial sabotage, low morale, etc.). Many obstacles can be found to trusting relationships, whereas the road to trust is narrow and difficult to navigate. We show that trust grows out of a shared interpretation of experience—a connectedness—between managers and workers. This stance requires sensitivity and skill on the part of everyone in the organization. We describe the value of the FJA process for empowering workers within a community of shared purpose, free communication, and nondependent trust.

Part II, which consists of chapters 7 to 9, describes the process of generating FJA data by the focus group method and connecting management goals to the FJA effort. Chapter 7 discusses how the HR specialist can produce an FJA task bank. Examples of the statements that make up a task bank are given. The task bank is the follow-through on the idea that the Task is the fundamental unit of analysis and thereby provides the basic information for HR interventions. The intent of this chapter is to present the FJA data gathering process—the focus group interview—in sufficient detail to serve as a study guide for anyone wishing to prepare to qualify as an FJA facilitator. Among the topics discussed are the planning and conducting of an FJA focus group, the group dynamics involved, the writing of the all-important task bank, and the skills required of an FJA facilitator (analyst).

Chapter 8 covers the consultation with management to arrange for the FJA focus group (time, place, subject matter experts [SME], facilities) and how the results (FJA task bank, observations concerning worker adaptations) might impact on the work organization. The consultation should seek to obtain an understanding of the purpose, goals, and objectives of the organization so that the outputs and results generated in the focus group can be linked to them. This information can be especially useful in advising management about its allocation of human resources to mission and maintenance goals. Often called strategic HR planning, this process is a crucial area for HRM to demonstrate the value it adds to an organization.

Chapter 9 relates FJA to the TQM movement that has captured management imagination in the latter half of the 20th century. We discuss the basics of TQM and then show how FJA, as a theory and methodology, fits seamlessly with this approach and offers a powerful means to pursue total quality goals within the work-doing system.

Part III, the FJA applications, begins with chapter 10. These applications draw directly on the FJA theory and concepts contained in Part I of the book as well as FJA methodology described in Part II. Each of the nine chapters in Part III describes an intervention that can be undertaken using FJA as a model. Chapter 10 shows how FJA can be applied to recruiting the best person for the job. We draw heavily on the capacity of FJA to provide job seekers with the information needed to self-select into positions that best suit their skills, temperaments, and interests.

Chapter 11 uses the FJA task bank to develop employment tests for assessing the capabilities of job applicants as an adjunct to the employment interview. Emphasis is given to two types of tests: work history/experience questionnaires and work samples. We show how FJA job analysis data meets the requirements of test development and professional psychology for reliable and valid measures. Some consideration is given to the use of FJA for generating criterion-related, construct-related, and content-related validation evidence in support of employment tests.

In chapter 12, we discuss the use of FJA concepts in the development of structured employment interviews for the hiring of new workers. The interview consists of behavior description and situational questions derived from task bank data collected during the job analysis focus group session. These questions are then built into a structured interview pattern capable of being scored. Example of interview questions are given along with suggestions on how to use these questions properly in the hiring process.

In chapter 13, the use of FJA for designing and delivering training is discussed. We show how the task bank data can be used as the basis for the design of training and development programs as they relate both to job content and job context. The task bank is especially useful for this purpose because it connects knowledges and skills required of the worker to the behaviors the worker must perform and the results he or she must achieve. It also indicates the performance standards and quality standards the worker and product must meet. Thus with regard to job content, FJA provides answers to the fundamental questions of trainers: What exactly am I to train for, where does it fit into the job assignment, and what are the standards to which I need to train? With regard to job context, the chapter points to the need for the organization to be sensitive to adaptive skill requirements and that such sensitivity builds a relationship that can drive the functional and specific content skills.

Chapter 14 is devoted to the use of FJA in performance assessment. Performance standards are easily derived from FJA task statements and can be integrated into the design of performance measurement systems, especially those requiring judgmental ratings of worker performance by peer, supervisor, or self.

Chapter 15 considers how FJA task data can be used in career development and coaching for individual employees. The intense competition associated with globalization has radically altered the outlook on careers. No longer does it seem feasible to count on a career with a single company or even on a single career. More and more individuals have to assume personal responsibility for their career and not be dependent on a single organization for career fulfillment. This means that counselors need to help individuals become aware of opportunities for skill growth in whatever position they are in and coach them in how those skills might transfer to positions both within the company and elsewhere. Using FJA task bank data, it is possible for workers to see both how they are functioning with relation to the specific content of the organization of which they are a part and how those functions generalize to other jobs in the labor market.

Chapter 16 shows how FJA can be used to reward worker performance and growth through the design of job evaluation systems. The objective of FJA-based job evaluation is to pay employees both *equitably* (based on "equal" or "similar" levels of skill, complexity, and training) and *fairly* (based on recognition of unique or exceptional factors in the work situation such as merit performance and environmental hazards). A detailed example is given to show how FJA-based job evaluation is applied to evaluating jobs.

Chapter 17 deals with the problem of job redesign from the FJA perspective. We begin with the premise that workers frequently exercise initiative to redesign their jobs often without management's knowledge. FJA can be used to build on this positive tendency by facilitating an ongoing dialogue between workers and managers about the job improvements needed to improve productivity and facilitate worker growth. The task bank, updated regularly and kept accessible to the work station, provides the basic tool for this purpose.

In chapter 18 we examine FJA and the law. In the present era of equal employment opportunity (EEO), legal concerns impact on much that HR technicians and managers do. In this chapter we demonstrate not only how FJA contributes to the legal defensibility of various interventions, but how it can be used proactively to meet the letter and spirit of important legislation and programs now impacting on HRM, including the Americans with Disabilities Act (ADA) and Affirmative Action (AA).

In summary, the 18 chapters present a systematic development and explanation of FJA, beginning with theory and concepts in the first six chapters of Part I, explaining FJA methodology in the three chapters of Part II and, building on the first two parts, with FJA applications in the last nine chapters. The result is the definitive work on FJA. This book is intended to continue and reinforce the use of FJA as one of the premiere HR tools available to business, industry, and government. More than that, it is intended to reinforce the concept of holism in the HRM field as well as the humane and informed management of people in this era of global competitiveness.

PART I

Learning and Understanding the FJA Model

Chapter 2

The Work-Doing System

A work-doing system consists of three interacting components—Work, Worker, and Work Organization. The interaction has its start in the purpose of the progenitor of the Work Organization whose aim is to produce a product or service. Workers are recruited to help, which they are willing to do because they have their own purposes, namely, to make a living and/or to promote their own growth. These several purposes meet in the work, the results of which are focused on realizing the progenitor's purpose. This purpose and those of the workers are most effectively achieved when they are merged and become a mutual endeavor. The systems approach is a methodology for meshing and disciplining these purposes so that both the work organization and workers achieve their purposes—optimum productivity and worker growth.

This chapter explores the concepts of the systems approach and discusses its advantages and limitations as they relate to planning for a work-doing system. This is followed by the FJA conceptualization of the three components—Work, Worker, and Work Organization—of a work-doing system, laying the groundwork for their elaboration in chapters 3, 4, and 5.

AN EXAMPLE OF A WORK-DOING SYSTEM

Early in 1989, as a result of a steady stream of inquiries and requests for a book Fine wrote about FJA 20 years earlier, he concluded there was a genuine interest in FJA. The book, however, was out of print and needed updating. He assumed the inquiries were part of the increased interest in the role job analysis was playing in equal opportunity litigation and also a recognition of the inadequacy of the job analyses done for test development. Practitioners were looking for a better mousetrap. FJA could be that mousetrap and he would provide it. Because he was retired, he could self-publish the book and perhaps earn a small profit. He also liked the idea of being in control of the publication and keeping the price down by avoiding middlemen.

He broached the idea to his wife, a publications specialist, and she supported the notion, especially by offering her technical help. He proceeded to research the feasibility of this idea. He first sketched out what the final product would be like (scope, number of pages, etc.), mentally deciding the amount of time it would take and whether he and his wife could handle it, given their other commitments—she had her job and he did occasional consulting and training workshops. He did not want to get involved with hiring outside labor.

He transformed his speculations into tentative specifications and obtained estimates from several printers about the cost to produce a small book in an attractive format. He also investigated costs for mailing the final product and for advertising in professional journals and by direct mail. With this information in hand, he had a pretty good idea of the capital needed and set up the TDP publishing company with an investment of $3,000.

Thus began his work-doing system. He had a clear short-term purpose, risk capital of $3,000, labor resources consisting of himself and his wife's technical help (editing and preparation of camera-ready copy), a computer and printer, an office in his home, a tentative list of subcontractors for printing and advertising, and his vision of and enthusiasm for what was needed. He was also aware that the work would have to fit in with the family (eight grown children and three grandchildren) and the work life of two rather active and busy people—there would be competing systems. He set a schedule, a publication date in October/November 1989, and went to work. The first thing he did was to use his training in a systems approach to plan his project.

ADVANTAGES OF A SYSTEMS APPROACH

This ordinary example of a small business venture has almost all the characteristics of a work-doing system and illustrates the advantages and limitations of a systems approach. The advantages can be summarized in two words: *focused effort*. The limitations of a systems approach inhere in regarding it as a panacea, which it is not, and in becoming too focused. This becomes apparent as the discussion proceeds. We begin with definitions of system and systems approach.

> **System:** A sequence or series of interrelated activities coordinated according to a master purpose and viewed as a holistic undertaking to process or convert inputs (resources of various kinds) into outputs (products or services).

Systems Approach: A conceptual tool used to organize and marshal resources (technologies, material, workers) to get work done with optimum efficiency and to achieve a master purpose that meets specified standards.

In both of these definitions, the central characteristics are: *a master purpose, the resources necessary to achieve it, an output that meets quality standards, and a coordinated effort that achieves optimum efficiency.* Let us consider each of these characteristics in turn, beginning with the master purpose.

Master Purpose: The master purpose is generated by its progenitor on the basis of perceived needs. Personal values and understandings of how those needs should be dealt with are brought to bear on those needs. The master purpose becomes the focus around which resources and effort are marshaled.

It is important to explore the master purpose thoroughly. After all, it has been abstracted, pulled out of a nexus of needs and associated values. It is thus inevitably intertwined with other purposes, other values. In the example, the recognized need was for availability of a handy desk aid version of the FJA scales for practitioners. However, almost simultaneously, another purpose intruded—production of some income. These two purposes were in conflict in arriving at a price for the publication. Sticking to the initial purpose helped to determine a reasonable price for any interested buyer and one that would also return the investment and yield a small profit. Underlying the pragmatic aspect of the two purposes were opposing values: service and greed. In this instance, service won out. Values such as these tend to play a hidden role behind statements of a master purpose.

Let us now consider the second major characteristic of a work-doing system: resources.

Resources: includes capital, raw materials, technology (machines, equipment, procedures), workers, and housing. Inevitably, along with resources, it is necessary to consider *constraints,* because rarely are resources sufficient or a perfect match for achieving the purpose within a given time frame.

It is helpful to break down the master purpose into the component parts and associated resources necessary for its realization. This results in seeing the work-doing system as an agglomeration of subsystems, all contributing to the realization of the master purpose. A printer was needed, advertising had to be arranged, and shipping and distribution provided for as noted in the example. Each of these components, although a subsystem for the master purpose in the publishing venture, is in fact a competing system, a master purpose to its own progenitor. Thus needs and values impose their own constraints on achieving the master purpose of the TDP publishing venture. (Anyone who has ever tried to do his or her own contracting when remodeling a house—a personal master purpose—and the lineup and coordination of various construction specialists necessary to achieve it, has had a first-hand experience with the relativity of master purposes and their competition with one another.)

The matter of components requires more attention. To a considerable degree the success of the system—the achievement of the overall purpose—depends on how well the components are defined and their performance characteristics fitted into the overall system. Because the master purpose defines the wholeness of a particular undertaking, it is essential to define the component parts as part of that wholeness. In the example, no matter how natural the component parts may seem—for example, printing, advertising, marketing—as far as contributing to the ultimate purpose of producing a publication, they have the potential of assuming a separate existence. This happens when components pursued independently present unexpected options that appear quite logical, even enhancing, but ones that are out of line with the stated master purpose. For example, if the printer of the planned publication suddenly came forth with proposals for a different paper stock, a different font, and a four-color job—meritorious in themselves—that would be totally out of line with where the project set out to go. (We return to the discussion of components in the context of the limitations of the systems approach.)

We now consider the third characteristic of the systems approach, achieving quality performance:

> **Fulfilling the purpose according to quality standards:** The output is a product or service. The quality standards of the output are both those that define the intrinsic nature of the product or service and those necessary to meet the competitive requirements of the market.

Actually, having a master purpose and lining up resources in relation to constraints to accomplish it are underlying conditions for achieving quality standards. In the example—producing a desk aid to facilitate the use of FJA Scales—the issue was: Could a quality product, both technically adequate and effectively communicative, be produced with the limited resources available? Breaking down the venture into components made it possible to see if the standards for each aspect of the project could be achieved and add up to the quality desired for the final result.

It is as important to specify standards as it is to describe resources. The standards become the basis for measuring progress toward goal achievement and the measurements make it possible to track failure by noting when projections have not been met. When this tracking occurs on a component-by-component basis, it enables *feedback* of information into the system and consequent correction of original specifications and standards. In the example, the original calculations of the volume of returns from direct mail advertising called for renting a post office (P.O.) box. The volume did not materialize and so the 6-month P.O. box rental proved unnecessary and was not renewed.

The final characteristic requiring elaboration is optimum efficiency:

Optimum Efficiency: This is the balance between efficiency and effectiveness in work-doing systems resulting in products and/or services at the most reasonable cost using the resources available.

The systems approach is frequently identified with efficiency. Because the systems approach is as much concerned with *effectiveness* as it is with efficiency, this is a mistake. Either efficiency or effectiveness can be pursued to the detriment of the other in an intensely competitive market. Nevertheless, efficiency gets special attention because of a prevailing suspicion most things are not being done as well as they could be, and are, in fact, being mismanaged. If there was a will, it is believed, there would be a way to reduce costs. This belief is held especially for tax-supported public services. Although it may be true that one or another activity could be run more efficiently, that is not the point. The point is whether the larger system, of which the activity is a part, can be run more efficiently and still deliver the product or service intended. And that is a matter of optimization.

In carrying out various activities of Fine's small publishing business, it quickly became apparent that he was sacrificing efficiency for effectiveness. For example, he is not an efficient word processor. Should he have contracted out his word processing? When he considered what was involved in finding a qualified word processor, getting the work to that person, retrieving it, proofing and correcting it, he decided that although his time may have been worth more, he would gain very little by subcontracting. Furthermore, he told himself, it was time he did something to improve his word-processing skills. (In a systems approach it is always necessary to watch out for these contaminating secondary purposes. Typically they are rationalizations. If he really wanted to improve his skills, he could have registered for a training course. That would have been more efficient, but it would have considerably dulled his enthusiasm and probably quashed his publishing venture.)

SUMMARY OF ADVANTAGES
OF A SYSTEMS APPROACH

On the basis of the discussion of these characteristics of a systems approach, we can now summarize its advantages. It channels vision, gives direction, provides a basis for organizing resources and measuring performance, and it helps to allocate work so the purpose can be achieved according to specified standards within a set time frame. In short, it unifies and focuses effort. We now proceed to a discussion of the limitations of the systems approach.

LIMITATIONS OF A SYSTEMS APPROACH

The fundamental limitation of the systems approach is its underlying and inadvertent "arrogance" (Churchman, 1968). Once set up it tends to assume exaggerated significance. It becomes all important to the point of minimizing other purposes, commandeering resources regardless of the needs of those other purposes.

Almost any defined and focused system is abstracted from some larger system in which it is embedded. The larger system is part of an environment that contains many variables over which the abstracted system does not have any control, and that of course, can have a great deal of influence on it. These variables present outside limitations. In addition, we need to reconsider the whole matter of the component breakdown of the system that is necessarily arbitrary. There are usually options in how the components are determined.

Environmental limitations: Environmental limitations of the systems approach include the larger systems of which they may be a part (e.g., the variables of the publishing world that could impact the production aspects of the publishing project); and of the professional world, where existence of competitive products could affect the need and values relating to the project. Another limitation is the overall economic environment (e.g., depression or prosperity), which could have an impact on the need for a system that is designed to improve HRM operations.

Component limitations: Sometimes the components that are decided on seem to be a natural choice, natural specializations. However, sometimes they are so specialized they go their merry way without proper consideration for where and when their particular output fits in. For example, in the book publishing enterprise, illustrative charts were needed. Similar charts were also needed for an upcoming training program. The two different needs became interwoven, seemingly becoming one goal: new charts. This, of course, slowed down the book's progress. To avoid further delay on the book, the two needs had to be untangled and two separate goals established. Instances like this can blindside the whole systems effort. Component or subsystem determination should be a team effort, particularly in large undertakings involving various component specialists and monitored by someone who oversees the whole project. One of the most vivid and dramatic examples of this team effort was the 5-year program of Boeing to build its latest transport plane, the 777. This team effort was documented in a TV miniseries for the Public Broadcasting System.

Hidden purposes: A master purpose is rarely the only purpose of a project involving the systems approach, regardless of how strongly it is asserted. The other purposes may be the personal ambitions of the participants involved in carrying out the project. Usually, however, there are other purposes, frequently associated with achieving power or satisfying greed. Problems arise when these other purposes are hidden. If the hidden purposes are not to become distractions or diversions of effort and resources, they must not be hidden. They must be considered among the possibilities at the very start of the project and provisions must be made to deal with them either by accommodation (e.g., special rewards), by transfer of disruptive individuals, or by spin-off of additional projects. In short, the systems approach must have a human face and deal with the realities of human functioning and aspirations.

SUMMARY OF LIMITATIONS OF A SYSTEMS APPROACH

The focusing aspect of the systems approach is the main source of its strength, but it can also prove to be its Achilles heel. It must not be blind to the fact it is abstracted from larger systems within its environment and also from social and economic contexts that involve significant variables that can impact on it. In addition, it must have a human face, sensitive to the reality that its master purpose can easily hide subsidiary purposes in conflict with the master purpose and divert resources from its achievement. This calls for continuous monitoring of the system and its component subsystems.

THE WORK-DOING SYSTEM IN FJA

FJA's use of the systems approach seeks to build on its strengths and moderate its limitations as much as possible. It brings into focus the significant elements relevant to HRM in a work-doing system. These elements are represented in the three components of the system, Work, Workers, and Work Organization.

These three components are not as clearly delineated in a small organization such as the example used here. Nevertheless they are there, largely embodied in one person wearing three hats. One hat is that of progenitor/ entrepreneur of the Work Organization. This hat involves providing the capital; establishing the purpose, goals, and objectives; arranging for the workplace and necessary equipment; and setting standards. The second hat, that of the Worker, includes the determination of being qualified to do the work that needs to be done to produce results. The third hat involves doing the Work, including the administration work (arranging for the flow of funds, lining up and negotiating with subcontractors, purchasing equipment and services); the HRM work of qualifying oneself and assistants; and the production work of researching, writing, and editing the proposed publication. Obviously, in a one- or two-person organization this means taking on quite a load of responsibility let alone the presumption of adequacy. (In a later chapter, we discuss this presumption of adequacy under adaptive skill.)

In the FJA theoretical framework, these three components are conceptualized as shown in Fig. 2.1. Work, Worker, and Work Organization—organized around the central purpose of achieving productivity with efficiency and effectiveness and satisfaction of worker growth—are present in all work-doing organizations, regardless of size. Each of these components of the system has involved a different discipline along with a different vocabulary and, in fact, has usually been taught separately. In our view, they belong together because they have significant complementary roles to play in a systems approach. (To the engineer working on the design of the technology of the work organization, this stance could be regarded as an arrogant diversion.)

The complementary roles of the three components is even more apparent when we examine their interplay in the work situation as shown in Fig. 2.2. Figure 2.2 shows what we believe are the natural and ongoing interactions between the components and support the systems conception proposed. Each of the components has interests in common with the other.

Workers and Work Organizations can benefit from conscious, informed interaction over matters of compensation, grievances, promotions, and compliance with legal requirements. Such interaction can promote mutual understanding and outlook on the crucial issues of productivity and profitability. Similarly, the interaction between Work Organization and Work can improve technological design and productivity. Job analyses have revealed that management is not as well informed as it may think it is about how work is actually getting done and how innovative workers can be. Workers typically experience flaws and inadequacies in standard operating procedure (SOP). Drawing on this experience, workers can often contribute to the state of the art in a particular area of work when there is a positive channel of communication between them and management. Finally, the interaction between Worker and Work can contribute to an im-

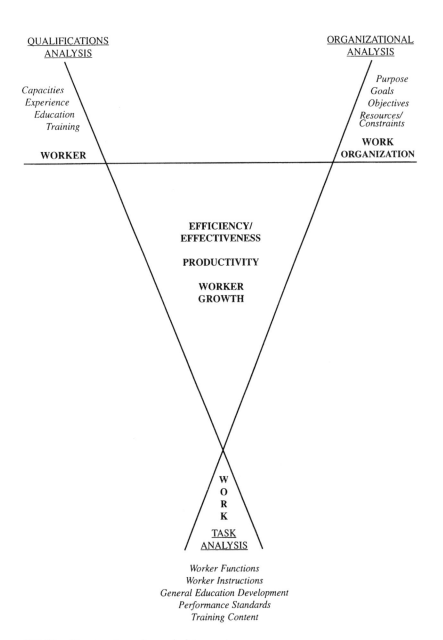

QUALIFICATIONS
ANALYSIS

Capacities
Experience
Education
Training

WORKER

ORGANIZATIONAL
ANALYSIS

Purpose
Goals
Objectives
Resources/
Constraints

WORK
ORGANIZATION

EFFICIENCY/
EFFECTIVENESS

PRODUCTIVITY

WORKER
GROWTH

W
O
R
K

TASK
ANALYSIS

Worker Functions
Worker Instructions
General Education Development
Performance Standards
Training Content

FIG. 2.1.   The structure of a work-doing system.

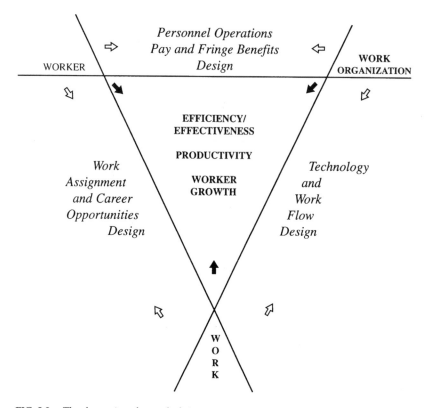

FIG. 2.2.   The dynamics of a work-doing system.

proved design of work assignments and a more-informed approach to career opportunities. The more workers are aware of the similarities and differences among job tasks, the more flexible they can be in adapting to changing technology and working conditions.

Although sometimes in conflict, as is perhaps inevitable in any bringing together of separate subsystems, the three components have much to gain from sharing information and concerns. The fact remains that these interactions are real and ongoing although often obscured by traditional adversarial relationships and competition for recognition and power.

SUMMARY OF THE FJA SYSTEMS CONCEPT FOR THE WORK-DOING SYSTEM

The FJA concept of the systems approach to work-doing organizations consists of three complementary subsystems—Work, Worker, and Work Organization. Although each has its own vocabulary and discipline, they belong together because in the real world of work-doing organizations they are always present, always interacting. Considering them together as parts of a single system engaged in realizing the same master purpose illuminates each, particularly in the specific ways they interact with each other.

In the next three chapters, we consider each of these components in detail.

Chapter 3

The Work Organization

The Work Organization is the brainchild of the marriage between need and enterprise, a vision embodied in a purpose. Sometimes it is also embodied in an individual with leadership potential, an individual who can initiate and inspire the start-up of an organization.

In a universe of infinite possibilities, the Work Organization is like a flickering point of light emerging from darkness, slowly gathering intensity, momentum, and direction. Everything—principles, policies, procedures, technology, public image—follows from its purpose as though determined by destiny. From the very beginning it needs to interface with the Work that needs to be done and the Workers who are called on to do it.

First the vision needs to be transformed into a mission with a destination—"a man on the moon in this generation," or, in this case, an FJA publication in the hands of practitioners by the end of the year. From that point on, the Work Organization takes form as a gargantuan undertaking, a one-person job, or anything imaginable in between. This form serves many goals, among them: housing the enterprise, attracting Workers, providing the Work, and ultimately serving as the touchstone for the achievement of the purpose.

In this chapter we want to understand the work-doing organization: how it organizes itself to become a system, its options, and the consequences of those options, and the environment it needs to create in order to provide feedback for both the Workers and the Work to flourish.

EXPLORATION OF RESOURCES AND CONSTRAINTS

Purposes of Work Organizations are not generally stated in specific terms as far as outcomes and time limits are concerned. Typically, the purpose is stated more in intentional terms. This is especially true of very large undertakings, for example, the purpose of a constitution and by-laws or the purpose of a new large enterprise. Even a small enterprise, such as the publishing effort described in the previous chapter, began with a simple statement of purpose: to publish a revised edition of the FJA scales in a handy format for everyday use by practitioners. In order to plot a course for the achievement of a Work Organization's ends, it is necessary to elaborate on the purpose. This elaboration typically begins with consideration of the resources available (e.g., money, technology, and worker skills) to achieve the quality product envisioned.

However, this is only the beginning in the exploration of resources, an exploration that leads to uncovering constraints, the other side of the coin. Inevitably, market considerations come up and force the issue of whether or not the presumed need is real. Assuming it is real, the corollary issues are: how to inform potential customers of the existence of the product (what forms of advertising will be used) and how will the product reach the customer (retail outlet, postal service, or courier)? Somewhere among these ruminations, a determination needs to be made as to where the product will be produced. Will the entrepreneurs do it themselves or contract it out? If undertaken as a self-contained enterprise, what will that entail as far as staffing, housing, and legal requirements are concerned? And when will the results of all this effort see the light of day?

These questions and considerations are enough to indicate that serious organization and coordination need to take place in order for the purpose to be realized. At this point setting goals and objectives can be seen as not only plausible but desirable. Practically every question that comes up has optional answers and varying costs and consequences. The time has come to generate hard data with respect to the options in order to make hard choices.

SETTING GOALS AND OBJECTIVES

Some authorities in the field of management by objectives (MBO; Patten, 1981) see no point to distinguishing between goals and objectives, considering them synonymous. Our inclination is to distinguish between them, allowing goals to include longer time periods and subsume the multiplicity of shorter term objectives necessary to achieve them. In the FJA systems approach, goals are described as 1- to 3-year efforts, each subsuming two or more objectives that achieve results in periods of time less than 1 year and as little as 1 week. Another option is to formulate goals to parallel the annual budgeting period of an organization and have the objectives realized in shorter time periods, permitting budgetary limits and restraints to serve as one of the measurements.

There is another subtle difference that tends to manifest although not in any formulaic manner. *Goals* tend to be more *ends*-oriented, closer to the end result implicit in the purpose. *Objectives* on the other hand, tend to be more *means*-oriented, more involved with the *hows* and technology necessary to achieve the purpose. This may be due to the fact that goals are stated in broader, more general terms, more akin to that of the purpose.

This difference between goals and objectives becomes important in managing the work organization, particularly if there are aspects of technology that tend to be incompatible with the avowed aims of the purpose and goals. The use of television in education is one example. Television can and has been used to teach the alphabet, and learning the alphabet has been incorporated as an objective in early childhood education. However, a goal of early childhood education is to teach children to be independent self-starters, able to use books and other materials in creative ways. Achieving the objective to some extent is in conflict with achieving the goal because passively watching television discourages active involvement with educational materials for many children. Preventing purposes and goals from being twisted out of shape by objectives is a continuous management problem. This problem is a major reason for using the systems approach in the application of FJA theory.

The primary reasons for defining goals and objectives are to:

- allocate resources in a manner most suitable to achieve the purpose.
- ensure that all the things that need to be done will be done or, if gaps in the resources available exist, make certain something is done to fill the gaps.
- have all the things that need to be done completed at a specified strategic date.

In the publication example described earlier, the goal was to have the publication ready in time for a professional meeting.

MISSION AND MAINTENANCE GOALS

Entrepreneurs soon discover that goals are of two types: (a) those pertaining to the mission (embedded in the vision represented by the purpose) and (b) those pertaining to the maintenance of the organization itself—the entity needed to put the "show on the road." These latter maintenance goals can stimulate a lot of irritation in unsophisticated entrepreneurs when they become aware of the resources that must be siphoned off to support them, resources they feel could be better used for mission goals. These maintenance goals are doomed to be under a shadow, tolerated as a necessary evil and frequently raided to support mission goals. When downsizing occurs, the resources they encumber are the most vulnerable. Yet these maintenance goals are the goals that include HRM—the recruitment, selection, training, and equipping of an organization's workforce.

One way of dealing with the inherent rivalry between mission and maintenance goals is to involve the workers in setting the goals and allocating the resources. There is a fundamental mutual dependency—one cannot exist without the other. This dependency can be actualized in teamwork starting at the very top of the organization, especially in setting time tables as to when services and material need to be supplied for the mission to be accomplished.

Typically, maintenance goals are grouped under administration. Administrative personnel, especially in very large organizations, are often situated some distance from the work of the mission. In organizations dealing with the extraction of raw materials, such as forest products and petroleum, extensive and continuous field work to learn the needs and problems of the workers carrying out the organization's mission can overcome the separation. If this is not done, bureaucracies that ostensibly exist to serve as communication channels often end up being mainly concerned with their own survival. When this happens, the mutual understanding that needs to exist between mission and maintenance breaks down and the organization becomes rigid and unresponsive, eventually failing. This is a familiar phenomenon in government organizations where the maintenance bureaucracy tends to become an end in itself. It has lost touch with the reason for its existence, namely, to serve as a vehicle that facilitates the execution of specific missions.

THE MEASUREMENT OF ACHIEVEMENT: FEEDBACK

Breaking down the purpose of a work-doing system into goals and objectives not only enables management to get the work done, it also facilitates the tracking of success and/or failure. Each goal and each objective is set up with measurable indicators of whether it is being accomplished. If this is all that is being measured, the systems approach would not be necessary. MBO would be quite sufficient.

But *this is not all.* For an organization to remain healthy and viable in today's world, it is equally necessary to determine how both Workers and Work fare in the pursuit of results. Workers and Work inevitably enter the equation for productivity. For example, are the results achieved with excessive overtime? Do they involve unusual stresses for the workers? Are the workers involved in setting the objectives and determining the measurement indicators? Is the work performed in the usual manner, or do the workers manifest innovative approaches to get the work done? Do these innovative approaches suggest new ways of planning the work in the future? Is teamwork involved? Is the technology appropriate for the quality and production goals anticipated?

These are more than humanistic, do-good questions. In fact, the failure to pay attention to these and similar questions and their answers had a lot to do with U.S. industry falling behind its European and Japanese competitors during the 1970s and 1980s. The reengineering of much of U.S. industry is prompted by these and similar questions. Hammer and Champy (1993) wrote:

> Companies need people who can figure out what the job takes and do it, people who can create the slot that fits them. Moreover, the slot will keep changing. In an environment of flexibility and change, it is clearly impossible to hire people who already know everything they're ever going to need to know, so continuing education over the lifetime of a job becomes the norm in a reengineered company. (p. 72)

Results from the tracking of success and failure in achieving the goals and objectives become signals for examining: (a) the planning and design process, (b) the quality and training of the workers, and (c) the design and assignment of tasks they perform. The feedback indicators that are tracked include times of completion, quality of output, number of rejects, and throughput (Goldratt & Cox, 1984). These indicators must be chosen in such a way that the whole system comes under scrutiny.

SENSITIVITY TO THE SYSTEM: THE FOUR "P"S

The systems aspects of the Work Organization are manifested in its principles, policies, procedures, and problems.

Principles

Organizations are set up to realize a purpose that presumably was formulated to meet a need, real or imagined. In either case, in the minds and hearts of the progenitors, values are associated with the purpose. These may be overt, but frequently they are not. An example of an overtly expressed value, is that of Schultz who "has masterminded an empire based on the notion that even though the term 'coffee break' is part of the vernacular, there's traditionally been no place to enjoy one" ("By Way of Canarsie," 1994). Schultz felt there should be such a place—"an extension of people's front porch." Starbucks, his company, owned 1,006 retail stores as of October 1, 1996 (amazingly, Starbucks had only 17 stores in 1987). Net sales for 1996 rocketed to $696 million, the ninth year in a row revenue increased by 50% or more (Balaban, Kieta, Lunger, Lutz, & Wachiralapphaithoon, n.d.).

Schultz continued: "My parents . . . gave me great self-esteem and a sense of what was possible. I always saw myself wanting to do something deemed successful and good at the same time. I never wanted to lose my thread to my past (a childhood in Brooklyn, New York). I understand where I came from." The article continued, "These are not just words. One reason for the smiles behind his counters is that Starbucks is the first company in the country to give its part-time employees (65% of its workforce) full health care benefits and stock options." We believe that this is a good example of a purpose imbued with values translated into positive principles for operating a business.

An example of hidden values and an issue in the news from time to time, has been the glass ceiling that affects upward mobility for minorities and women in the ranks of management. Similar hidden values show up when a choice has to be made between profits and quality, or profits and ties to a community. Frequently, profits are given first priority in these situations. This value gets translated into principles, stated or not, and sends a subtle message to workers, giving them permission to cut corners in the quality of their work or their integration in the community. The point is the principles are there and typically show up in the policies of an organization.

Policies

These are the written statements declaring the rules by which the organization will operate. They derive from the principles. In the case of Starbucks, the matters of health insurance and profit sharing are stated policies. In the case of the hidden values, they do not necessarily appear in a policy statement. They may simply be part of the informal culture of the organization and only discovered when a problem manifests. This seemed to be the case for Denny's, one of the largest restaurant chains in the country. The management of a number of its restaurants, particularly in California, were allegedly discriminating against selected minority groups, demanding payment for food in advance and, in some instances, refusing to serve them. Finally, following protest demonstrations at some of the sites, top management entered the situation, insisting it was not a policy of the chain and claiming there was a misunderstanding. Negotiations followed, a policy of nondiscrimination was declared with the insistence that it was a principle of management. Disciplinary measures were meted out to the offending restaurants and minority ownership of some restaurants was provided. Not until problem-arousing massive consumer feedback emerged did a clearly stated principle and policy become part of a negotiated agreement.

Organizations have volumes of policy statements. These policies are, in effect, its operating system and pertain to every aspect of its operations, for example, housing (buying vs. leasing), purchasing, accounting, depreciation of equipment, consulting services, outsourcing of various production operations, printing, hiring, reimbursing travel, taking leave (sick and vacation), covering health insurance, compensation, parking, taking work breaks, and working overtime. These policies are usually on loose-leaf paper and stored in binders with dates on every sheet. Policies are constantly being revised.

Policy setting has to do with mission and maintenance goals. As an activity, it is established close to the very head of the organization where a person or group receives the feedback of the functioning of all the organization's subsystems. On the basis of this feedback, a determination is made if things are happening as they should, and if not, why not, and what revisions in policies and procedures are necessary to make them happen. These persons must be highly aware and sensitive to the purpose/values/ principles—sometimes referred to as the *culture* of the organization—if they are to respond promptly and consistently to the feedback.

In one-person undertakings this requires that the entrepreneur wear a special hat labeled "honesty and objectivity" that, when worn, enables him or her to evaluate what is going on and ruthlessly take required action. This is clearly a very difficult thing to do and may partially explain why many small undertakings do not survive.

Procedures

These are the day-to-day operating instructions that follow from the policies, often, if not always, specifying the technology that is to be used in achieving the desired results. Procedures define what an organization does to establish uniformity, consistency, and predictability in its operations.

For example, when an organization declares the generally accepted accounting principles (GAAP) to be its basic bookkeeping policy, certain fundamental procedures, understood by any auditor can be expected to be in use. These procedures are referred to as standard operating procedure (SOP) for that organization. Some of these procedures are more or less universal, such as the GAAP. Most procedures are, of course, specific to the organization—performance appraisal comes to mind—although they may have many similarities to what goes on in other organizations. Organizations almost always have a policy of appraising the performance of their workers but typically have their own unique procedures for carrying this out.

Procedures need to be understood as *instructions,* management's way of distinguishing between prescription and discretion, telling workers what they want done and how they want it done. They are provided to workers during orientation and specific job training. It is one of management's ways of providing leadership, particularly if the procedures and their method of presentation and follow-up are consistent with policies and principles and do not have hidden jokers. Hidden jokers refers to the oft-repeated adjuration to use judgment (discretion) at critical places in the work—meaning only correct judgment—without specifying what that correct judgment might be.

To effect the standardization and control for which procedures are de-signed, they are presented in a specific format conveying information for a particular action to be taken. The action may be only one step in a series of steps or the entire series. Once formalized in this manner, procedures need to be followed explicitly to achieve their objectives. Hence the rigid-ity of bureaucracy. Sometimes exceptions may be made to a formalized procedure, but in that case the manner of making an exception is also for-malized.

In a systems context, a procedure is like a hard-wired circuit. It ensures predictability. Therefore, procedures should be carefully tested before being introduced, usually on cases representing the extremes of the situ-ations for which the procedure is designed. However, it would be naive to imagine that procedures, no matter how well-thought-out, can anticipate all possible contingencies. Computer programs are a case in point. In the main they are extremely well-thought-out and tested for "bugs." Never-theless they need to be constantly monitored.

Problems

Problems are inevitable; they are endemic to any system. They are best re-garded as contingency feedback and constructive failure and reflect the simple fact that an organization cannot anticipate everything likely to go wrong. As Murphy's Law states, "Whatever can go wrong, will." Here are some of the problems that are sure to occur.

Principles/Policies: As indicated, the progenitors of purpose are certain to have values that not only inhere in their production or service purpose but are characteristic of their persona and may have little to do with the business they have organized. Progenitors are concerned with their vi-sion, with seeing ahead, with enlisting support—it is what makes them leaders. They cannot do everything and in any case they cannot do everything well. One of the things they need help with is formulating policies that are indeed consistent with their principles. Yet anomalies and inconsistencies develop and require constant surveillance of feedback. This may be truer of relations with customers and suppliers outside the organization because such customer relations involve some greater subtleties with far less control. There may not be second chances in a highly competitive environment. Mistakes can be very costly.

Principles/Procedures: This is an insidious problem area that occasionally occurs in customer service. The feedback indicates that procedures were used that were contrary to the principles of the organization and could be very costly, for example, the Denny's situation described earlier. Often this problem occurs when there has been a failure in communicating how procedures are based on fundamental principles. Workers lose their temper with irate customers and take a swing at them. This violates the "customer is always right" image of the organization around which it has built up its customer service reputation. There is a definite policy on how to deal with intemperate customers and a procedure to follow—but incidents happen. Such breaches could occur for a variety of reasons—extreme stress, inexperience of salespeople, poor selection of salespeople, and so forth. Problems of this sort call for a hard look at existing procedures in several areas—selection, training, security, communication—and might even call for some adjustment in the principles and their inherent values.

Policies/Procedures: This involves the interface of goals and objectives. As already noted, it is very possible to inadvertently formulate objectives incompatible with policy. For example, the procedures for negotiating bank loans can inadvertently violate policies of confidentiality and privacy by trying to get too much information from customers, or, create trouble by getting too little information in the pursuit of certain classes of business. Nowadays policies direct more responsibility to line personnel and equip them with portable computers to facilitate the exercise of this responsibility. This, of course, creates a whole slough of problems with regard to how much access should be allowed to the enormous data banks that on the one hand can be the basis for innovation and on the other, for mischief. This can be a real challenge to procedure writers.

Policies/procedures problems occur whenever new technology is introduced. One large area of such problems concerns easing workers into the new technology with a minimum of resistance. Depending on a variety of factors such as time pressure, competition, the nature of the labor force and its morale, and experience in accepting change, procedures can be prepared that either reflect a policy of patience or a policy of take it or leave it. Obviously, principles at the root of the policies are also challenged. In any case it is likely the procedures may have to be altered from time to time to meet reality.

SUMMARY OF FJA AND THE WORK ORGANIZATION

A Work Organization is a manifestation of purpose and values, elaborated through its goals and objectives. The goals and objectives are the means for determining the resources and constraints that make the organization fly. They are the first step in measurement because the goals and objectives must comprehend—add up to—the purpose. In addition, a criterion for the usefulness of each goal and objective is whether it provides measurement indicators to track achievement. These measurement indicators are the means for monitoring feedback. Although most of these aforementioned considerations need to be part of the initial planning process for the Work Organization, not all of them can be anticipated. This makes it imperative for planning to be a continuous activity, especially responsive to measurement indicators and feedback monitors. The Work Organization also needs an operating system within which the goals and objectives can be implemented and the impact on Workers and Work can be tracked. Principles that reflect values, policies that implement principles, and procedures that implement policies are the day-to-day nitty gritty of the operating system. A conscious recognition and means must exist to resolve the problems that inevitably occur between the various components of the operating system.

Chapter 4

The Worker

WORKERS ARE WHOLE PERSONS

In FJA, workers are viewed holistically. Although individuals as workers have their particular purpose in a work-doing system—worker growth as well as productivity—they are more than just workers. They are consumers, family persons, spiritual beings. In each of these incarnations, they have different purposes and are part of different systems. But these systems are not totally separate. They are entwined in one another, spill over into each other, and impact a worker's performance.

As a result, a conscious and deliberate effort is made in FJA to avoid using language that would partialize workers, see them only in their instrumental form to be analyzed in terms of factors, traits, or the like. Instead, workers are viewed as whole persons, steadily accumulating knowledges, skills, abilities, and experience (KSA/E) in order to enable them to function and adapt to the job–worker situation.

This holistic concept is depicted in Fig. 4.1. At the center is the worker's performance in the job–worker situation. This performance is based on the experience of the worker at any given time and represented by everything in the surround. The upper portion of the surround includes the KSA that contribute to the instrumental and technical skill of the worker and focus on job content. These skills encompass the worker's *functional* and *specific content* skills—the know-hows and how-tos. The lower portion of the surround includes the worker's adaptations to self, to instructions, to responsibility, and to the overall environment and encompasses the worker's *adaptive* skill focusing on job context. All of these components—KSA/E— are always intertwined in performance.

KSA/E is comprised of terms common to all players in the HRM system—workers, managers, technicians, and professionals. These terms are as useful to describe work requirements as they are to describe worker

FIG. 4.1. A holistic concept of performance skill requirements.

qualifications. There is, therefore, no need to resort to abstract, recondite terminology (factors, traits) and statistical manipulations to establish a relationship between them for HR purposes. Furthermore, KSA/E contain the validity of recognition, the "knowing more than we can tell" (Polanyi, 1983) validity of tacit knowledge in explaining what appears self-evidently to be true—what workers know and what they can do. Terms relating to psychological dimensions such as intelligence, interests, and temperament, or to physical capacities such as height, weight, agility, and visual acuity can be useful analytically to understand aspects of performance. However, to use them as primary explanations of performance is likely to be a distortion of what actually is the situation.

People engage with and function in the real world—the world of the family, work, community—as whole persons. They observe, they learn, and they enlarge their physical, cognitive, and interpersonal behavior.

They bring to the real world and its situations all their proclivities at once, coping and/or innovating as the situation might demand.

They also adapt. Over time, people build up a repertoire of adaptive behavior—adaptive skills—that reflect their behavioral style. For example, they move toward, away from, or against people; they develop preferences for instructions that are predominantly prescriptive or discretionary; they gravitate to authoritarian or participative social situations.

In their functioning they do not often dwell, if at all, on which part of themselves is really dominant or primary, although their situation can call for a primary effort in one or another part of themselves. When they shovel snow to clear a path in front of their houses, they are no doubt aware of major physical exertion, but their minds might be dwelling on other things they have to do, perhaps on something creative in which they are engaged. When they sit at a desk writing a report, they may be mulling over a troublesome family situation, wondering how to deal with it.

People develop a sense of self, who they are and what they want as they grow. Some have a stronger, clearer sense of self than others, but to one degree or another, this sense of self is the basis for workers' decision making during the course of their work history. This sense of self is what influences them to pursue one line of work rather than another, to take a job because of need, to change jobs because of dissatisfaction with where they are, and to undertake further skill training in order to obtain a better job.

KSA/E

Because the terms knowledge, skills, abilities, and experience come up repeatedly in this and the next chapter, we define them here.

Knowledge: Knowledge relates to information and ideas, the *know-hows* and *how-tos* involved in getting work done. *In FJA, both are named by using the gerund form of the verbs, e.g., welding (know-how) and precision working (how-to).* Sometimes the same gerund names both, e.g., writing (know-how) and writing (how-to). *Know-hows* have to do with knowing the parts (nomenclature), structure (how things fit together), dynamics (how things work together), and theory (the principles of how they work). *How-tos* have to do with operations, for example, machines and procedures and the skills for executing them. It is possible to have know-how about things in great detail, for example, automobiles and how they are driven, without being able to operate them. On the other hand, it is possible to have the how-to for operating things without knowing much about them, for example, an electronic copying machine. Knowledges show up as objects of actions (skilled behavior) and are either *things,* for example, tools, machines, and materials; *data,* for example, information about how things work, what to do in given situations and for different problems; or *people,* for example, consumers, customers, clients, patients, or students.

Skill: Skill involves acquired competencies, ranging from relatively simple to relatively complex behaviors, as they relate to TDP objects in the job–worker situation. These behaviors occur in concrete situations involving *specific* know-hows; they do not exist in the abstract. However, these behaviors can be perceived as occurring generally in a variety of concrete situations in which case they are referred to as *functional* how-tos. These generalized behaviors apply to the use of tools, machines, equipment, and materials in various combinations appropriate for achieving a purpose; to behaviors involving data to produce more data and/or to solve problems; and to behaviors involving interaction with and responding to people to satisfy their needs for information, treatment, advice, guidance, or agreements. *In FJA these behaviors are the know-hows and how-tos expressed as gerunds (verbal nouns) and referred to as functional or specific content skills.*

Skills also involve *adaptations* to self and environment. These adaptations involve *willingness* to deal positively with the conditions that come with the job–worker situation; *willingness to* precedes the particular condition to which an adaptation needs to be made as in "willingness to abide with confidential security conditions." Adaptive skills are also expressed as performance requirements.

The person who wishes to acquire more skill needs more information and training to deal with the multiple problems that can develop, more experience to achieve specified levels of accuracy, and more opportunities to exercise the judgment/discretion necessary for achieving a desired result. The more skill a person acquires, the larger number of variables and the greater the variety of situations he or she has to deal with. (A further discussion of skills follows the definition of ability and experience.)

Ability: Ability is concerned with level of performance or how well a person executes a task. Levels of performance are determined by and/or evaluated in relation to the specifications of the output required and what is known about or determined to be the standards appropriate to the techniques/methods/ processes for achieving the outputs. The terms for expressing these levels of performance are (a) adjectives or adverbs that describe a result in relation to a standard or compare a result in relation to other relevant results or (b) numbers that represent a scale from low to high in some characteristic that reflects quality or quantity. For example, a word processor is described as being "very accurate" (adjective) and/or "able to produce 75 words a minute" (number). Ability is the result of total person functioning, the interaction of skill, knowledge, effort, responsibility, and work conditions.

38

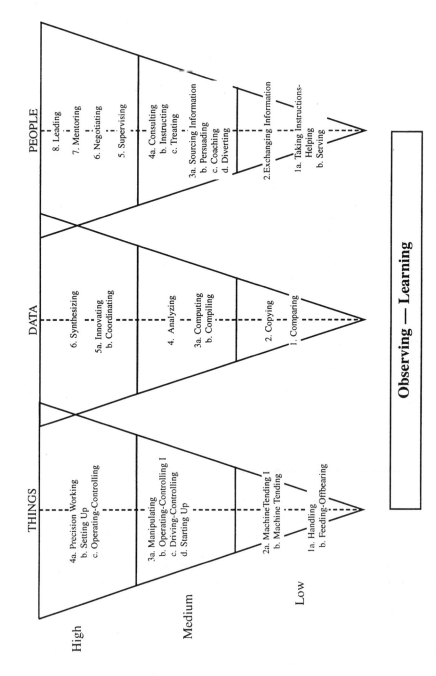

FIG. 4.2. Worker function chart.

Experience: Experience involves a personal database consisting of the performance of assignments according to procedures in which trained and learning that actual assignments/events typically present unique aspects requiring the stretching and bending of rules/procedures through use of judgment to get work done. This personal database supplies the worker with clues for dealing with unique events that are not yet ready for generalization into new rules.

THE JOB-WORKER SITUATION CALLS FOR THREE KINDS OF SKILLS

Three types of skill have been referred to in the previous discussion of skill: *functional skills* and *specific content* skills that are focused on the specific content of the job–worker situation and *adaptive* skills that are focused on the context. Are they really different? Yes they are in (a) how they are acquired and (b) their role in transferability—moving from one assignment to another. Let us look at them more closely.

Functional Skills: competencies that enable people to appropriately process TDP on simple to complex levels, drawing on their physical, mental, and interpersonal resources. They are expressed as gerunds and shown in Fig. 4.2, the worker function chart. *Functional skills are acquired from the moment we are born and start exercising our human potential with relation to the TDP in our immediate environment.* For example, manipulating tools and utensils, following multistep instructions, and listening with attention become functional skills. Later, they are sharpened in school, in play, and in the pursuit of hobbies. They are the generalized behaviors that enable people to pick up the specifics of new situations.

Specific Content Skills: competencies that enable people to perform a specific job to predetermined standards using specific equipment, technology, and procedures and relying on functional skills. Specific content skills are also expressed as gerunds reflecting specific content areas, for example, welding, riveting, carpentering, bricklaying, filing, recording, nursing, healing. Sometimes they are expressed in terms of broad processes such as assembling, researching, and marketing. There are as many specific content skills as there are unique specialties. *Specific content skills are learned on the job in connection with specific tasks or focused self-study to accomplish specific objectives.*
    The *context* of the job is a challenge to individuals' behavioral style, to the management of their personal selves as they affect effort and responsibility and relate to the Environment (Fig. 4.1). This style is embodied in adaptive skill.

Adaptive Skills: Competencies that enable people to manage themselves in relation to the demands of conformity and/or change in particular situations.

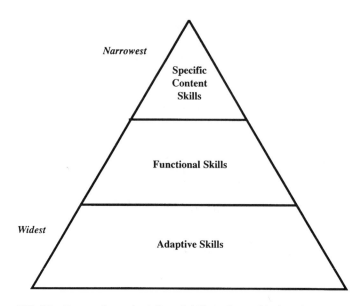

FIG. 4.3.   Range of transferability of skills in the world of work.

*Adaptive skills are acquired in the course of life experience, particularly early child-
hood, on practically a subconscious level.* They are integrated as the values, attitudes, and manner of responding to the physical, social, and environmental
circumstances in which persons find themselves. They are expressed as the
willingness to adapt to, for example, time, space, people (moving toward,
away from, or against), prescription and discretion in instructions, impulse
control, authority, initiative, and resourcefulness. They are crucial in activating functional and specific content skills.

Figure 4.3 illustrates the FJA concept of transferability when the job–
worker situation changes markedly, particularly when it involves a change
in environment. Essentially, Fig. 4.3 shows that the most transferable skills
are people's adaptive skills, the skills that characterize their behavioral
style. Unless the person is transferred to the same work in a different workplace, the least transferable skills are those relating to the specific content
of the job. If the needs of individuals, as reflected in their adaptive skills,
are met in the new workplace, then their functional skills can be effective
in tackling the specific content of the new job–worker situation.

CHOICE PROCESS FOR EFFECTIVE PERFORMANCE

The three kinds of skills—functional, specific content, and adaptive—are
present and interacting simultaneously in a total skilled performance.

They are simply different aspects of the performance, drawing on different personal resources. They tend to play significantly different roles in making choices about taking a position and whether or not to stay in it.

Readers can best evaluate the FJA theory by applying it to themselves, particularly by reviewing how they came to select the job in which they are presently employed. According to FJA theory, the first step is to select a field where the specific content is relevant to one's background, interest, or experience. The second step is to evaluate specific job offerings for appropriateness to one's adaptive skills, one's willingness to put forth the effort called for, take on the responsibility demanded, and adjust to the physical, social, and environmental circumstances of the job. If, following this evaluation, the person reacts negatively—the combination of adaptations required make a negative impression—then the person leaves the field and starts over. If, on the other hand, the person comes away with favorable feelings, he or she accepts the offer. This is when functional skills come into play, engaging the specific content of the new job–worker situation. If the favorable impression is validated on the job, the person grows into the position or even grows "up" in it. On the other hand, if it fails to fulfill its promise, the worker tends to detach from the position, functional performance becomes sporadic or deteriorates, and the worker looks further afield.

THE WORKER AS COGNITIVE PROCESSOR: THE GED SCALES

Central to the worker's observing and learning is the acquisition of cognitive (data-oriented) skills, skills built around reasoning, math, and language. Cognitive skills are central because human beings have advanced into complex societies, including their work-doing components, largely on their ability to think in symbolic terms and process the resulting data. Although physical and interpersonal skills have a significant cognitive element, cognitive skills do not necessarily involve either physical or interpersonal elements.

One of the requirements in the Functional Occupational Classification Project (FOCP) begun in 1950, was to establish the general educational requirements (General Educational Development, GED) for specific jobs. At that time, it was felt that indicating these requirements by grade completion would not serve the purpose satisfactorily. The variation in ability among individuals represented by grade completion was too great. Opinions were sought from personnel people in government and industry and from educators as to the level of reasoning, math, and language required in each of a sample of 250 job descriptions. On the basis of these opinions, three scales were constructed—one each for reasoning, math, and language—consisting of examples taken from the sample job descriptions. These scales were then used to rate 4,000 job descriptions in the *Dictionary of occupational titles.*

As is evident in Appendix A, these are ordinal scales of the same nature as the TDP functional scales. These scales can be used to rate both the job requirements and the worker's experience. A review of the scales reveals that the definitions of the various levels relate to job content and are behavioral anchors. Even more significant may be the fact that although these behaviors may be learned in school they need not be. They can be self-taught and/or learned through life experience. For qualification purposes, the worker needs simply to describe experiences involving the behavioral anchors and performance results.

Cognitive skills play a crucial role in an increasingly technological society. They are the specific vehicle for defining and communicating the variables that enter into technology and for mastering its language and instructions. They are particularly adaptable to school training through the medium of books, computers, and other audiovisual materials. Sometimes, they overshadow the role of physical and interpersonal skills that require more interactive training and experience in simulated or real situations in order to be effectively learned. Interpersonal skills tend to be as heavily influenced by cultural traditions as admonitions concerning "correctness" or "appropriateness." Although the cognitive factor is important in the learning of physical and interpersonal skills, there seems to come a point where it needs to be set aside to allow the total person—nonverbal, instinctual, physical, and cultural—to take charge.

THE WORKER AND JOB DESIGN

One of the most misunderstood and neglected areas of HRM has been the role of the worker in job design. What is this role and how has the neglect come about?

Essentially, the role of the worker in job design is to allow him or her—once oriented and trained—to take over *ownership* of the job–worker situation. This means that workers need to be *trusted* to do their best to achieve the objectives of the organization, not only to follow prescriptive procedures but to use discretion and take risks without fear of reprisal. Those risks include adaptation and innovativeness that usually occur after becoming familiar with a situation. Human beings enhance their self-concept when they take responsibility for themselves in everyday life, at work or elsewhere. If they feel responsible, competent, important, likeable, they will be more likely to express those parts of themselves (Patten, 1981).

Why has this been so poorly understood? We believe it is due to the HRM field being intent on matching persons and jobs. Practitioners of HRM see staffing as a task for specialists who believe they have superior knowledge about people and jobs and what is good for workers and the work situation. With all due respect to what has been learned through testing research in the field of industrial psychology, this view falls far short of what common sense and understanding of the whole person teaches us about human capacity and motivation. Only recently, in part as a result of the recognized inadequacies of matching practices, and in part due to intense competition from Japan and western Europe, have we begun to take seriously the findings of our systems and holistic thinkers—MacGregor, Maslow, Bennis, Argyris, Katz, and Kahn. As in Deming's case, these thinkers seem to have made a greater impression abroad than in their own country.

What are the consequences for HRM of adopting the holistic point of view? To begin with the holistic point of view places far less emphasis on the matching hypothesis for bringing jobs and workers together. This hypothesis seeks to establish parallel dimensions for job requirements and worker qualifications and then match them for a theoretical good or even "perfect" fit. Although industrial psychology has defined some 50 or so dimensions of this type (Fleishman & Quaintance, 1984; Fleishman & Reilly, 1992), it has never been successful in knowing which ones and how much of each to combine for a good fit. The reasons for this failure are inherent in the weakness of the assumptions of this concept. The assumptions are that the individual is a constant, the measurements are valid, different combinations of the measurements will have no significant effect on the final score, and the requirements for the job are constant. Jobs are notoriously fluid and inconstant—some more, some less. Workers likewise, depending on the environment of the job–worker situation and the extent to which the worker is met halfway by management, are quite flexible in their willingness to put themselves out to achieve the standards of employers. Consequently, the whole process of matching on the basis of these assumptions and measurements is highly questionable.

A positive result of taking the holistic point of view in the practice of HRM has been the increased use of *team building*, a configuration that draws on the whole person for getting work done. Team building reveals potentialities of the individual that tend not to emerge on individual analysis. A precondition for effective team building is a management that has the integrity to proceed with commitment and independence and "stay the course." Patten (1981) described it as follows:

> The psychological contract is constructed out of reciprocal expectations, shared norms and standards, and mutual commitments. Managers enforce it through their power and authority in the organization. Employees enforce

it by influencing the organization or withdrawing all or part of their participation and involvement. In some ways the psychological contract resembles
a collectively bargained contract, but it is not written and exists in the minds
of the participants because it has been negotiated in a teambuilding atmosphere. In building a team with such a contract, goals are understood and
supported; the sense of belonging to a group is strong. Trust and openness
are present in communication and in relationships. The resources of the
team members are tapped and used well. Leadership is shared. Procedures
are developed to cope with problems and solve them. Sensitivity, flexibility,
and creativity are present in group process work; and the group can steadily
improve its processes. (p. 88)

SUMMARY OF FJA AND THE WORKER

FJA views workers as whole persons—as consumers, family persons, and
spiritual beings—in additon to being workers. Each incarnation involves
unique purposes that are entwined with one another. To reflect this wholeness, FJA uses holistic language to describe qualifications and job requirements. This holistic language involves the KSA/E related to objects in the
real world—TDP—that in turn involve the worker's physical, mental,
and interpersonal potential. This is the basis for recognizing and defining
the functional skills that are used to relate to specific job content and get
work done.

In addition, workers develop adaptive skills to manage themselves as
whole persons in relation to the context (effort, responsibility, and work
conditions demands) of their job–worker situations. The adaptive skills
play a crucial role in a worker's choice process in selecting a job and deciding whether to stay or leave. Despite the importance of cognitive skills in
our technological world, the worker's whole person functioning—nonverbal, instinctual, physical, and cultural—needs to be considered as crucial in the learning and adaptive process.

The FJA approach to understanding the worker in the work-doing system is well-illustrated in job design. Using the FJA approach, a qualification process based on KSA/E is used, and once workers are selected, oriented, and trained they are allowed ownership in their job assignment
and trusted to do the job that needs to be done to achieve the goals of the
organization. A technique that best illustrates the results of this approach
is team building and teamwork, a job–worker situation that draws on the
potential of the whole person.

Chapter 5

The Work

As used in this book, *work* is a human effort expended to achieve a result. In work, two things happen simultaneously: a worker is doing something and something is getting done. What the worker is doing is functioning in some way in relation to an object. The object can be a Thing (something that is tangible), Data (information, ideas), or People (or live animals). Simultaneous with the functioning of the worker, a procedure/technology is being followed to produce a product or perform a service. *The recognition of this duality is the bedrock of FJA.*

This fundamental duality manifests in the different vocabularies used to express what the worker does and what gets done. These two vocabularies are based on a difference in perception. *What the worker does* is the vocabulary of behavior, of worker action. *What gets done* is the vocabulary of results and reflects technology. In no way can we understand human behavior at work by using the vocabulary of results. This was the major problem with the 1940 edition of *The Dictionary of occupational titles*; its job definitions were almost entirely in the language of results. Thus when counseling workers according to their behavioral experience and presumed potential for placement, there were no satisfactory behavioral indicators to validate a match. An intensive study of the kinds of inferences being made from the descriptive language of results led to the recognition of the duality.

This chapter describes the results of the analysis of the language used to describe jobs and how sorting out the different vocabularies helps our understanding of work. The language of worker behavior, what workers do, was the basis for the formulation of worker function scales that reflect the inherently ordinal nature of skill. These scales proved to be a powerful analytical tool for describing work. The concept of worker functions also led to the definition of tasks as the basic modules of work.

THE LANGUAGE OF WORKER BEHAVIOR

In the job descriptions of *The Dictionary of occupational titles, 2nd Ed. (1940)*, some of the verbs used in those descriptions were of a different nature from the rest of the dictionary's language. In hundreds of descriptions of drilling, machining, shaping, planing, routing, boring, and the like—all of which described end results of technology—there were the terms *feeding, tending, operating, setting up*, which were not associated with something getting done. Instead, these terms expressed what the worker was doing. When the usage of these verbs was carefully examined, it was found they consistently referred to characteristic behaviors of the worker in relation to the machine. What was more, they spelled out a continuum of behavior from simple to complex. These behaviors could be defined as levels of an ordinal scale where any particular level included all the simpler levels below it but was excluded from the higher levels. In short, the definition for tending included feeding but was excluded from operating-controlling (see Fig. 4.2).

This linguistic finding had immediate usefulness in assembling groups of jobs that have different content but involve similar worker behaviors. Could similar concurrence of worker behaviors identified in jobs with different content thus lead to more effective recommendations for transferability and training?

A vast research endeavor was undertaken to answer this question. The next logical place to look for verbs associated with what the worker was doing was among jobs that also involved things but did not obviously require machines: assembling, carpentering, plumbing, bricklaying, inserting, folding, packaging, and the like. A hierarchy of skill was found among these jobs, from crude laboring to skilled crafts, and descriptions of physical behavior (reaching, handling, fingering, feeling, climbing, balancing, etc.) but no ready-made terminology that had the same qualities as those found for machines. Therefore, terminology had to be adapted and invented to serve in the same way as the verbs used to describe worker relationships to machines. These terms were *handling, manipulating,* and *precision working*, which were defined to describe hand–tool work from relatively crude to precise use, use of a few tools to use of those of an entire trade, and the use of increasingly complex measurement. In effect, two parallel scales were developed for which the objects were Things. At the same time *driving-controlling* (of vehicles) was separately distinguished from *operating-controlling* and defined.

With regard to Data, there was also a dearth of terms that applied strictly to worker behavior. However there were verbs in job descriptions of clerical and professional work that could be used to formulate a hierarchy of functions. As it happened, they closely corresponded to the evolution of how a person learns. These terms were *comparing, copying, computing and compiling, analyzing, coordinating,* and *synthesizing.* The definitions were basically out of *Webster's* with modifications to have them conform to an ordinal scale.

The biggest problem occurred in the search for terminology that would naturally fall into a scale of functions that applied to People. Part of the problem was that the terminology describing worker relationships to people was not quite as mature. The jobs were newer and appeared to cluster at very low or very high skill levels. Also, in the 1950s when the developmental research was taking place, there were not as many job descriptions involving a relationship to people as there were to Things and Data. Nevertheless, a scale was developed that worked, although it involved inventing and defining some terminology that would make up an ordinal scale. The terms were: *taking instructions-helping and serving, exchanging information, coaching and diverting and persuading, consulting and treating and instructing, supervising, negotiating,* and *mentoring.*

Experience in working with the People scale has indicated that despite the definitions of the functions to represent ordinality, the ordinality of this scale does not work quite as well as the Things and Data scales. The reason may be that there are two qualitatively different types of interpersonal relationships represented in the scale: subjective and objective. The serving-helping, coaching, treating, and mentoring functions express an empathetic, caring dimension while the remainder of the functions in this hierarchy seem to involve conveying and transacting information in relatively impersonal, increasingly formal relationships.

In the 45 years since the worker function scales were created and used in countless projects all over the world, the need for only seven additional functions has manifested. Three of them were for the Things scale and to some extent reflected the technological revolution that took place during these years. They were a breakdown of tending into *machine tending I* (material products processing) and *machine tending II* (data processing and duplication); a breakdown of operating-controlling into *operating-controlling I* (stationary machines and equipment) and *operating-controlling II* (machines and equipment operated in multidimensional space); and *starting up* (complex mobile equipment).

Only *innovating* was added to the Data scale. This was added to help clarify the confusion that occurred in the clamor for creative workers when companies wanted workers to be innovators and not necessarily creators.

Three were added to the People scale: *sourcing information,* which also could in part be attributed to the enormously increased role of information and its dissemination in the last 50 years; *treating,* which in part could be attributed to the proliferation of health care work; and *leading* (apart from managing), which is a function that rarely appears in job descriptions but shows up as a requirement in the search for chief executive officers (CEOs) and similar positions.

All of the functions appear in Fig. 4.2 and are defined in Appendix A.

THE SIGNIFICANCE OF WORKER FUNCTIONS

The original 26 worker functions seemed like a very small vocabulary to describe all the relationships of workers to the work that they did. However, they were not 26 independent and isolated descriptives. They were organized into three ordinal scales and the definitions within each scale did define, from simple to complex, the skills involved in relating to TDP. Furthermore, because it was planned to use them to classify the kinds of behaviors involved in work, it became apparent that a complete picture could not be attained by selecting only a dominant function to describe a worker's relationship to the work that got done. It was necessary to select one function from each hierarchy—TDP—that best suited a job description and then give each function an estimated proportionate weight (the three proportions had to add up to 100%) reflecting the function's proportionate involvement in the job. Weighting of functions according to their involvement with TDP was called a job's *orientation*.

Designating function level and orientation of a job turned out to be a powerful classification device, conveying a tremendous amount of behavioral-relevant information for counseling and placement. In fact this became the basis for the occupational classification systems of the United States and Canada.

Readers can quickly test the significance of these two measures—functional level and orientation—by applying it to themselves. Suppose you are a trainer for an organization, and have a well-equipped training facility that includes an overhead projector, a 35-millimeter projector, a VCR and television, flipcharts on easels, and the like. And suppose you work from curricula that have already-prepared teaching manuals and corresponding trainee workbooks but that require modification on your part from class to class. Further suppose that your major involvement is with trainees, but you also have some involvement with colleagues and managers. This can be expressed in functional language as follows:

	Level	*Orientation*
Things	Machine Tending II	15%
Data	Innovating	30%
People	Instructing	55%

The full interpretation of these measures includes the aforementioned descriptive material but in addition indicates that you are primarily responsible for the standards associated with instructing, secondarily with those associated with innovating, for example, modifying the lesson plans, and finally with tending the audiovisual equipment. The orientation percentages reflect different degrees of responsibility. Note that innovating also includes the analyzing that you do when you evaluate the work of your trainees.

THE TASK AS FUNDAMENTAL UNIT OF WORK

Despite accurately characterizing the highest functions of the trainer, the previous analysis was unsatisfactory in an important respect. It did not provide for an understanding of the range of the trainer's activities. In analyzing the work of the trainer, or any other job for that matter, it was evident the job was composed of a number and variety of elements that also needed to be recognized for such reasons as: what occupied the worker's time, and how were the worker's skills and knowledges involved? Complete analysis of a job revealed the elements that made up a job also involved functions and orientations and could be quite varied. On further analysis of many jobs, these elements were found to reappear in job after job. They had a greater stability than the so-called job, particularly the job title. The term available to designate these elements, a term that had been casually used for that purpose was *task*. *Task* could now be given a more focused definition.

The definition of a task was formulated as follows: *A task is an action or action sequence grouped through time, designed to contribute a specified end result to the accomplishment of an objective, and for which functional levels and orientation can be reliably assigned.* The task action or action sequence may be primarily physical as in operating a drill press, primarily mental as in analyzing data, or primarily interpersonal as in consulting with a client.

THE TASK AS A SYSTEM MODULE

The functional and orientation concepts emerged when sorting out the language of description as found in the job definitions in the *Dictionary of occupational titles*. During this developmental process, the challenge was: Could these concepts now be put to practical use to make original observations? The answer was *yes* and the starting point was the English sentence formulated to answer basic informational questions. Figure 5.1 shows the model that was used and the questions it was designed to answer.

Who?	Performs what action?	To whom or what?	Upon what instructions? (Source of information)	Using what tools, equipment, work aids?	To produce/achieve what? (expected output)
Subject	Action verbs	Object of verb	Phrase	Phrase	In order to...

FIG. 5.1.   Model sentence work sheet.

Item 1. *Who?*—is the subject of the task statement, answering the question, "Who is doing the work?" It is, of course, always the Worker and does not call for a particular answer for the generic job analysis. However, when the job analysis is being done in a particular workplace, especially when the issue is job design, the name of the incumbent is very relevant because the task might be reassigned and redesigned to improve productivity.

Item 2. *Performs what action?*—calls for a verb or verb sequence that is as specific and descriptive as possible about what the worker is doing. Chapter 7 goes into greater detail concerning the choice of such verbs including the ones that can easily entrap the analyst. The significant thing about these verbs is that they must be classifiable into worker functions and assigned a level in the scales. Because there is a dearth of such clear-cut descriptive verbs to describe worker actions, it is often necessary to use two or more verbs in a tandem arrangement.

Item 3. *To whom or what?*—calls for an object of the verb(s). The object is a TDP noun in a job–worker situation. Things verbs naturally call for things objects; Data verbs call for data objects; People verbs call for people objects. A commonsense naturalness needs to be followed here, otherwise unacceptable incongruities result. This tends to take care of itself except where the verb used for worker action is overly general and meaningless, for example, "processes information" instead of "sorts/compiles classified information."

Item 4. *Using what?*—calls for the designation of tools, machines, equipment, measuring devices, or work aids used to implement the work action. If several things are listed, then this may be a signal that more than one task is being performed. This can be significant because the different tasks may call for different skills and knowledges.

Item 5. *Upon what instructions (sources of information)?* —calls for the non-tangible enablers (as opposed to those in Item 4) of the action. This is a rather involved item. The instructions can be verbal or written, specific (prescriptive) or general (discretionary), proximal to the assignment or distal, delivered in person or in writing as a work order. A common way of designating instructions is by saying, "following SOP," which indicates that it is part of the knowledge and training of the worker. Another common way is to say "depending on experience (DOE)," which indicates that following procedures is not enough and that the skill derived from learning about the ways to deal with special cases (exceptions to procedures) is involved. It is important to indicate the balance between prescription and discretion required in performing the task. To some degree this becomes evident by specifying the sources of information that can vary from very specific (tables, scales, etc.) to very general, and in certain instances, sources that need to be researched and discovered.

Item 6. *To produce/achieve what?* —calls for an indication of the result. Again, the result needs to be consistent with the action and the object, for example, Things actions need to have things results. An additional concern is that the result must be of the same or similar magnitude as the action verb. The result of a task is usually only a partial contribution to a larger objective of the organization or technology. It usually takes the results of several tasks, linked in a systematic way, to achieve an objective. For example,

> writes a letter of transmittal of the annual report for the president's signature . . . in order to acknowledge the addressee's special interest in the college.

is preferable to

> writes letters for the college president's signature . . . in order to enhance the college's communication process.

The first task is likely to be only one of many contributing to a college's communication process.

A SIMPLIFIED VERSION OF THE TASK MODEL

Although effective for analytical purposes, the just-described model needed to be altered for common everyday use. The model adopted is shown in Fig. 5.2.

To facilitate obtaining the information for a task from SMEs and recording it for their perusal, the following additional devices are used in the order indicated:

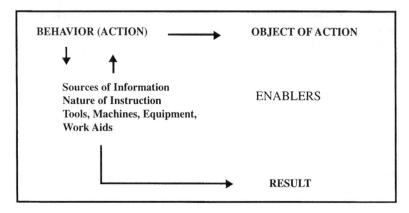

FIG. 5.2.   Simplified version of a task model.

- enablers relating to tools, machines, equipment and work aids are preceded by the term *using*.
- enablers relating to knowledge are preceded by the phrase *drawing upon*.
- enablers relating to skills are preceded by the phrase *relying on*.
- if the instructions are SOP, use *following SOP*. If the instructions are more complicated, they are woven into the narrative of the task action at an earlier point, preceding knowledge and skill.
- results are preceded by the phrase *in order to* abbreviated as IOT.

These devices serve both the FJA facilitator in obtaining all the necessary information and the SME by providing them with enough structure to critically evaluate the information elicited.

THE INSTRUCTIONS TO DO THE WORK

The worker function scales were first tried out in a scientific research laboratory in 1959. It was found that although they worked well in gathering and summarizing the information about job content, information relating to the initiative with which the incumbents went about their work was lacking. Numerous interviews were conducted with incumbents and supervisors and the determination made that the initiative inhered in the variety of instructions workers were given. The instructions given to the workers at different levels (laborer, technician, assistant engineer, engineer, scientist, manager) were then studied. These varied in the amount of responsibility given to the worker as reflected in the knowledge they were assumed to have and the amount of judgment they were expected to exercise. An 8-level ordinal scale, similar to the worker function scales, was formulated to express these different levels of responsibility. The initial FJA job descriptions were reanalyzed and given additional ratings for worker instructions. This seemed to fill the bill. The FJA ratings plus the worker instruction ratings now fully described the jobs and the differences between them.

At about this time Jacques' (1956) book on *Measurement of responsibility*, which described responsibility in terms of the prescription/discretion mix in job instructions, made an impression on the developmental work. Because this classic book covered the same ground as the worker instructions (WI) scale, the scale was modified to bring it into accord with Jacques' work. The present scale is the result (see Appendix A).

At the lowest level the scale reflects a situation that calls for a willingness to accept overwhelmingly prescriptive instructions, instructions given to the individual by management along with the technology for achieving the specifications required. Very little discretion or judgment is required. Also, as Jacques points out, the time span for seeing the result of an action is very short, practically immediate. The corollary behaviors are obedience and submission to the requirements of a system that has been developed to the point where such prescription is possible. The worker needs to be able to suppress judgment lest it disturb the repetitive results for which the system has been designed. Work designed for such instructions requires very little training, a great deal of self-discipline, and partialization (limited use) of the person. In fact, work such as this is ready to be automated or robotized, and frequently is. It is really not fit for humans who wish to be acknowledged as whole persons.

At the highest level of the scale, job instructions are for work that requires major decision making such as for a CEO. Very little is prescribed except for the limitations placed on authority and the returns expected on investment. In fact, the prescriptive aspects emerge incidentally during the decision-making process. Picture the manager of a household who must establish a budget and make decisions every day about meals to be served and ingredients to be obtained; recipes to be followed; how the house will be decorated including the types of furniture and accessories that will be procured and arranged for maximum effect; how the children will be cared for, dressed, disciplined, and educated; how the household help should be motivated, disciplined, and rewarded if there is such help; and finally how a positive, pleasing, wholesome ambience in the household should be realized as though it was the most natural thing in the world. This situation calls for a fully functioning, dedicated, holistic human being willing to use judgment constantly, take risks, and stretch skills to the limit. The time span for achieving competence at this level is of course quite long and indefinite.

Level 4 represents the behavioral context of a craft person, one fully trained in a trade or craft, as in an apprenticeship, and in full control of the technology available. Although required to follow certain SOP and conform to local codes, craft persons use their judgment in dealing with the problems that come up in a particular assignment, drawing on experience.

Level 5 is similar to Level 4 except that in this instance the instructional background includes theoretical training and professional literature that can be drawn on to understand and solve problems in a particular technological field.

In the WI scale, we have an extremely powerful tool for describing behavioral requirements. The behavior described is essentially an adaptive skill, one of many skills concerned with how people manage themselves in relation to conformity and change. It correlates with the ratings on the data, reasoning, and language scales thus showing its underlying cognitive component.

Experience has shown that the preference individuals have for a level of instruction is often a good indication of their need for structure in the work situation. Persons who need and/or prefer a great deal of structure and a minimal amount of responsibility are quite content with instructions on Levels 1, 2, or 3. Persons who seek independence in their work situation and are willing to assume responsibility, aspire to Levels 4, 5, and 6. Level 7 represents the situation preferred by potential explorers, inventors, and researchers who structure their own world of work. Level 8 calls for a strong leadership drive wherein the person not only structures his or her work situation but inspires others to realize a master purpose or vision.

SUMMARY OF FJA AND THE WORK

Work needs to be understood as a duality of workers doing something to get something done. Each part of the duality has its own vocabulary. This is fundamental to distinguish behavior from results. The behavioral vocabulary of work falls into three ordinal hierarchies of TDP functions. The functional hierarchies are a base for defining fundamental units of work, namely tasks, which are far more stable than jobs. Selecting one function from each hierarchy and estimating the percentage of involvement with each on the basis of the relative importance of the standards (orientation), provides two measures that are powerful and reliable descriptors of work. An additional measure is obtained from a scale of WI, the levels of which serve as indicators of the prescription/discretion mix involved in the task. The tasks are the fundamental building blocks of the work-doing system.

Chapter 6

Reducing Friction in the Work-Doing System

In the previous chapters we developed a frame of reference and described measures that enable practical, proactive HRM to deal with the turbulent, dynamic changes in the global economy. We have drawn a picture of workers as whole persons accommodating to the purposes, goals, and objectives of a work organization to get work done. We have shown that the overall work-doing system consists of three components, each with its own intrinsic dynamic—worker growth for the workers, productivity for the work organization, and efficiency and effectiveness for the work—and that these components are mutually complementary and dependent on one another to achieve the most beneficial results. In the long run, the work of an organization is effectively accomplished and attains optimum productivity (and hence profitability) when the workers are satisfied with their growth as persons from the standpoint of income, skill, and security.

The reality, of course, is different than the ideal picture we have drawn. The reality is often one of great friction, often destructive. All too often single components of the work-doing system strive to realize their potential independently, and even at the expense, of the others—efficiency for its own sake, productivity/profitability to satisfy a bottom line, worker growth without regard to the survivability of the work organization. One force driving the organization is competitive pressure from other firms seeking hegemony in the market. Another force is constant internal rivalry among the three components. A third is an adversarial tradition between management and labor in North America.

These forces place the system under constant threat to come apart at the seams. Because it is a dynamic system—great forces actively engaged— enormous energy can be released in a terribly destructive manner, as in a strike, if the self-centered forces of the components are not held in check, are not meshed in dynamic equilibrium. Something is needed to reduce the friction among these self-centered forces that do not exist in a vacuum. The key to reducing this friction is realizing that all these forces are person-centered. Workers are persons; work organizations are managed by persons; the work is performed by persons. These persons are all created out of the same mold. They all have the potential for self-centered alienation. They also all have the potential for self-realization through cooperation as well as competition. Is there a lubricant that can facilitate the components of the system to work together? There is. It is in effect today in many places and can definitely be extended to many more. Improbable as it may seem, *it is mutual trust growing out of mutual interest and personal responsibility.*

TRUST? YOU CAN'T BE SERIOUS!

The mere mention of the word *trust* in these times of rampant downsizing of people who have spent their lives identifying with and being loyal to a corporation is probably enough to raise the reader's gorge. This is why we hasten to clarify what we mean by trust and disassociate it from blind loyalty to an impersonal corporation. By trust we are referring to something that most of us rely on to make life tolerable and livable. It has two simultaneous aspects: (a) the risk and associated vulnerability of believing in the honesty and integrity of friends, neighbors, vendors, employers, and family (Mayer, Davis, & Schoorman, 1995), and (b) the common sense of not surrendering to naivete and instead recognizing that one's first responsibility is to oneself (Morin, 1990). The latter aspect is simply a matter of dealing holistically with the risk and vulnerability of the first aspect.

William J. Morin, a principal in the outplacement firm, Drake Beam Morin, explained:

> In the workplace, our first loyalty has to be to our own needs. I come first. You come first to yourself. We all come first for ourselves. It sounds selfish, but it's really an expression of selfness, the cornerstone of what I call non-dependent trust. Nondependent trust takes our natural desire to trust others and fits that inclination to the business environment. (Morin, 1990, p. 29)

Morin (1990) writes, when push comes to shove, the implicit or informal implication existing in the relationship between the worker and work organization is that the last word belongs to the work organization. A worker's supervisor has the responsibility to act in the best interests of the company. Morin (1990) notes several common situations in which the supervisor must ignore his or her personal feelings of caring for the individual.

> What can happen? Your manager promises you a raise, but a corporate wage freeze is announced, and now she (*sic*) can't deliver. You expect and

deserve a promotion, but your manager tells you that, because of an employee downsizing, you might be lucky to have *any* job next month. Your manager hears about upcoming cutbacks, doesn't inform you because of a management directive demanding secrecy, and leaves the company for another job. None of these actions is the work of an unethical, unworthy person. Yet they reinforce the value, or perhaps the necessity, of putting your own interests first. (p. 31)

Fitting our interests to the business environment means taking responsibility to analyze the situation and make decisions based on that analysis. To take the boss' directions without question may be loyal, but it is totally irresponsible.

Morin has some sage advice for employees based on his years of experience in the outplacement business but more particularly, on a survey conducted by his firm for a billion-dollar company.

The majority of employees stated that they believed in the values of their corporation. But 70% of the respondents said that they didn't trust management to run the business properly. A majority also felt very confused about what was expected of them. (p. 32)

He advises individuals to ask themselves the following questions about the tasks they are asked to perform.

- Does the instruction make sense to me?
- Is this instruction compatible with similar tasks I have done in the past?
- Do I understand the instructions well enough to complete the task?
- Do I know how my performance will be measured?
- Do I understand how my performance will be rewarded?

These practical questions are those of a responsible and independent worker—some would say, an *empowered* worker—and represent a search for information that reenforces nondependent trust. The dialogue that could be initiated by such questions would have the effect of reducing the risk and vulnerability and reenforcing the first aspect of trust. For such a dialogue to occur, we need to pause and consider a whole set of assumptions.

ASSUMPTIONS ABOUT THE NATURE OF PEOPLE: CAN THEY BE TRUSTED?

What are management's assumptions about workers? Rush (1971) cited a personnel manager for a large electronics firm engaging in job design for worker motivation:

The biggest hurdle we had to overcome when we started to build job enrichment into some routine jobs was changing attitudes of our supervisors.
The real problem wasn't so much in finding ways to enrich the lower level
jobs as in challenging the assumptions the supervisors had about the *people*
who perform these jobs. Somehow it was assumed that people who do menial
work have different needs and values from people in more highly skilled
and prestigious jobs. Until we did some intensive organizational development with our supervisors we had little hope of succeeding in job enrichment. (p. 25)

Such attitudes still appear to be widespread. Despite the fact that "probably the most crucial individual in making non-dependent trust work is
the front-line manager," the most common management failure is "forget-
ting that a company's lifeblood rests with individual employees and their
ability to analyze, criticize, and be creative" (Morin, 1990). The tide may be
turning. Extensive adoption of teamwork and quality circles have shown
management the extent to which they have ignored and overlooked their
human resources.

What is the worker's viewpoint of management? Not very favorable!
Elaine Kamarck, policy advisor to Vice President Albert Gore on reinventing government, describes visits to online workers in government agency
after government agencies (Kamarck, Goddard, & Riback, 1988). The workers detailed the inefficiencies and wastefulness of government procedures
that they had to follow because they were part of the system. These same
workers described how the work they were doing could be done more effectively, even when it meant that their own jobs would be eliminated.[1]

These illustrations highlight the mutual distrust workers and management have for each other. In a sense, workers and management have more
or less come to regard each other's untrustworthiness as a given. McGregor (1960) referred to management's beliefs in this regard as *Theory X*. This
belief system manifests itself in the work-doing system as managerial "direction and control through the exercise of authority" (p. 49). He con-
trasted this with a *Theory Y* belief operating under the central principle of
integration, which McGregor describes as "the creation of conditions such
that the members of the organization can achieve their own goals *best* by
directing their efforts toward the success of the enterprise" (p. 49). The opposing assumptions of Theory X and Y are summarized in Table 6.1.

---

[1]This disillusion and mistrust parallels these same feelings and disgust for government,
elected representatives, and even leaders of corporations that exists among the general public at the time of this writing. Poll after poll indicates the public feels the trust they have put
in these people to do the right thing has been betrayed. The aroused public appears to be
ready to "vote out the rascals" (as far as government is concerned) and presumably vote in
those who will restore their trust.

TABLE 6.1
McGregor's Theory X and Theory Y Assumptions

Theory X Assumptions
1. The average human being has an inherent dislike of work and will avoid it if he (*sic*) can.
2. Because of this human characteristic of dislike of work, most people must be coerced, controlled, directed, threatened with punishment to get them to put forth adequate effort toward the achievement of organizational objectives.
3. The average human being prefers to be directed, wishes to avoid responsibility, has relatively little ambition, wants security above all.

Theory Y Assumptions
1. The expenditure of physical and mental effort in work is as natural as play or rest.
2. External control and the threat of punishment are not the only means for bringing about effort toward organizational objectives. Man (*sic*) will exercise self-direction and self-control in the service of objectives to which he (*sic*) is committed.
3. Commitment to objectives is a function of the rewards associated with their achievement.
4. The average human being learns, under proper conditions, not only to accept but to seek responsibility.
5. The capacity to exercise a relatively high degree of imagination, ingenuity, and creativity in the solution of organizational problems is widely, not narrowly, distributed in the population.
6. Under the conditions of modern industrial life, the intellectual potentialities of the average human being are only partially utilized.

Note. Adapted from material reproduced from D. McGregor, 1960, *The Human Side of Enterprise.* Copyright 1960 by The McGraw-Hill Companies. Reproduced with permission.

From our experience in conducting hundreds of job analysis workshops with workers, we know their assumptions about management are as unflattering and unrealistic as Theory X assumptions about workers. But can conditions be set that reduce mutual suspicion, build trust, and set the stage for worker growth and enhanced productivity? In restating this question, Porter, Lawler, & Hackman (1975) asked whether an "optimal state of affairs" can exist consisting of:

a job . . . designed so that an employee could gain important personal satisfactions in direct proportion to the degree that he (*sic*) worked efficiently and effectively toward the goals of the organization. . . . If jobs could be so designed, it might be possible to have simultaneously both high productive efficiency for the organization and high personal satisfaction for employees. (pp. 284–285)

We believe that this is indeed possible. But who would design the jobs? Would this still be left entirely to management? Our view, drawing on McGregor's Theory Y assumptions of workers as trustworthy and creative as well as our own experience, would be to invite the workers' participation in the design of their jobs.

Significant research supports this view. Miller and Monge (1986), for example, in their review of the research literature on participative management located 47 studies containing "quantifiable estimates" of the relationship between participation in decision making and either job satisfaction and/or productivity. Their intensive examination of the results of these studies showed the effects of participation were greatest when the workers genuinely experienced it in the workplace and when participation was extended as widely across the work unit as possible. Miller and Monge described this as an *affective* result of participation, one that satisfied workers' higher order needs for growth and for positive motivation on the job in line with Theory Y assumptions.

There is, of course, ample anecdotal evidence for this type of positive worker reaction in the workplace. Morin (1990) related an experience of walking through an antiquated printing plant on its final shut down. After the last shift had departed he looked over the old fashioned and outdated machinery.

> But I noticed something else, too: a variety of chewing-gum and baling-wire improvements that employees had apparently dreamed up on their own to improve operations, or perhaps just to keep the plant running. I thought, if management had recognized the effort that had gone into these Rube Goldberg inventions, and had supported that effort with real resources, I wonder if this plant would have closed down today? (p. 6)

Donald Petersen, former CEO of the Ford Motor Company, states the following about his experience with worker participation.

> At Ford, our employee involvement program started slowly and had its ups and down. but ultimately it was one of the driving forces behind the company's comeback in the 1980s. By late in the decade, easily two-thirds of Ford's employees were participating in an employee involvement team of one kind or another. They contributed tens of thousands of highly worthwhile ideas, year in and year out. (Petersen & Hillkirk, 1991, p. 25)

We can personally attest to the fact that this is a common experience. In at least half the plants in which we have done job analyses, we have found improvisation and innovativeness, typically unacknowledged by management. In fact, it is our view that workers must be involved in the design of their jobs, if the maximization of human potential that McGregor talks about is to be achieved.

ORGANIZATIONAL IMPLEMENTATION OF A THEORY BASED ON TRUST

The implementation of Theory Y assumptions could at the very least result in a truce in the conflict between management and labor. In any case, surely it is evident that an enormous amount of debilitating stress, for both workers and managers, would be eliminated and trust would become a possibility. Patten (1981) noted:

> In the world of complex organizations . . . personnel managers, training directors, and human resource experts who function as change agents, seek strategies, models, and approaches from the behavioral sciences for consciously altering the *status quo* in the direction of greater individual, organizational and social health. Words such as trust, authenticity, openness, innovativeness and a problem-solving, confronting attitude are repeatedly mentioned as missing from much of everyday organizational and industrial life. (p. 60)

Patten goes on to point out that these change agents typically address the deficiencies in their team-building and organizational development (OD) efforts using group dynamics. Group dynamics techniques help individuals develop awareness of the extent to which they are open about themselves and their relations to group members, the kind of facade they use to keep group members from knowing who they are, and the ways in which they accept and use feedback from group members about their interactions.

> As the level of trust increases in a group, the arena (the shared awareness of knowledge) exhibited by the various group members also tends to increase. . . . The more one participates in a group, the more blind spot data (individual behavior of which the self is unaware) are displayed to others. In this way individuals become off guard and reveal themselves and place themselves in a position for getting feedback about aspects of themselves of which they are not aware. (Patten, 1981, p. 23)

The use of group dynamics builds on the assumptions that people can be trusted, and that trust, like distrust, is a learned experience.

OBSTACLES TO ACHIEVING TRUST

The obstacles to achieving trust are legion. In addition to the kinds of Theory X assumptions noted in Table 6.1, there are the circumstances of an individual's experience and search for identity in a complex world. We can list only a few of these obstacles before discussing another approach that parallels team building, draws on group dynamics, and helps people "lost in familiar places" learn to overcome distrust (Shapiro & Carr, 1991):

- The changing nature of the economy from an industrial mix that accommodated persons with relatively little skill and education to one that has become a knowledge economy requiring considerable basic reasoning, math, and language skills. (Persons lacking these basic skills are in effect rejected by the economy.)

- The tremendous increase in competitiveness among and within organizations that results in job uncertainty and insecurity. (Good work and loyalty are no longer a guarantee of job security.)
- The pressure to achieve identity through affiliation with some sort of group frequently requiring surrender of a part of one's personal beliefs. (The group can be a gang, a religious cult, a political party professing a particular ideology, and/or a social group through which one attains a particular status. Some measure of brainwashing is usually associated with the affiliation.)
- Political campaigns, advertising, and media that brazenly promote half-truths or untruths that make winning the be-all and end-all no matter the cost. (This particularly undermines faith in negotiation and most sources of information dissemination.)
- The widespread corruption of public servants and elected officials along with plea bargaining in the judicial system. (This contributes to the ability of skillful and expensive lawyers to use the legal system to win freedom or at least light sentences for wealthy persons accused of criminal behavior, thus undermining trust in it.)
- Rampant careerism whereby managers are opportunistic and self-interested to the exclusion of worker welfare, the work organization, and society at large. (This undercuts faith that others have in individual managers to do anything other than promote their own careers.)

Obviously, it is a difficult challenge to foster trust in this kind of an environment, which has a shattering effect on our relationships with others and on our beliefs in their integrity and trustworthiness. Nevertheless, it has to be done.

A METHOD FOR BUILDING TRUST

Shapiro and Carr (1991) described an approach that complements team building and is perhaps a precondition for team building to occur. They first describe, from their point of view, the condition in which we find ourselves.

> Our individual lives are lived in a series of groups. Some of these groups are obvious and immediate—a family, a club, a class at school, a neighborhood, a work organization. Others are more amorphous—a nation, a religious tradition, a professional association. . . . Within these groups individuals are faced with the task of defining themselves, adjusting their distinctive personalities, and establishing identities-in-context, identities that can stand for deeply (and often unconsciously) held values and beliefs. This task is made

more complex by the variety of changing roles we are required to adopt in our social institutions. . . . Awash therefore, in a sea of complex and over-lapping contexts, we tend to lose hope of being able to grasp anything at all. A sense of personal significance and meaning eludes us in a swirl of social change. (p. 4)

How is one to achieve trust in a world strewn with obstacles to it? How shall trust manifest in a work organization in which a downsizing is being contemplated? Let us picture the workers faced with this dreaded contingency, workers whose "sense of personal significance and meaning" is suddenly threatened by a catastrophe for which they may not at all be prepared. How can the threat of downsizing be handled by management so that individuals "faced with the task of defining themselves can adjust their distinctive personalities and re-establish an identity-in-context" (Shapiro & Carr, 1991)?

Shapiro and Carr, following in the group dynamics tradition, propose a method aimed at restoring connectedness among people they call *shared interpretation of experience*. This is not an easy thing to do. Shapiro and Carr ask: "Can we develop a shared interpretation of experience? And if so, how?" They go on to describe a group experience involving three basic components of equal importance:

1. the use of individual experience, the irreducible basis on which we all operate,
2. the collaborative testing of reality by sharing individual experiences, and
3. the discovery of a larger context to which the participants' linked experiences relate.

To understand what Shapiro and Carr are getting at, it may be helpful to follow through with our suggested example—downsizing in a large organization. (To some extent, the validity of this example depends on the culture of the organization. It is not likely to be considered as a viable approach in a highly authoritarian organization.) Suppose top management decides that downsizing is the path to take to achieve certain goals. Suppose it further arranges for small group meetings prior to taking action. These groups of no more than eight persons could more or less correspond to the organizational structure by department or by functional team. Each group would include a facilitator trained in the basics of group dynamics and whose role would be to listen, to serve as a resource with regard to the measures management is contemplating, and, on occasion, to feed back to the group what is being said.

The purpose of the group would be to provide an opportunity for individuals to share with the others what downsizing and the possible loss of their job means to them—they could vent their anguish, their bitterness, their disappointment, and question the very need for the downsizing and its magnitude. Some might voice proposals for countering the action with new or revised technology, new or revised procedures, or willingness to make sacrifices of one sort or another in order to save their jobs. The point is they would have in this shared experience a common basis for connecting with one another, and ultimately, with the top management of the organization.

To connect with the highest levels of management, each group would select one person to meet with other similar selectees in groups of eight, each selectee reflecting and expressing the sentiments of the original group. In this manner of successive groups of eight, everyone who would be affected by the downsizing could be heard from. Individuals have the opportunity to explore the trust (risk and vulnerability) they invested in the organization. Through the shared experience of connecting with one another and expressing and exploring options, they will also have some possibility of recovering their independence (nondependent trust).

There is no reason to believe that these measures will necessarily lead to a happy ending for the great majority of downsized workers. What is occurring in business and industry is a historic upheaval and inevitable painful transition, especially for those who lose their jobs. It is unlikely that management will ever be able to offer lifetime jobs to those who work hard and play by the rules. Global competition is too intense for that. What can be hoped for is that management will handle the transition with honesty and integrity so that it can still be trusted in the conditions that seem to be shaping the future.

It is not possible to place an absolute value on the approach just described or to predict exactly what impact it would have. What does seem evident is that the organization would be doing what it believes necessary to survive while also making an effort to obtain input from those who would be most affected. Carrying out this extensive venting and listening could possibly contribute to constructive transfers of skills within the organization as well as establish a basis for outplacement carried out with grace. The remaining employees would gain a clearer picture of the organization in which they are risking their vulnerability and a more informed basis for fostering their independence—their responsibility for themselves. Some commentators suggest that younger workers are already adopting these values of independence, counting only on their own skills for employment security.

Nolan and Croson (1995) described a six-stage process for transforming the work organization to make it viable in the competitive environment of the 21st century. Two components at the core of each of the stages are: communication throughout the organization and the integration of technology in the management of the organization. In Stage 2 (which follows the first downsizing stage), they describe the flexible, continuous negotiation needed to achieve a dynamic balance among stakeholders: employees, suppliers, customers, and shareholders. This can be achieved in part, they assert, by all organization members having open access to information. Nolan and Croson described this need:

> The volume, accuracy and timeliness of information are vastly different than what they were even five years ago, with the trend continuing toward cheap, perfect information in real time. It is extraordinarily important that management fully comprehend this new reality, and act on it. The days of relying on holding back information to create strategic advantage in bargaining are over; advantage now comes from revealing that you are informed. (p. 28)

Extensive flow of information enables management and labor to participate and correct problems using informed discretion to equitably distribute the benefits of downsizing, the firm's surplus, to stakeholders.

Further supportive evidence for the method proposed by Shapiro and Carr, appears to be borne out by an independent study conducted by Heckscher (1995), in which he takes a close look at what happens to management loyalties during corporate restructuring. He interviewed 250 middle managers from 14 firms, among them AT&T, Dow Chemical, DuPont, General Motors, Honeywell, and Pitney-Bowes. Ten of these companies were considered "troubled" and four "dynamic." In the troubled companies, Heckscher found a traditional community of loyalty riddled with crisis. Although most of the managers in these companies felt a high level of overall support for the need to downsize and restructure, those with high sustained loyalty were found to retreat into an inward-looking immobility. Three to 5 years after the downsizing, managers were found to lament that there was even more bureaucracy than before. For example, a frequent complaint was a lack of sufficient communication from top management down. Although communicating persistently about strategy, these top managers were not creating a context that gave their people an understanding of how to do something about strategy. Therefore, strategy remained disconnected from day-to-day implementation issues faced by middle managers.

On the other hand, traditional loyalty was largely rejected by managers in dynamic organizations. Heckscher found that these more successful organizations, many of which underwent the biggest changes, took the time to reevaluate their corporate values. They tried to foster independence rather than obedience, show respect for the personal needs of their employees, encourage honest dialogue between employees and their managers, and help employees gain the skills and knowledge needed to maintain employability. Managers in these organizations attempted to maintain a delicate balance without moving to either the bitterness of unrequited loyalty or the cynicism of unrestrained individualism.

Heckscher sought to formulate some rules that would characterize these "professional" managers in dynamic organizations. Neither the traditional organization and loyalty "contract" nor a free agent (opportunistic self-interest) and its alternatives will motivate people to cooperate under current conditions of rapid change and downsizing. He proposes instead the concept of a *community of purpose*. A community of purpose is defined as the voluntary coming together of individuals with commitments and an organization with a misssion. It is the shared commitment to the accomplishment of a mission or task without a permanent and dependent relationship of employee to employer.

Heckscher draws two pictures for us. One is of the more traditional organization in which employers felt a moral obligation to honor the implicit contract with employees by offering them employment stability in return for their loyalty. The second is of the more adaptive organization in which the main moral obligation of both employer and employee was to be above-board in discussing interests and commitments.

Perhaps we are stretching it a bit, but to us it seems that Morin (1990) and his concept of nondependent trust, Nolan and Croson and their description of a flexible environment with a free flow of communication, and Heckscher and his derived common denominator of an adaptive, dynamic organization having a community of purpose, all describe different aspects of the need for a shared interpretation of experience as set out by Shapiro and Carr. *We regard this as mutual trust growing out of enlightened self-interest leading naturally to a leveling of power in the work organization and to greater worker participation.* This is what we have in mind as the lubricant for the successful functioning of the work-doing system.

How does FJA enable this lubricant to work? Spreitzer (1996), in research on empowerment, suggested some answers to the question. Her work with 397 middle managers of a Fortune 500 company shows that empowerment is enabled by a work unit environment where the following conditions are met:

• Every position (and job) should have a clear set of responsibilities providing explicit guidance and direction. (The FJA task statement documents the worker's perception of the prescription and discretion assigned to them in executing their functions. This enables tracing miscommunication among workers and between workers and supervision.)

• Supervisors should manage with a wider, rather than narrower, span of control so that workers do not feel that someone is always looking over their shoulder. (FJA enables this by revealing the extent workers use other sources of instructions and information, for example, networking or self-study, and are innovative.)

• Empowerment is enabled when workers believe that they have support—endorsement or legitimacy—from others in the organization, especially higher management. (FJA mobilizes this support by generating a shared interpretation of experience among workers and with management.)

• Empowerment is further enabled through access to information especially to how each worker's work contributes to the objectives and goals of the organization. (FJA accomplishes this by explicitly relating, task by task what the worker does to get work done and by identifying the resources, task by task, used to do so.)

• Empowerment can only happen if management establishes a participative climate in the work unit as noted earlier in the Ford example. (FJA promotes a participative climate by involving workers and management in a reciprocal undertaking namely the FJA focus group—see chap. 7.) There is a crucial element of "surrender" that takes place insofar as the workers are sharing what they alone know—how they do their jobs—and management is confessing a degree of ignorance: "we need to know what you alone know to achieve our production goals."

We see some research support for the rationale underlying the basic FJA process as a means of empowering workers. This empowerment works together with, and in fact draws on, the strengths present in a community of purpose between management and workers, activated by nondependent trust and free-flowing information.

FJA: A TECHNOLOGY BASED ON NONDEPENDENT TRUST

FJA is a conceptual system and practical procedure in which nondependent trust is a cardinal feature. It includes the following propositions:

1. Workers, including managers, are whole persons.
2. Incumbents are SME. They know more about their jobs than their supervisors and information about those jobs can and must be accessed directly from them.
3. SME in a focus group session, guided by a facilitator using FJA language controls, can and will provide reliable and valid information about their jobs.
4. The statements/language provided by SME about the KSA required in their work, can be depended on for determining job requirements and worker qualifications.

Within this framework, FJA defines units of work—tasks—in terms of the levels of skill and the demands made on physical, mental, and interpersonal potentials.

FJA is oriented to efficient and effective productivity. Efficiency is best achieved through a systems approach that focuses on results and that values and conserves resources. Effectiveness means meeting the needs of consumer, capital, and workforce. In the case of the workforce it means contributing to worker growth, the fundamental premises of this orientation being:

- work involves whole persons and is best designed for whole persons.
- workers are most willing to work in environments that meet them halfway in making adaptations.
- workers are most likely to feel satisfied with their compensation when it is responsive to their performance and need for individual growth (training, more challenging work).

These propositions are expanded on and elaborated in subsequent chapters.

SUMMARY OF REDUCING FRICTION IN THE WORK-DOING SYSTEM

Although the FJA and Systems Approach (SA) that we have described as a foundation for HRM provides understanding and measures for proactive operations, it is in dire need of a lubricant to overcome the natural and ever-present friction in the work-doing system. We have described this lubricant as nondependent trust that is based on the free flow of communication at every level of a work-doing system. Such a free flow of communication and information make possible the shared interpretation of experience, the operative construct for trust to occur. FJA, in its theory and practice, embodies the nondependent trust that tempers the risk and vulnerability associated with the belief in those we feel care for us.

PART II

Generating the FJA Data

Generating Task Data
With Workers:
The FJA Focus Group

THE CHALLENGE

An FJA focus group is an exercise in communication, group dynamics, and creativity. The job analyst—or as we prefer, the facilitator—is challenged in the most profound sense. Training, skill and sensitivity to feelings are on the line. The facilitator is called on to be a conductor of human behavior and to produce music with a very sketchy score. The music is in the psyches of the focus group participants. The analyst, functioning as a facilitator, accesses this music by applying understanding of *the human need for acknowledgment, recognition, and acceptance.* The analyst as facilitator creates an environment in which experienced workers express personal knowledge they alone have and "jointly interpret shared experience" (Shapiro & Carr, 1991).

Much of the workers' knowledge is conscious, obtained in schools, training, and/or on the job. But much of it is also subconscious, a distillation of experience in which personal solutions to problems encountered in the course of the workday may or may not have worked. The environment created within the focus group is one in which the conscious knowledge of the participants comes together, and insights are expressed that may be new or may have only existed under the surface. The facilitator, through FJA, provides a shared frame of reference, "a partial shelter from ambiguity and uncertainty" (Shapiro & Carr, 1991). As he or she leads the workshop, an emerging pride is evidenced by the participants in the KSA they use to do their jobs to the standards required for quality performance.

THE INVITATION

Five or six participant SME receive an invitation from management to attend a group workshop to describe the work they do in their jobs. It is rather formal indicating management's purpose and the employment of the facilitator to assist them in achieving that purpose. SME also receive a letter from the facilitator thanking them for their willingness to cooperate, explaining in a few simple sentences how they will function as SME about their work and that the workshop will take approximately 2 days. The letter also notes that the method used is FJA, which requires job information obtained directly from experienced incumbents.

SME have been selected because they more or less hold the same job (usually the same job title), are members of the same project team, and are experienced, mature workers in the work they are doing. If in the same job, to the extent possible, they represent the range of assignments in that job category. The information they provide is used as foundation data for HR operations such as selection, training, performance appraisal, and/or career planning.

THE SETTING

In front of the room, there are two easels with large pads to write on. The names of the workshop and the facilitator are written on one. In addition, the facilitator may use the other pad to list the five questions around which the workshop is conducted, sample tasks for later showing, and perhaps a model of the FJA task statement. (Sometimes an overhead projector and prepared transparencies are used for this purpose.) The primary use of the pads is to record SME responses to the questions. The pages on which the answers are written are then taped to the walls of the room so that they can be added to, altered, and referred to throughout the workshop. The cumulative effect of this procedure is to reenforce the fact that SME are being listened to and that there is a lot more to their jobs than even they believed at the start of the workshop.

> *Note: The remainder of the chapter combines guidelines with the narrative flow of the work of a focus group. In this context it is preferable for the reader to identify with the role of the "conductor." Therefore, instead of referring to the "job analyst or "facilitator" throughout, the voice of the narrative has been changed to involve you, the potential facilitator.*

INITIAL PRESENTATION TO FOCUS GROUP

Following introductions on the morning of the first day, you ask participants if they have any questions or desire clarification before the work starts. At this point the workshop situation is quite ambiguous and uncertain for SME, for it seems like many other similar experiences initiated by management. Usually, no more than a few questions are asked, primarily along the lines of:

1. *What is the real purpose of the workshop? Does it have anything to do with staff reductions?* The purpose, mentioned in the letter to participants, is repeated and as far as you know the workshop does not have anything to do with staff reductions, although management could be making such plans without your knowledge.

2. *Why doesn't management use existing job descriptions or information?* Existing materials were not created by incumbents but rather by personnel specialists or industrial engineers of some type and usually have little resemblance to what is actually going on in the job.

3. *Have you done this kind of job analysis with other workers and/or more particularly workers doing the same work as ourselves?* You need to answer this question in the most straightforward manner that applies to you. However, you may note that FJA has been conducted with job incumbents at every level, from low skilled, for example, janitors, van drivers and postal clerks, to skilled professionals such as managers, executives, engineers, social workers, physical therapists and so forth. They have also been conducted with several types of blue-collar workers including continuous process chemical plant operators, heavy equipment operators, and bus drivers. All types of office jobs, for example, programmers, data analysts, data administrators, secretaries, and word processors, the entire police profession, and most occupations in health and human services have also been analyzed using FJA. If you are a new facilitator, your training included observation and supervision in one or another of these occupational groups.

During this period of information giving and clarification, it is usually possible to feel the skepticism, disbelief, and distance of the invited SME. Their attitude can also be characterized as one of noninvolvement or "show me." This is quite understandable. Being asked to spend 2 days talking about their jobs has never occurred before. No one has ever invited them to be consulting experts about what they know best: their jobs. Furthermore, when dealing with personnel operations, typical experiences of incumbents involve a lot of paperwork that has no immediate use to them in their work. You need to be accepting, tolerant, and nondefensive about this attitude without calling attention to it. As the workshop progresses, this attitude changes from skepticism to one in which the participants develop a "negotiated interpretive stance" (Shapiro & Carr, 1991). "This stance contains three basic components, of equal importance: the use of individual experience . . . the collaborative testing of reality; and the discovery of a larger context to which our linked experiences relate" (p. 8).

Immediately following this question-and-answer period, you explain how the workshop will be conducted. You make this presentation from two separate flip charts, one listing the five questions around which the focus group is conducted and the other describing the structure of an FJA task statement. The five questions and what they yield are as follows:

1. What do you get paid for?   OUTPUTS

2. What do you need to know
   to do what you get paid for?   KNOWLEDGES

3. What Skills/Abilities do you need
   to apply your knowledges?   SKILLS & ABILITIES

4. What do you do to get work done?   TASKS

5. What standards do you work toward,   PERFORMANCE
   yours and your organization's?   STANDARDS

The structure of the task is shown in Fig. 7.1.

This presentation takes very little time, perhaps 15–20 minutes. In conclusion you can point out that the first three questions will probably be answered by the first morning break and that everything SME have to say will be noted on the flip charts and then taped to the wall so they can be added to as occasion arises. This concludes the presentation except for answering any questions that might come up.

THE START OF THE FOCUS GROUP CONTRIBUTIONS: OUTPUTS

You write "OUTPUTS" on a blank flip chart and alert SME that it is now their turn to do what they were assembled to do.

The workshop is likely to get started slowly. The approach being made to SME is, to say the least, unusual, and as already noted, they are likely to be skeptical. After all, they feel you should know what they are being paid for. One of them may even say so. At which point you could say:

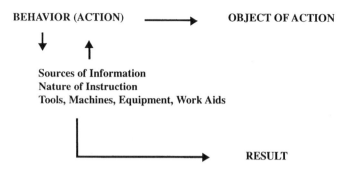

FIG. 7.1.   Structure of a task.

> Yes, of course, I have an idea what your work is. But as we said in the letter inviting you here, we want to hear it from you and note it in your words. You are the experts. In general our experience has been that there is much more to what people do than appears in their job descriptions.

You may need to tolerate a few moments of silence, but this passes. Someone will speak up. Others follow to amplify, specify, and/or correct. One of the things that happens is SME are stimulated by the different points of view they hear about their work. Although the start of the workshop may involve some awkwardness, the strategy proposed is intended to strengthen your credibility as well as the role of expert for SME.

It is important to note on the flip chart what SME say as they say it. They tend to be quite general and, almost in the same breath, propose particulars for the same general statements. Nevertheless, note them as offered. Remember, you are not the SME and therefore you are in no position to correct them. Your categories are not their categories. The only intervention necessary is to ask for clarification where what is proposed is vague, expresses an intention, or relates to one of the later questions. Remember again, this is the SME initial exposure to the idea that the workshop belongs to them, and its purpose is to record things in their words. You need to reenforce this idea especially early on. It rapidly ceases to be an issue as SME generate the answers to the five questions. If some of the things they say they get paid for are too vague or duplicative, this emerges later when they start describing the tasks they do.

The SME proposals as to what they get paid for need to be noted until they feel they have covered all their work (in the perspective of FJA, "all" is 95%). The list usually contains 5 to 10 categories although on a few occasions there have been more or fewer. You can mentally note whether "everything" has been listed by considering whether both *mission* and *maintenance* categories have been included. When finished, as mentioned earlier, the flip chart containing the list is taped on the wall.

KSA

For the next step it is practical to have two flip charts to work on, one headed KNOWLEDGES and the other SKILLS/ABILITIES. Proceeding in this manner avoids the need for SME to make the distinction between the two. Although knowledges are typically nouns and skills/abilities typically verbs or verb phrases, SME tend to think of them simultaneously, and it is best for you to sort and list them as proposed without major editing. SME usually grasp the difference between the two as you sort and list. This has the effect of cementing the communication between you and the SME. Again, you continue listing the KSAs until SME feel they have exhausted the possibilities. It is not advisable to prompt SME on the basis of personal knowledge because to do so would break the understanding that they are the experts. One exception, where relevant, would be to bring up reading, writing, and calculating, if they have not been mentioned. These KSAs tend to be universal and taken for granted and can be listed on both charts. (In case someone asks what the difference is between skills and abilities, for the purpose of the workshop, it has been found advisable to say, "It's largely a difference in how people have been accustomed to identify them. We will simply note them together. So long as you think it is a matter of skill or ability, we will list it."

SME are likely to mention things in broad subject categories, for example, "the law" in the case of policemen or "electronics" in the case of service engineers. In all of these instances, you should ask for a clarification/ specification of what SME have in mind. It may be useful to ask: "What do you have in mind with regard to the law or electronics? Is it what a lawyer or an electronic engineer needs to know?" Such questions usually elicit the desired specification, for example, "layman's understanding of the law," "local, state, and federal statutes relevant to criminal behavior," "the rights of detained suspects" in the case of the law, or "printed circuitry for specific electronic functions," "the use of special test equipment such as oscilloscopes and the meaning of certain wave forms" in the case of the service engineers.

The objective of this form of questioning is to attain specificity useful for training and to help SME remain grounded in reality. It also demonstrates active listening and positive interest and helps establish your credibility. This is further enhanced when you ask for some explanation of technical terminology or jargon when it comes up. If the explanations proffered become too technical, this should be indicated promptly to help establish the language and technical level at which subsequent dialogue will take place. It is important in establishing the level of discourse that (a) you do not appear to be testing SME knowledge and skills and (b) you are not in training to do what SME are doing. Actually, the desired level of discourse is established without any conscious effort simply by being straightforward about the information desired and being clear about the informational objectives of FJA.

The inquiry about KSA continues until SME seem to have exhausted the subject. You can then say: "Well, let's tape what we have to the wall and get on with our work. We can always add to the lists as we go along. That is what usually happens."

GENERATION OF TASKS

As already noted, the KSA part of the workshop will be completed by the morning break or shortly thereafter. You can now proceed to the major work of determining the tasks performed for each output. You say:

> We are ready to undertake our major work. We will use the list of Outputs, the things you get paid for, as an agenda. The question to be addressed is: What do you do, what tasks do you perform, to produce these outputs using the KSAs you have listed? Which output would you like to start with?

Usually the group will start with the first one, but this is up to the group. Quite often they select the one, wherever it is on the list, that they consider represents the major thrust or mission of their work. Listen for consensus. It quickly manifests without any special act on your part such as calling for a vote, *always to be avoided*. Getting started is typically slow. Remind the group once again of the structure of a task statement, reviewing the model on the flip chart shown earlier, and urging them to be as specific as possible about the actions they perform.

List the output SME select on top of the flip chart, numbering it according to its place on the list. If first, it will be numbered 1.0 and the first task will be 1.1, the next task 1.2, and so forth. The number of tasks for each output will vary. There is no way to predict how many. Frequently the tasks enumerated for the output that represents the major thrust will be expanded to include tasks originally thought of as belonging to another of the listed outputs. Paperwork tasks are a common example. You can call this to the attention of SME and ask:

> Do you wish to include these tasks here, or would you rather have them in a separate output? It does not matter. The choice is yours. The objective is simply to capture all the tasks you do. We can always rename the output.

Capturing the tasks and putting them in FJA format is the most difficult and complex part of the FJA workshop. It is essentially an exercise in active listening. SME sometimes have difficulty knowing where to begin. When this manifests, you can say: "It doesn't matter where you begin. If it turns out you began in the middle, we can work backward before we go forward. Things usually come full circle." If there appears to be an impasse at the start, you can ask:

> Does work on this output start with an instruction or work order of some kind? If so, where does it come from, and what does your response have to be? Or is a batch of semi-processed material brought to you for continuation of the processing?

These observations, or simply the interaction among SME (one starts talking and then another picks up the conversation) gets the process started. You must listen to pick up the behaviors (actions of the workers) and distinguish them from the end results of the behaviors. SME typically focus on end results and take behaviors for granted. In sorting out behaviors from results, you may need to persistently intervene with the question: "but what do you do to get (such and such) work done?" Look for the work accomplished being a determination, a recommendation, or a result leading to another behavior (action).

The following devices have proved helpful to the facilitator and the SMEs in both eliciting and organizing the information:

• Ask SME to provide a sequential outline of all the tasks performed to accomplish the output. This may be a sequence or simply a group of tasks. Jot down for yourself (this can be done on one of the blank charts of the pad you are working on) the keywords in the order you will elicit the task data. This device establishes a direction for both you and SME without a hard and fast commitment to the tasks proposed, allowing room for change to occur as the full task data is generated.

• Roughly divide the flip chart into four sections, top to bottom. The top needs to allow enough room for the action and the bottom for the result. In the second section you write *"drawing upon"* allowing enough room for the sources of information (knowledges), and in the third section *"relying on"* for the skills/abilities required to apply the knowledges.

The effect is to provide SME with a format and rhythm for generating the task information. It also facilitates comparing the tasks for level and orientation.

The most difficult part of the listening/sorting out process is to avoid getting too detailed in capturing the task, as in a time and motion study, or too general as in using verbs that are very broad and obscure what is going on. The latter can easily happen because frequently several different behaviors feed into a single outcome or result. If you find yourself starting to write a task on the flip chart with the verbs: *conducts, performs, directs,* or verbs similarly broad and vague this is a signal for you to ask: "Please give me some detail about what you do when you conduct, perform, etc.?" The object is to get specific behaviors that can be readily translated to the definitions of the Worker Functions scale. It is quite acceptable to use a string of two or three verbs to capture an action at the start of a task, thus: *responds/questions/informs* or *reviews/analyzes* or *tends/fills/empties.* In such instances you need to take care not to glob together behaviors that call for very different KSAs.

It is important to be aware that the functional behaviors do not occur by themselves but are invariably part of specific content. Before moving on from one task to another, you must be sure the behavior (action) that starts each task is one readily translatable to a level in the functional structure. Specificity is the key to ultimately making a reliable rating of the functional level during the editing of the task bank. Attaining this specificity may require some careful, persistent querying.

Some outputs have a natural, progressive sequence describing an activity from a logical beginning to its end. Manufacturing sequences, processing a contract or loan, diagnosing and repairing a mechanical or electronic device, or following through on a request for help are of this type. Other outputs such as paperwork, self-development, and some managerial outputs tend to be a miscellany of tasks without a repeatable sequence. Once started on an output that has a sequence of tasks you may find yourself asking SME as they conclude a task: "Then what do you do?" Do not be surprised if some SME follow one sequence while others follow another. Do not attempt to consolidate or rationalize various sequences into one. Instead give every sequence equal respect and note the different tasks performed. Explain that when SME get the final task bank they will be asked to check off the tasks they do. They are not all expected to perform the same tasks. Individual differences in getting a job done are common. The task bank should allow for the various possibilities.

Performance standards are nearly always brought up during the formulation of tasks. Because performance standards (described with adjectives and adverbs) are not included in the task statements, they must be acknowledged. This is done by accumulating them on a separate flip chart headed "Performance Standards" with an explanation to SME that they will be separately considered under the last item on the agenda.

The criteria for knowing at what point you have a task statement are:

- the action or action sequence is specific enough for functional levels from the scales to be reliably assigned,

- the action clearly contributes to the result, and
- the KSAs and instructions drawn upon are quite explicit.

If you find yourself having to write a great deal of KSA material, this is a signal something is wrong. Probably you have more than one task and need to seek refinement of the action.

No matter how much experience you have, it is easy to find yourself, prompted by the input of SME, starting a task statement with some form of the end result (outcome) and concluding it with another form of the same end result. This happens because the vocabulary of end results (what gets done) is far richer than the vocabulary of what workers *do* to get the work done. When this happens, you need to back off and start the task statement over again, refocusing on a specific action being performed.

MAINTAINING MOMENTUM

As you proceed, it is helpful to check off the outputs for which SME have completed generating task statements. Because task generation for the first output is likely to take well into the afternoon of the first day, some anxiety may be expressed by SME about having enough time to develop tasks for all the outputs. You can assure them there will be enough time, and because you know they have already covered the main thrust of their work, most likely they have far fewer tasks to describe for several of the other outputs. They are also likely to have noticed that, as they move along, they are producing tasks with increasing ease.

If it appears you cannot finish generating tasks in the time allotted, cut off this activity about 1 hour before the scheduled conclusion of the second day in order to allow time for discussion of performance standards. Remind SME they will receive a draft copy with only minor editing of all the material they have produced. The instructions accompanying the draft requests they modify or correct the material as they see fit. At that time they can add whatever they feel has not been adequately covered. They need only to express this in their words and they will be contacted by you if additional information is needed.

TAKING NOTE OF ADAPTIVE SKILLS

As SME interact and describe the specific content skills of their work and, by inference, the functional skills (behaviors) required to get the work done, they invariably report on the context of the work and the obstacles they need to overcome—particularly to achieve the standards most important to them. These obstacles can be organizational, personal, or environmental. They can refer to problems with receiving supplies or services, problems in communicating with supervisors, coworkers, or customers, and/or problems with air quality, extremes of temperature, lighting, or traffic. They might not have an immediate relevancy to the content of work but are relevant to its context. Frequently, personal situational problems are brought up such as the stresses caused by overtime and shift work and the impact of these stresses on family life.

In all of these instances, SME adaptive skills are revealed, that is, the ways in which they manage themselves in relation to conformity and change—manage the dynamics inherent in their work situation. You can list these along with the content oriented skills and abilities, making a mental note of their effect on the achievement of performance standards and the quality of the work. These adaptations are commonly discussed with accompanying laughter and comments while you write on the flip charts. You can regard this as a sign the workshop is going well, relationships are probably being formed, personal experience is being shared, and you have succeeded in creating a positive environment, one in which, as noted earlier, the interpretation can be negotiated and sense of reality shared (Shapiro & Carr, 1991).

ATTENDING TO THE FOCUS GROUP ENVIRONMENT

What does it mean to create an environment in which experienced workers can express personal knowledge and make sense of their reality? It means to trust SME, to respect the role of expert consultants with which they have been entrusted, and that they alone have the information and knowledge that you, as facilitator, are seeking. It means understanding that the focus group situation is likely to be totally new and, in the experience of SME, suspect. Previous encounters with management have most likely been experienced as "we" versus "them." An initial problem that you have as an FJA facilitator is to win the confidence of SME. You have done this throughout the FJA focus group procedure by deferring to the language of the SME. You must be careful not to intervene with wording or knowledge suggesting you have greater sophistication with the work than the incumbents. Your task is not to supply the words or information, "the notes of the score," but to pick up on what the SME provide, organize it, and achieve maximum clarity using the theory and techniques of FJA. After writing a task you need to read it back slowly to the group for their approval. The group is the final arbiter of its accuracy.

WRITING PERFORMANCE STANDARDS

The questions to be addressed under the Performance Standards heading are:

> What do you attend to, watch out for, when getting a job done? What do you expect to see so you can say and feel "a job well done?" Is what you expect of yourself more or less demanding than what management expects? What do you do to put quality into your work?

Performance standards are adjectival or adverbial in nature. They modify either the knowledges (nouns) or the skills/abilities (verbs). They are either descriptive or numerical or both. When numerical, they usually are dimensional tolerances, time specifications, or dollar amounts. When descriptive, they are expressed in subjective, qualitative terms that may be understood in a particular work situation but are not readily transferrable.

The discussion of performance standards can begin by presenting the flip chart on which standards have been accumulated during the formulation of tasks and asking the question: "Which of these are your own and which required by management?"

Some SME respond by referring to the standards used on the official performance appraisal forms (if there are any). This, of course, is quite acceptable, but it is necessary to go beyond them. Usually SME will do this on their own initiative, perhaps expressing themselves negatively about the official standards that may tend to be general and abstract. Frequently, there is a more spontaneous reaction in which a mixture of personal and organizational standards are described. These standards are mentioned along with the constraints which exist to achieve them. These are discussed back and forth by SME with considerable banter and humor, particularly whether or not they are realistic, how they affect their work, the stress they may involve, and how some of them may be inconsistent. In the course of this discussion, SME will probably bring up, directly or indirectly, the adaptations they have made to achieve the standards. Once again, you need to listen carefully to pick up the adaptations SME are willing to make to perform effectively.

SUMMARY OF FOCUS GROUP PROCEDURE

Conducting a focus group is a quintessential FJA facilitator experience. It is the place where theory and practice come together. As a job analyst/facilitator, you need to be at your best in applying understanding of human behavior and group dynamics in a very specialized situation—conducting a focus group with SME. These experts usually do not know each other but have come together to create a common product that they will all ultimately validate.

Sensitivity to different personalities, for example, those who talk too much and those who let others do the talking for them, needs to be dealt with and, of course, there is more than one way to deal with them. For those who tend to dominate, it is vital that you avoid a put down of any kind. Groups are likely to rally behind a slighted member and fight against you regardless if the slight was justified or not. After all, there is no getting around the fact that the FJA facilitator is the outsider. What you can do is, with utmost courtesy, sometimes indicate that time is at your heels and you must move on. For the quiet ones you might occasionally ask them whether a task you have just written corresponds to their experience.

Active listening in this focus group means to write down, with clarification, what you hear, and read it back to the group for their confirmation. It also means acknowledging and thanking each SME for the word, phrase, idea, or whatever that adds to the formulation of a task.

In addition to attending to the group dynamics and interpersonal behavior, you must constantly check out how well the functional structure is working. Before moving on from one task to another, you must be quite sure the behavior that starts each task, attached as it necessarily is to specific content, is one readily translatable to a level in the functional structure. In any case, enough information, verbs, and verb sequences, must be recorded to allow for a reliable rating of the functional level of the task during the editing stage.

You experience a great reward in conducting a successful FJA workshop. The reward is seeing the change in the attitude of SME during the course of the 2 days. Little by little the skepticism tends to melt away. There is growing wonder at how much more there is to their jobs than they originally thought—how much more knowledge they draw on and how many skills they have and need, to get their work done. Also, you see any doubts they may have had about the procedure for obtaining the information dispelled. Frequently, at the end of a focus group, when it is time to leave, SME will linger and thank you for a rewarding experience.

Chapter 8

Consulting With Management to Introduce FJA Into the Work-Doing System

TWO ASPECTS TO THE INTRODUCTION OF FJA

There are two aspects to introducing FJA to management. The first and primary one concerns arranging for the basic accommodations necessary to conduct FJA focus groups. The second involves demonstrating the wider implications of FJA for HRM in today's highly competitive environment. No matter how small the problem originally presented, working at it with FJA ramifies to other areas of the organization because it contains all the basic elements of the work-doing system. The original problem usually will be an HR bread-and-butter issue such as those discussed in chapters 10 to 18 on FJA Applications. The challenge for FJA is to stay focused on the immediate problem, although the information and insights being gathered have broader ramifications. Seeing how FJA works in dealing with immediate problems can sometimes stimulate the curiosity of management to discover how it would operate in other situations. This would be the time to present the wider usefulness of FJA, for example, for such major undertakings as downsizing, reengineering, and TQM. Following through on the original problems can, on a small scale, involve a reappraisal of work assignments for which the task analysis produced by FJA is the fundamentally needed information.

However the analyst needs to be sensitive to the culture of the organization using FJA. FJA is unabashedly oriented to Theory Y assumptions and it would be exceedingly inept for the job analyst to be confrontational if management hews to Theory X. The results of FJA speak for themselves, demonstrating the efficacy of worker involvement. The very first focus group demonstrates that the workers have something of value to contribute to the understanding of the work they are performing and that they are doing a lot more than management is aware of to achieve quality production.

ENTER FJA

The FJA response to initial inquiries or a request for a proposal, points out that FJA solutions to problems are based on detailed information gathered from incumbent workers (i.e., SME). This is done by means of focus groups with the SME, usually six in number for each classified job, held over a 2-day period in a location removed from the workplace. A training facility often serves the purpose quite well.

In addition to SME, the FJA facilitator requests the participation of at least one person, usually from the HRM staff, to learn enough about FJA to help implement the findings of the focus groups with a minimum of outside assistance. Whether the initial need is a selection procedure (test and/or structured interview), performance appraisal, training program, or job design, someone needs to be available to follow through on the developmental activity. The more the person participates in the developmental activities, the more that person is likely to be certified to conduct FJA focus groups on his or her own. (See Appendix B for information on selecting functional job analysts and Appendix C for a discussion of their training and certification as FJA facilitators.)

COOPERATION FROM MANAGEMENT

Conducting an FJA focus group within an organization requires significant cooperation from management because of the staff time and coordination involved. Desirable, if feasible, is a preliminary consultation with the responsible managers to explain how an FJA focus group works and to answer questions as to why things are done as they are. (This may be a clarification of some of the information provided in the response to the original request for a proposal.)

The purpose of this consultation is to achieve a meeting of minds, a mutual understanding of the problems of management and the potential of FJA for addressing those problems. Topics of discussion would include a review of the organization's need for a job analysis and the factors that attracted management to FJA. The FJA consultant asks what management would like to see as the end result of the job analysis effort and how they expect to use it. The consultant should be able to demonstrate how the detailed task data produced by an FJA focus group deals with the problem they have in mind. The task data shows the connection among level of skill (functional level), enablers (specific knowledge, level of instruction, and tools, machines, and work aids), and the result (product or service). This is the information that makes up the task module of FJA and the basis of its usefulness for HR managers. Some managers may assert that they already know these connections, which to a significant degree may be true. But more to the point is: Do they see and understand them from the workers' point of view?

If the ambience of the meeting seems suitable, the advantages of a focus group can also be presented, particularly how a focus group exemplifies trust in the workers. It may also be useful to explain how an FJA task bank differs from the product of other job analysis methods, such as checklists, particularly if the organization has had previous experience with checklists.

Management needs to be informed that the focus group is a 2-day workshop involving six SME with identical or closely related assignments. A variant could be SME having somewhat different assignments but working as a team on a single project. In addition, SME need a couple hours to validate the task bank, either individually or in a group. The SME selected need to be as representative as possible of incumbents in the particular position(s) being studied. A letter to SME from management requesting their participation and indicating the objective of the workshop needs to be sent to them about 2 weeks before the date of the focus group. Immediately thereafter they receive a letter from the FJA facilitator anticipating their cooperation, thanking them, and indicating that they will have an unusual experience insofar as the person conducting the workshop will be learning from them.

ARRANGEMENTS FOR THE WORKSHOP

The focus group requires a training type room with enough space for the participants to get up, stretch, and walk around if they need to. If possible, the room should be remote from the everyday workplaces to avoid the tendency of participants to visit them during breaks. Two easels with flipchart pads are needed in the front of the room along with several markers of various colors (mainly black) to record the comments of SME participants. As the remarks of SME are noted, the flip charts are torn from the pads and taped to the walls of the room. Enough tape should be on hand for this purpose. Usually, by the end of the workshop, the walls are filled with the charts, "wallpapered" as the participants usually say, reflecting their hard work.

Sometimes it is helpful to have an overhead projector available for the facilitator to show prepared sample tasks, the five questions around which the focus group is conducted, and the model of an FJA task statement. Another option is to write this material on some of the charts before the workshop and show them as needed.

Mid-morning and mid-afternoon coffee breaks are scheduled and in the afternoon, soft drinks are usually provided. Lunch is scheduled for the usual time. It is best if the eating facility is on the premises or arrangements are made to have lunch brought in. These breaks help to promote the camaraderie that develops during the work of the focus group and in which the facilitator can participate if it occurs in the normal course of events

EDITING TASK BANKS

After the workshop is completed, the facilitator collects all the charts from the walls and edits them. Sometimes it may be easier to edit them while they are still on the walls. Editing is not so much for content as for punctuation, phrasing, and occasional wording to facilitate reading (see Appendix D for a detailed discussion of editing the FJA task bank). The task bank is then keyed into a word processor in standard task bank format, printed, and sent to SME by office mail for their editing and validation. SME are asked to read the task statements to ensure that the task statements describe what they do to get things done in their jobs, to change the task statements where necessary to more precisely express what they individually do, and to indicate which tasks they do and which tasks they do not do. The SME are also asked to add whatever knowledge, skills, performance standards, and tasks they may have overlooked in the workshop. On the last sheet of the task bank, SME are asked to sign off that the task bank covers 95% of their assigned work. (An optional validation procedure is to meet with the SME as a group to review the task statements one by one and to make the suggested changes.)

When the validated task banks are returned to the facilitator, changes and additions to the individual task banks are integrated into a master task bank. The task bank is now ready to be evaluated and discussed with management and whatever technical personnel (training, selection, etc.) are immediately involved with the problem at hand.

CONFERRING WITH OPERATIONS PERSONNEL

The first topic of discussion concerns the application of the task bank to the presenting problem, the problem for which FJA was employed in the first place. The task bank produced by the focus group is the new element in the picture. An initial query to management might be: Does the task bank present them with any surprises? Do they see the job differently? Were they aware that the job involved the range of KSA that have been asserted by the SME? Are the results produced in the tasks those expected by management and do they contribute to the objectives management is planning for? In short, is there basic agreement between management and the SME as to what the job is all about?

It is not unusual for the task bank to present management with a new perspective about the job. Frequently it is found that SME are doing more than was originally called for in the job description, especially in meeting unanticipated contingencies.

REINVENTING WORK

In the current turbulent HRM scene a number of rather imposing and portentous phrases have gained currency, such as "downsizing, "restructuring the workforce," "reengineering the corporation," and "reinventing work." All of them, as far as we are concerned, are merely euphemisms for the dynamics that have always existed in the workplace—the redesigning of work assignments in response to changes in technology, competition, workers' innovations on the job, and the adaptations industry and workers make to evolving social requirements. What is different today is the frequency of these changes and the greater cataclysmic effect for the individuals involved.

But a simple fact remains: At the point where work gets done, workers are functioning at various levels of skill and knowledge and adapting to a variety of physical, social, and environmental conditions to perform tasks to specified standards. Those tasks must be documented and understood by HR specialists so they can apply their measures, generalized tools, and consulting skills to help select workers, train them, appraise their performance, give them constructive feedback, and adapt their environments to achieve optimum productivity and worker growth.

In this context, FJA has a special role to play. To begin with, its task formulations come directly from SME in their own words. They are revealing as no checklist can be because they link the essential information that must be linked—behaviors, KSA, and results. This is the information necessary to understand the work-doing system and manage its HR dynamics.

SUMMARY OF MANAGEMENT ACCOMMODATION

FJA requires significant cooperation from management in order to make its contribution. It involves the participation of six SME for each occupation studied in a 2-day workshop with arrangements that include space, training equipment, and facilities for breaks and lunch. In addition, continuous involvement of an HR staff member to implement FJA findings, and if feasible, to extend its application to other occupations, is desirable. FJA does its best work in organizations sympathetic to the HR assumptions of Theory Y and those willing to view themselves as open systems. Although the findings of FJA may have ramifications beyond the immediate problem for which initially employed, it is wise to keep focused on the particular problem and the ways in which FJA contributes to the solution.

The Use of FJA in TQM

FJA, in its assumptions, is part of a paradigm shift in industrial and organizational psychology that has been gathering momentum for at least a generation. It may be that it is climaxing now at the verge of the 21st century because of the intensity of global competition and the emergence of the preeminent criterion—both internal and external customer satisfaction.

Enormous restlessness in organizations is reflected in downsizing and reorganization and the intensive search for the elements that make for total quality. This is the climate with which FJA must deal when it is invited to come into an organization. FJA not only is in tune with this climate but in its own way has been part of the paradigm shift taking place. It is not a gimmick or flavor of the month. It is a conceptual approach that is part of the groundwork and infrastructure of the new paradigm. It represents a whole different set of assumptions from those of traditional management.

WHAT IS QUALITY?

Quality is touted by many as the savior of U.S. industry in an age of fierce global competition. This lesson was driven home by Deming whose promotion of quality control in Japan after World War II helped to drive its economic renaissance since the 1950s. (Recall the 1950s and early 1960s when Japanese goods were considered to be inferior junk. How times have changed!) Now North Americans pursue TQM with the same intensity.

But what is quality? *Quality* is a protean concept—that is, quality takes different forms and means different things every time we use the word. It defies any simple, all-encompassing definition. To get a better understanding of the shifting definition of quality, consider what quality means for:

- A new car ("Quality Is Job One" was Ford's slogan for years) sold to the final consumer. The car is durable with low maintenance costs and high reliability. It outlasts most other makes for the price. It has no defects in body, finish, or equipment.

- Automobile parts purchased from a subcontractor by a major car manufacturer. The parts are built to specifications within very low tolerances. They are delivered on time and there are no defective or damaged parts in the order.
- A quality painting purchased by an art collector. The artist is well established or a promising new talent. The work is aesthetically pleasing and meets all technical and artistic criteria for the artist's style, which may be unique in its own right.
- A quality fiction manuscript reviewed by a publisher. The plot is well developed and has an inventive new twist. Characters are appealing, novel, and interesting, not caricatures or stereotypes. Dialogue flows naturally and heightens reader interest throughout the book.

Quality matters to the customer or client who consumes the product or uses the service—it is what differentiates the product or service the company or individual has to offer from what the competition has to offer. For businesses selling products and services in the marketplace, quality determines whether a buyer will come back again. In today's global economy linked by the Internet and other means of instantaneous information (fax, telephone) a willing competitor can be found literally at a moment's notice to provide a product or service, sometimes at a better price. The imperative for quality has even made inroads to government and nonprofit organizations offering public services that were often nonresponsive to demands for quality in the past.

HOW IS QUALITY ACHIEVED, AND HOW CAN FJA HELP?

FJA offers a practical way for managers and workers to reach the shared interpretation of experience needed to trust each other and work well together. Quality management extends this envelope of shared interpretation to include the client or customer who purchases the product or uses the service to bring them "into the loop." Of course, this does not mean that the client or customer takes part in the FJA focus group. Rather, workers and managers adopt a genuine listening stance toward the desires and needs of their clientele. In response to what they hear, they adopt a goal of continuous improvement of both business process and results. They must strive to understand the meaning of quality from the perspective of those purchasing their product or service, then faithfully capture this understanding in the results and performance standards documented in the task bank. This must be an ongoing effort and requires constant attention. As customer or client needs change, the task bank must be rewritten to reflect the new realities as understood by both workers and management. These perceptions might even be directly cross-checked with customers periodically inviting them to comment on the suitability and accuracy of results and performance standards impacting on their experience of product or service quality.

Partlow (1996) emphasized this need for customer perspective in TQM as "The primary focus of TQM is not so much on quality as it is on the customer who defines that quality. In other words, TQM is concerned with quality because quality is the customer's concern" (p. 68).

Partlow goes on to describe how empowerment is used in the hotel industry to help initiate and maintain a TQM culture throughout the company. He reports the results of his study of eight leading TQM hotels, where some of the hotels he studied asked employees to participate in advisory groups that raised quality concerns to, and exchanged views with, management. He reported:

> Omni Hotels and South Seas Plantation use employee focus groups, called "employee exchange communication meetings," as a means of providing employees an opportunity to address their concerns or give input about upcoming issues. Similarly, Opryland's Employee Communications Council provides each employee a forum to discuss problems and concerns on any topic from pay to parking. (p. 71)

These examples from the hotel industry capture the flavor of the reciprocal process we are advocating, where FJA becomes an integral part of the ongoing discussions between workers and management. Where we have conducted FJAs in TQM organizations, the various elements of TQM are directly written into the task statements in a clearly identifiable way (as they should be if FJA reflects the worker experience of the job and total quality is an integral requirement of that job). This assists workers and managers together to focus their quality efforts on the objective realities of the job, and not on irrelevancies that do not serve the cause of total quality.

It is tempting to think that focusing on the customer—the recipient and assumed beneficiary of work efforts—will unequivocally confirm that he or she is being provided with high quality results. Realistically, newly opened communication channels will convey mixed opinions and views, some of which are less complimentary than hoped for or expected. It takes a personal stance of courage and brutal honesty to avoid being defensive, to genuinely listen, and to hear and accept the bad as well as the good news. If managers and workers achieve such equanimity of mind, FJA opens powerful possibilities to improve the work processes leading to quality improvement efforts. Stamatis' (1996) book, *Total quality service: Princi-*

ples, practices, and implementation, stated: "after determining where the problems are, the worker or manager must then 'take the initiative for the appropriate action'" (p. 30) to improve quality. For this to happen, the source of variation in quality must be correctly attributed to the actions of either the worker or the manager. The source of quality variation will be one of only two types: *common or inherent causes,* which are attributable to the work organization and under management's control and associated with problems remediable solely by management. *Special or assignable causes,* which are attributable to factors under workers' control and due to special (rather than systemwide circumstance) and must be resolved by the workers. In this book, we propose detailed procedures by which the worker and manager can use FJA to sort out inherent from assignable causes and initiate actions to address them in furtherance of quality. (Chapter 13 on Performance Appraisal is especially informative on this matter.) This approach involves a detailed discussion of the task bank by workers and management to pinpoint causes and take appropriate actions.

Quality goes well beyond technicalities and cannot be fully achieved through finger pointing, the application of the "right" methodologies and techniques, and/or indications of what went wrong to correct problems in the work place. Most fundamentally, quality is a matter of a shared interpretation of experience, a positive attitude—high morale, personal commitment, and the willingness to make the extra effort that quality demands of workers and managers. These positive attributes find their expression in the adaptive skills people bring to the workplace as they are encouraged in their expression by an open and trusting stance on the part of management. Without these adaptive skills in place and encouraged by management, a quality control effort becomes a paper exercise without heart or soul. Fine, in an FJA project with field engineers (FE) who service complex medical equipment on clients' premises, identified a number of adaptive skills associated with service quality on that job. He called these the "the character backup of quality." They included the willingness to stay open to the requests of customers, take time to observe customers' problems and patiently question them, and stay with the repair until the equipment was working reliably and satisfactorily (persevere until the customer was satisfied). Quality cuts to the very core of work and is the reason why people take pride and put their toil and sweat into what they do on the job.

DOES STANDARDIZATION OF PROCESS AND RESULTS LEAD TO QUALITY?

The strict application of scientific management has led managers to attempt to exhaustively detail in their policies, practices, and procedures what appears to them the "right" way to produce a product or deliver a service. Their intention is to leave nothing pertaining to quality or efficiency to chance. Although management attempts to catalogue the most efficient procedures as with time and motion studies, these efforts are doomed to failure in all but the least complex jobs, such as those in which people are being replaced by robots. Many jobs in today's rapidly changing technologies require high levels of worker skill and training. In jobs of moderate to high complexity where management wants to produce a standardized product or deliver a standardized service, the quest for quality through total prescription of worker activities can prove to be a chimera. Workers must exercise their discretion. It is up to management to learn where and how discretion naturally occurs and to support its expression (including training) in those areas where workers are in control. Management's proclivity for prescription should be limited to aspects or work where management is in control. The FJA WI scale quite precisely captures this distinction between managerial and worker control.

The FJA focus group illustrates the impossibility of prescribing all aspects of procedure beforehand, although prescription of results desired can be spelled out. Consistency and uniformity of results are achieved from the FJA focus group because the facilitator uses the right mix of prescription and discretion for the tasks performed (see Appendix C in the Fine & Getkate (1995) *Benchmark Tasks for Job Analysis*, for the tasks of an FJA facilitator). However, for the facilitator to use this discretion to achieve a high quality FJA task bank, he or she must have the proper training and experience combined with knowledge of FJA theory and methodology, and the required functional and adaptive skills. Each focus group has its unique challenges. It is as if each focus group of job incumbents has its own personality—a unique way of dealing with the facilitator and the situation represented by the focus group. In this context the facilitator must guide the group through the 2 days, drawing on all of his or her potential as a whole person and wisely using discretion to extend the FJA model and philosophy in specific situations where exact guidance is not given in this book or during training (e.g., "Now it's time to move on the next task!" "I'd better ask Joyce a question—I think she has something to contribute but appears too shy to say anything."). In this sense, the work of the FJA facilitator, and the adaptations he or she has to make, have much in common with the adaptations by the focus group participants when they resume their regular duties.

THE ROLE OF HR MANAGERS
IN ACHIEVING TOTAL QUALITY

Organizations seeking total quality should, and usually do, enlist the services of their HR managers. Because much of the expertise in FJA resides in the HR function, HR managers must take a lead role if FJA is to be used to its full potential in achieving total quality. But FJA will be at its best only if HRM itself has a culture that promotes, and is consistent with, the best of total quality practices. What does this total quality (TQHRM) culture look like?

Cardy and Dobbins (1996) provided a description of the TQHRM culture in their article, then summarized the differences between the traditional and the TQHRM approaches by focusing on the process and content with which HRM deals. The main supportive arguments of TQHRM include nine assertions that describe the face of HRM required for successful total quality management. The close parallels between TQHRM worker involvement characteristics and the FJA model presented throughout the first two parts of this book can be easily recognized.

TQHRM Personnel Perform a Consulting Role—Traditionally, HRM personnel function as staff experts who analyze problems brought to them by management, decide on a strategy drawn from their professional training, determine what is needed and/or desired to deal with the problem, and more or less unilaterally implement it. In the TQHRM model, HR personnel function as consultants, get involved with customers (online if internal to the organization), and work out solutions directly with them including methods of implementation. This approach has the wisdom of capitalizing on the experience of the workers (a notion very consistent with FJA) and reducing barriers to implementation. It also has the potential of eliminating the traditional hostility between line and staff.

TQHRM Must Decentralize—Decisions concerning various HRM functions such as job analysis, selection, compensation, and termination, instead of being made centrally in "headquarters" (HQ) would involve constituent groups such as customers. For example, selection from a customer-driven perspective may emphasize interpersonal skills and fit with the organization more than ability to do a particular job. Line personnel would be empowered to make decisions concerning hiring, pay, and firing.

TQHRM Aims to Release Worker Potential—In the traditional HRM model, management must motivate. (This, of course, is consistent with Theory X.) The assumption is that workers will not do things on their own: they must be provided with special training and incentives. With the TQHRM model, performance improvement is a matter of removing system barriers. Working with line personnel, causes of performance problems, dissatisfaction, and turnover are identified and system measures undertaken to improve overall performance. That is, "TQHRM helps management and workers to identify inherent causes of systems problems" (Stamatis, 1996, p. 29), which management then takes responsibility to fix. The FJA task bank, as noted, is an especially useful information source for this purpose.

TQHRM Takes on a Developmental Role—HRM's traditional focus is on record keeping, measurement, and data gathering to objectively decide who gets a raise, is promoted, gets sent to training, and so forth. TQHRM is developmentally oriented with the needs of the constituents as the driving force. "The process emphasizes the broadening of skills in the workplace so that flexibility and adaptability are maximized" (Cardy & Dobbins, 1996, p. 12).

TQHRM Managers Think Pluralistically—In HRM there is the one best way demonstrated by the search for coefficients of validity for selection and appraisal. TQHRM relies on many approaches in the search for excellence, manifested in different adaptations to different constituencies. "The organizational culture, the work team, and various customer groups may determine important predictor and criterion measures. Some of these measures may focus on speed and others on interpersonal and problem-solving skills" (Cardy & Dobbins, 1996, p. 14).

TQHRM Thinks About the Organization Holistically—HRM is reductionistic; there is a breakdown of work activities into jobs and tasks and a systematic narrowing of perception as to what the work units are in order to facilitate HR functions. It is the practice to break down jobs into their component parts so that selection, training, appraisal, and compensation can be measured separately. The problem is that the parts do not necessarily add up to satisfactory performance. In TQHRM there is a move to fewer job descriptions and a more integrated view of the work process. The team rather than the individual worker is the focus. Overall performance and satisfaction of customers is the criterion.

TQHRM Is Cognizant of System Causes—HRM focuses on individual characteristics and their influence on performance; this is an aspect of the reductionism mentioned in compartmentalization. TQHRM operates on the assumption that responsibility for performance depends 85% on system factors 15% on person factors. This approach looks first to improvements in supply, technology, training, methods of observation, statistical control, and information gathering before scrutinizing the workers. Its appraisal of the workers is to identify only the exceptionally high and low performers for specific actions. In the TQHRM organization, improving the average level of productivity is based largely on system improvements not on incentive plans, feedback to workers, and merit pay.

TQHRM Collects and Uses Information About Worker Satisfaction—Whereas HR focuses on employee performance ratings typically made by supervisors, TQHRM focuses on employee satisfaction, organizational commitment, organizational citizenship behavior, and customer (internal and external) satisfaction—all treated as important with primary emphasis given to the last. Continuous improvement does not occur unless employees are committed to the organization and satisfied.

Worker Compensation Is Skills-Based Rather Than Job-Based—The widespread reliance on job-based compensation by industry, business, and government demonstrates the traditional HRM dependence on the reductionistic approach. The organization pays workers on the basis of a job's compensable factors, selects workers on the basis of job specifications, and appraises workers on the basis of behaviorally anchored rating scales for the specific job, ignoring the organizational context. In TQHRM all of these operational functions are person-based. "Selection is based upon the extent to which the applicant is perceived to possess the characteristics important for success in the organization, including cognitive ability, general technical characteristics, commitment, receptivity to learning, and a team orientation" (Cardy & Dobbins, 1996). Workers are paid on the basis of the skills they possess and acquire and have the potential of benefitting the entire organization. (See chap. 15 for a holistic approach to compensation.)

SUMMARY OF THE USE OF FJA IN TQM

TQM is here to stay. One indication of this is the increasing number of U.S. firms becoming certified in the International Standards Organization (ISO) process (e.g., ISO 9000)—a step in quality management now required to do business with much of the world. FJA has its role to play in achieving and improving the quality of products and services because it helps bring the people, technology, and organizational goals/objectives into alignment *by drawing extensively on the vast reservoir of worker skill and experience often left untapped by Theory X management practices.* It provides a systematic and comprehensive language for pinpointing those production factors that lead to (or detract from) quality, as well as a means to direct managers and workers to improving quality within their respective spheres of responsibility. When used within a Theory Y style of management and a trusting relationship between managers and workers, FJA provides the additional tools to open and sustain the highly focused dialogue between managers and workers needed to make total quality the driving force in situations as diverse as producing car parts on a production line, teaching students in a classroom, or selling products in a department store.

PART III

Using FJA in HRM Applications

FJA is a concept and method for gathering job analysis data, the basic data for HRM. It would seem obvious that the operations and activities of HRM can only be as effective and efficient as the quality of the data on which they are based. FJA data are designed to be qualitatively superior to data gathered by other methods. The superiority of these data is based on the theory supporting their derivation (presented in the first section of this book) and the respect and trust accorded to workers, along the lines of MacGregor's Theory Y. The combination of these two approaches results in data that are truer because of their direct origin from workers, more stable because of the controlled definitions of the terms used to define tasks, and more comprehensive with regard to the range of worker skills covered.

Throughout the applications chapters the following themes from FJA theory and practice, supplemented by the theories of MacGregor and Shapiro and Carr, are reiterated as a leitmotif necessary to achieve successful execution.

- The individual worker must be seen and treated as a whole person, not reduced to an incidental instrument of production.
- The worker must be viewed as an integral part of a job–worker situation that includes both job content and job context.
- The job–worker situation is a system module, a place where interaction among worker, work, and work organization is occurring all the time. The system is always there.
- Performance is always the result of the interaction of three kinds of skills: functional, specific content, and adaptive.
- The demand for quality performance from the worker must be matched by quality performance from the employer, which requires

a listening stance and reasonable accommodation to worker concerns and needs.

Practices that run counter to these themes are probably, in the long run, cutting into both productivity and profitability.

Chapter **10**

Recruitment—
Attracting a Workforce

THE ENGAGEMENT OF WORKER AND
WORK ORGANIZATION

If you are an employer, what kind of person do you want as an employee? Experience suggests you want a person who has the capacity and the motivation to be productive in doing the work that needs to be done. Such people are most likely to be motivated if they are interested in the products or services you produce and share your values. An added bonus would be their potential to grow with your business.

If you are a person looking for work, what kind of organization do you want to work for? What kind of place do you want to work in? Again experience suggests a place where you feel the employer deals fairly with you as far as earnings and benefits are concerned given your level of knowledge and skill. In addition, if you are interested in the product or service and share the employer's values, you will more likely be motivated to put forth extra effort. And if the employer offers training and educational opportunities to improve your performance as a worker and if the environment is physically pleasant and not unhealthful, so much the better.

In short, the engagement of employer and employee offers an opportunity for both. Both have something to offer and something to gain from commitment to each other. It is important to examine several aspects of this engagement in greater detail because first impressions often characterize and determine future relationships. Inevitably both worker and employer, reflecting their expectations, formulate hypotheses about each other which they seek to affirm. Because it is unlikely they have all the information about each other they would like to have, to some extent the engagement of worker and employer is a gamble. However, the odds favoring a fruitful engagement are better if basic information is exchanged between an employer and a potential employee.

In order to consider this basic information in some depth, it has been organized into six areas. These six areas derive directly from the expectations of the worker: (a) a description of the opening and the workplace in which it occurs; (b) the vision and mission of the organization and the goals that flow from its purpose; (c) the functional performance levels needed to accomplish the outputs of the organization; (d) the working conditions—physical, environmental, social, as well as effort, responsibility, and type of supervision—in which the work will be done; (e) the growth opportunities including training, educational support, promotion, and compensation; and (f) the accommodations the organization is prepared to make for disabilities, day care, flextime, and the like.

Putting forth this information does not imply that worker and employer approach each other with a checklist in hand to ensure that information is forthcoming anymore than lovers check each other out for all the desirable characteristics they ultimately would like to see in each other. Rather this is the information that sooner or later becomes pertinent in affecting a decent relationship between employer and employee in the workplace. On the whole it is better if it is forthcoming sooner rather than later.

DESCRIBING AN OPENING

Openness and trust begin with the initial contact of worker and work organization. Although some organizations have been sensitive to this fact for a number of years and have been evolving a practice to reflect this sensitivity, it is still a new idea. In some instances it may even throw both employers and prospective employees off balance. Employers may balk at the idea of indicating some of the unfavorable aspects of particular jobs in their establishment. Prospective employees may be surprised to hear that some things are less than perfect in the job they are contemplating (although they are not really totally unaware of them). Nevertheless, it is with this kind of sharing that openness and trust begins.

Openness requires enough information for people to evaluate what appears to be the advantages and disadvantages of employment in a particular organization. This information includes a description of both job content and job context—the total work environment to which workers need to make an adjustment. It is this information that enables people to decide if they are suitable for an announced opening and therefore willing to cast their lot with a work organization. It is described in greater detail in the following sections. When this kind of information is provided to prospective employees, they are in position to mull over whether the organization meets their needs and hopes, whether they can weave their life into that of the organization and make the kind of commitment the organization would like from them.

COMMUNICATING VISION AND MISSION

"A leader articulates a vision and persuades people that they want to become part of it, so that they willingly, even enthusiastically, accept the distress that accompanies its realization" (Hammer & Champy, 1993, p. 105). New employees should not have to wait until after they are employed to learn the vision of the organization to which they have committed. A statement of vision embodies values and prospective employees need to know right from the start if they can identify with the values of their future employer.

Harry Quadracci, president and founder of Quad/Graphics, a Midwest printing company that has grown at a phenomenal rate, places emphasis on building and maintaining trust. About his employees, Quadracci said: "We trust them. But we hope the mistakes will be small ones" (Levering, 1988, p. 188). A management statement on "Trust in Trust at Quad/ Graphics" defines trust as falling into five areas: Trust of Teamwork, Trust of Responsibility, Trust of Productivity, Trust of Management, and Trust of Think-Small. The statement defines Trust of Teamwork this way: "Employees trust that together they will do better than as individuals apart." The Trust of Think-Small definition reads: We all trust in each other: we regard each other as persons of equal rank; we respect the dignity of the individual by recognizing not only the individual accomplishments, but the feelings and needs of the individual and family as well; and we all share the same goals and purposes in life" (Levering, 1988, pp. 187–188). This "heart on the sleeve approach" helps prospective employees to decide if Quad/Graphics is a place where they want to work.

Today, as a matter of policy, it is common for organizations to advertise their vision and mission. In their annual reports, many organizations stress the importance of their human resources. These glossy reports often relate the diversity that exists among their employees and pictures them in responsible positions. They also often include a statement that their prosperity and competitive position could not possibly have been achieved without their "excellent" human resources. An organization's recruiting literature needs to include this information because it is in these representations that an organization's values inhere, particularly as they relate to accommodating themselves to the needs of particular segments of the work population. This information allows prospective employees to decide for themselves whether they can identify with these stated values and is therefore an important element in enabling self-selection.

FUNCTIONAL LEVEL OF WORK TO BE DONE

Much of the work that needs to be done requires a range of skill from low to high, from relatively little training and experience to a great deal. The experienced craftsperson moves easily from one level of skill to another in getting a job done. In some instances more work can get done, greater productivity achieved, if skilled workers have assistants who can help out with the less skilled work. Actually, most complete jobs in any field consist mostly of low- and medium-skilled work and a considerably smaller proportion of highly skilled work. Persons doing the lower skilled work can be allowed to do the more skilled work if properly coached and supervised. That is how people grow in their jobs. However, the reward system —pay, bonuses, promotions—must fairly and equally reflect this.

Employers are finding they can achieve greater productivity by having a flexible workforce rather than depending on specialists to perform specific work. Achieving this greater productivity requires management to contract with workers in good faith to maintain pay, benefits, and working conditions commensurate with their increasing value to the organization. In such a work situation workers grow naturally to achieve greater skill and experience. Flexibility, thus, can be an advantage to both worker and employer.

More and more organizations are departing from rigid job descriptions that box employees into specific work tasks to which pay scales are attached. For example, Jim Morrison—HR director at Mercury One-2-One, a cellular telephone specialist company—points to his company's performance-related pay scheme whereby a collective bonus is awarded to employees based on overall performance against targets. "If the company is successful in meeting its growth targets, then employees should have a share, because without them the company wouldn't succeed" (MacLachlan, 1995, p. 24). Morrison's approach reflects an increasingly common phenomenon, management willingness to go beyond job descriptions to achieve greater efficiency and higher productivity. Workers who use the it's-not-in-my-job-description excuse reflect the traditional approach that often results in inefficiency and negative productivity. The notion that every little thing that needs doing in order to get work done must appear in a job description is, of course, quite impractical and ultimately can destroy initiative.

In order to make flexibility a success, employers must understand that flexibility cannot work unless trust exists in the organization. Employers must constantly demonstrate to workers that as they become more valuable to the organization, they are compensated accordingly. Flexibility also depends on the employer having a cadre of trainers and senior workers prepared to give on-the-job training and coaching to less skilled workers when needed. Finally, at the time of recruitment, workers must be made aware that this flexibility is an employment condition—they need to be willing, from time to time, to accept the challenge of doing work that is new and different from what they have been initially hired to do.

WORKING CONDITIONS

Employers typically announce in their recruiting literature that they are equal opportunity employers (EOE). Essentially this means they have provided a level playing field for all candidates regardless of race, gender, disability, and other traditional reasons for discrimination. This policy recognizes the crucial importance of a job in the lives of individuals so they can function as whole persons. Nowhere more than in working conditions does an employer demonstrate allegiance to this credo. The challenge is not only to provide a level playing field for all applicants but also to meet the challenge of mutuality between employer and worker.

Working conditions challenge individuals' adaptive skills, their *willingness* to engage with the job context. Qualified workers may reject a work opportunity if the conditions do not suit them. These conditions include *physical, environmental, and social* over which an employer has more or less control.

> **Physical:** These conditions include the requirements to use one's physical capacities such as reaching, handling, fingering, feeling, climbing, balancing, seeing, smelling, talking, hearing, creeping, crawling, crouching, and the like. Some of these are inextricably bound up with the functional skills for getting work done. For example, a painter or paperhanger who is unwilling to climb ladders for whatever reason will not find many opportunities in the job market. Similarly for a plumber unwilling to crouch and crawl or a word processor who will not finger or handle.
>
> On the other hand, employers can often find ways to adapt a work environment for qualified individuals with disabilities. Most often these accommodations do not have to be expensive or complicated—common sense, a willingness to be inventive, and the involvement of the disabled worker in seeking appropriate accommodations may be all that is needed. To illustrate, Morfopoulos and Roth (1996) reported the following results of a survey by the Job Accommodations Network:
>
> > 20% of the accommodations suggested by qualified consultants resulted in no cost at all—a fact of which employers may be unaware. In 70% of cases, the cost of making the accommodation was under $500, and 81% of the time the investment was under $1,000. Examples in-

cluded installing ramps on stairs and handrails in bathrooms for individuals affected with mobility impairments, rearranging files or shelves for better access, or supplying a tape recorder to a police officer with dyslexia for dictating reports. (p. 69)

Environmental: These conditions include the need to adapt to unusual and/ or extreme environmental conditions such as extremes of heat, cold, odor, oil and grease, dust and dirt, exposure to the elements, and the like. It also includes hazards such as traffic, unstable ground, exposure to storms, dangers from hostile populations, or failures of technological safeguards, for example in nuclear power plants and refineries.

Although some of these conditions go with the territory as in the case of physical requirements, most can be controlled and at least made as safe as the state of the art permits. The work being done to control pollution is indicative of what can be done. In some cases the measures taken need to be quite drastic as eliminating smoking in the workplace. In other instances, such as the introduction of equipment to clean effluent before being discharged into the environment or to exhaust dangerous dusts at the point of origin as in woodworking plants, the technology involved is integrated and meshed with the production machinery.

In still other instances a great deal of responsibility needs to be assumed by the workers themselves as in wearing safety glasses or other special safety clothing or practicing certain safety routines as in nuclear power plants.

This is a prime area where, through the introduction of technological safeguards or the support of individual responsibility, an employer demonstrates that human resources are truly valued.

Social: This condition relates to a number of different areas, some of which cannot be definitively described in a recruitment announcement. For example, is the work environment authoritarian or participatory? While something may be said generally about management's preference in this regard, it cannot predict how individual managers or supervisors may conduct themselves or what the sensitivities of individual workers may be in this regard. This is an area where management needs to remain open and allow for a training and grievance procedure to ameliorate situations and redirect them in a preferred direction.

Much of the movement toward workforce diversity can be credited to legislation prohibiting discrimination against groups previously disadvantaged in U.S. society. For example, the Americans with Disabilities Act (ADA) of 1990 mandates employers to ensure that their workplaces, policies, and procedures are nondiscriminatory toward the disabled. In our public lives, overt discrimination is forbidden and officially frowned on. Whereas in private life individuals can sequester themselves in whatever way they choose, in the work environment they need to be prepared to work in very mixed groups of people, depending on the size of the enterprise. To maintain harmony, workers should be informed at the start what management's policy is on diversity and discrimination and perhaps be given some indication of the racial, ethnic, gender, and disability mix of its workforce. If individuals have strong prejudices, one way or another, they would thus have the opportunity to select themselves out if what they hear is not to their liking. Nevertheless, because all types of situations cannot be anticipated and the ramifications are very complex, management must have an administrative mechanism to deal with complaints and grievances. Dealing with diversity is a prime area for training in the 21st century for both management and the workforce. Both management and labor have much to learn.

GROWTH OPPORTUNITIES

Growth opportunities are the rewards employees earn for good work. There are three main areas of growth for all workers: compensation, skill, and status. Although frequently occurring together, they are not necessarily bound up with each other and in fact are separate areas of motivation for individuals.

Compensation: Compensation can occur as wages or salaries paid in agreed-on time periods of work (hourly, weekly, or monthly) or as piece work, X amount per item produced. In either case there may be bonuses or premiums paid for specified amounts above standard production. Bonuses are paid quite differently for hourly and professional workers. Frequently there is a starting salary and then an indication of increments paid for satisfactory work after specified periods of service. The amount of compensation is usually market driven by compensation surveys. There is also a ceiling for particular job classifications.

Information about starting compensation, the range that exists for a particular classification and whether or not bonuses are paid for performing beyond standard, should be part of the information provided to prospective candidates.

For some individuals compensation is all they care to know about growth. Their interests are centered elsewhere than the work situation, for example, their church or family. Their work effort may be simply to develop enough skill to earn the optimum return for the job they are in so they can focus on their other interests.

Skill and Knowledge: This is, for some individuals, a primary concern. Their first interest in their employment search is whether the work opportunity will allow them to grow and develop to the maximum of their ability. Compensation and status are secondary interests. They want to know the specific kinds of work they will be doing and the challenges they will have to meet. They also want to know what technology they will work with and who their colleagues will be. Usually they want to work with persons who are senior to them who can help them grow in their work. They will inquire as to the training they will be given and whether the organization supports off-the-job educational opportunities. Their interest in status is of a professional nature—to become known as an expert or authority in their specialty.

Status: Status has to do with achieving a position of power as well as one of respect. In fact, power may be the real ambition behind the desired respect. Power is concerned with being in a position to establish values, policy, and direction and also to realize the privileges associated with power. Status and power should not be confused with leadership. True leaders are initially visionaries interested in implementing a mission they believe will change things in a preferred direction. Often, when they realize the opportunity to implement their mission, they become enmeshed in the complexities of the implementation and are corrupted by the power they have attained. Persons concerned with status are mainly focused on where any particular position or association will lead. Compensation and skill are incidental to their drive to achieve status and promotion to higher positions of power.

Providing applicants with the kind of information just described tells them that the organization respects their ability to self-select. It also communicates a degree of trust through sharing organizational information with a person who is still a stranger. If this type of communication is sustained, the groundwork for loyalty is established.

ACCOMMODATION TO WORKER NEEDS

Employer accommodation is the flipside of worker adaptation. When workers adapt, they make concessions and experience the stresses and strains of squeezing themselves into the organizational mold. When employers make reasonable accommodations, they reciprocate the concessions made by employees and, in so doing, acknowledge that the employer–employee relationship is a two-way street and one that matters to them. Willingness to accommodate is a concrete demonstration that the employer values workers in their diversity as well as their individuality.

Accommodation happens as a response to government legislation (e.g., ADA) or as a voluntary act. Accommodations are best worked out in cooperation between management and the individual workers affected. An example of accommodation is building ramps in the workplace to allow workers confined to wheelchairs to move about freely when doing their work. Another example is the introduction of various types of lifting devices in many establishments to minimize the importance of physical strength and thus allow women to hold jobs formerly held by men. The result is a more diverse workforce (for some organizations diversity is needed to meet affirmative action goals) and a larger pool of qualified and interested applicants from which hiring can take place.

Recruitment materials should clearly demonstrate the extent to which management has gone, and is willing to go, to accommodate employees. A description of such accommodations as flextime, cafeteria style benefits, day care, and work aids may encourage persons with special needs to apply. For some job seekers (e.g., women with small children, workers with physical limitations), information about accommodations contained in or missing from recruiting materials will have a major impact on their self-selection and whether or not they pursue the job search with an organization.

TRADITIONAL RECRUITING

Traditional recruiting, by newspaper ad or word of mouth, provides only rudimentary information to the job seeker, hardly enough to permit the self-screening that could lead to effective self-selection. This is especially true for low-skill jobs where a newspaper ad might read: "Delivery driver required—knowledge of city essential." The come-on is basically a job title with some reference to specific content. Job seekers must guess what is really wanted and then squeeze themselves into the slot represented by the job title. This type of recruitment frequently results in probationary placements that do not work out—an expensive and wasteful employment process.

It is notable that as the level and the salary of the job rises, (e.g., professional jobs), media ad space also increases along with the amount of information provided. This additional information frequently provides some background about the organizational environment, permitting candidates to make a stab at self-selection and to consider whether their adaptive skills will fit. This approach correctly reflects the fact that providing comprehensive information can help avoid hiring individuals who are not productive and need to be replaced.

The difference in the approach to low-skilled workers as compared to professionals points to the validity of the FJA approach, which provides comprehensive information for all levels of workers. FJA makes this possible through its integration with outreach recruiting and the use of the pre-employment questionnaire (PEQ) described later.

OUTREACH RECRUITING

Outreach recruiting requires organization representatives to go out into the larger community, personally contact potential employees, and communicate the nature of the job opportunities to them in a forthcoming and knowledgeable manner. A good example is the career fair held on many college campuses. Employer representatives make personal contact with students, inquiring into their interests and expectations, and exchanging information with them concerning the available opportunities. They might even establish a strong contact with students who appear outstanding to them, interviewing them in-depth, and tagging them for employment after graduation. In recent years, during periods of high employment, similar fairs for job opportunities requiring lesser degrees of preparation have been conducted in community colleges and even in high schools.

Outreach recruitment can work especially well for members of racial minorities or groups with special needs by allowing the organization to take the first step and carry the message of EEO directly to them. Much of the discussion with EEO groups centers around the adaptations individuals need to make and the extent to which the organization is willing to make the necessary accommodations (e.g., ramps to accommodate wheelchairs, lifting devices to accommodate individuals unable to lift heavy weights, day care facilities for single individuals with small children). Merely entering such discussions indicates an organization's sensitivity, flexibility, and willingness to meet halfway groups with special needs. This is where the FJA task bank with information on job context as well as job content is especially useful to the recruiter. Consider also the value of such information passed on to third party recruiters (e.g., executive search organizations who know little about the jobs and the environments of the organizations that employ them).

PEQ

We live in an age of tests; we seem to prefer a score obtained from the administration of an instrument developed for a specific purpose rather than judgments made on the basis of interviews and self-report information on applications. In doing so, test limitations and erroneous use of test scores are often overlooked. While judgments made as a result of interviews are subjective and are frequently inconsistent, much can be done to improve their objectivity. At present, let us face the fact that both approaches, tests and interviews, continue to be used and that the real issue is how to improve their effectiveness.

The PEQ is much like a test. It was developed by Fine in collaboration with Myers (Myers & Fine, 1985) to help an organization sort thousands of applicants into good, better, or best bets in terms of its needs. At the same time it was intended to help applicants self-select, that is, decide whether they really wanted to do the kind of work for which they were applying. It was also seen as an effective basis for follow-up interviews with applicants after they were given occupational information concerning the job opportunities available.

The PEQ is based on the assumption that successful workers in specific job families have certain personal characteristics in common—some combination of functional and adaptive skills gained from personal qualities and life experience. This is the same assumption on which the usefulness of biodata is based (see Stokes, Mumford, & Owens, 1994, chap. 1). This same source provides considerable data on the validity of biodata for a number of personnel functions. The rationale for both the PEQ and biodata is summed up in the famous epigram, "What is past is prologue," and presumes that individuals who have excelled in certain work in the past are likely to do so in the future.

But is there really a unique pattern of human qualities associated with doing one kind of work as distinct from qualities associated with another kind of work? The answer, of course, is yes and no, or better still, it depends. Because there is considerable belief and some evidence that these patterns do exist, research was undertaken to establish what these patterns were for seven nonprofessional job families in a very large communications corporation (see Table 10.1). The PEQ was designed to discover if indeed these patterns existed.

The PEQ instrument is a questionnaire consisting of 150 to 300 items, depending on the job family, selected by a panel of experts (experienced incumbents, supervisors, and personnel workers) from a master list of 500 items. The master list consists of items more or less associated with success in a variety of job families. Drawn from the life experience, education, and training these items represent the widest possible background within the domain of the applicant population. They include the background and experience of women and minorities—hobbies, sports, school, and domestic activities—so their relevant life experience could also be tapped.

In general, three types of items occur in the questionnaire: (a) specific job-related items, for example, "installed, repaired, or replaced any type of PBX or telephone switching equipment"; (b) general task-related items, for example, "compiled lists from standard information sources such as telephone directories"; and (c) items that concerned adaptation to working and environmental conditions, for example, "met urgent time pressures and delays" or "performed repetitive activities without interruption for long periods of time" (Myers & Fine, 1985).

TABLE 10.1
PEQ Job Families in a Communication Corporation

Major Categories	Subcategories	Representative Title Examples
1. Operator	TSPS Directory Assistance	Operator
2. Clerical	General	Entry/Semi-Skilled/Skilled Clerk Dial Office Clerk
	Special Skills	Typist, Stenographer, Key Punch Operator, Data Entry Clerk
	Technical	Drafter, Engineering Clerk
	Customer Contact	Teller, Repair Clerk, Customer Clerk
	Data Processing	Business Machine Attendant
3. Service Representative	Residence Service Representative Business Service Representative Public Service Representative	Service Representative
4. Technical	Installation/Repair	Station Installation/Repair Technician, PBX Installation/Repair Technician
	Construction	Outside Plant Technician, Cable Splicing/Repair Technician
	Central Office	Frame Attendant, Switching Equipment Technician, Power Technician, Transmission Technician, Central Office Equipment Technician
	Testing	Test Dial Technician, Toll Testing Technician
	Assignment	Line Assigner, Estimate Assigner
5. Maintenance	Automotive	Mechanic, Garage Attendant
	Building	Building Equipment Mechanic
	House Service	House Service Attendant
6. Sales	Outside	Market Administrative, Coin Telephone Representative, Directory Advertising Sales Representative
	Inside	Directory Sales Canvasser
7. Other Support	Coin Collection	Coin Collector
	Motor Messenger	Motor Messenger
	Supply	Supply Attendant

For each job family, a rating scale measures the job relevancy of the background item. A specific item can have a different relevancy weight or none at all, depending on the job family. An example of such a relevancy scale for the operator job family is given in Table 10.2. Job applicants respond to the questionnaire appropriate to the job family in which they are interested. They check off all items that apply to them. The questionnaire score is the sum of the weights of the items checked. This score indicates the degree to which applicant's backgrounds correspond to successfully employed workers in the job family for which they are applying.

Applicants applying for jobs in any of the seven job families are first asked in which job family they are interested. (As a practical matter, only one job family is publicized as having vacancies at any particular time.) Applicants are given the occupational information—descriptions of the work involved and the advantages and disadvantages inherent in the jobs—for that job family. They are told the PEQ is not a test of ability but rather an instrument to better understand the background applicants bring to the job. The PEQ asks them to check off the items with which they have had experience. Completed PEQs are collected, scored, and sorted into high, medium, and low qualification groups. (The scoring is a simple addition of the relevancy weights assigned by SME). The applicants are told they will be informed of specific opportunities when they occur.

TABLE 10.2
Relevancy Rating Scale for PEQ Items Within the Operator Job Family

Relevancy Weight	Definition of Background Item	Example
3	*Highly relevant*—Experiences involving work behaviors that are either the same as those performed by operators or at least highly similar in content	Operated any kind of switchboard
2	*Moderately relevant*—Experiences involving work behaviors that are different in content but closely related to the work performed by operators	Answered telephone, took messages and relayed calls
1	*Slightly relevant*—Experiences that, although different than the work of an operator, involve attributes and characteristics that are similar to the work and might indicate potential candidates without a great deal of experience	Classified books in a library
0	*Not relevant*—Experiences not relevant to the job	Climbed ladders and worked aloft with hand tools

SUMMARY OF RECRUITING

Effective recruiting, recruiting that results in qualified applicants who have self-selected to become employees of a particular organization, depends on a fair exchange of information about both job content and job context. Employers need to share with prospective workers both the advantages and disadvantages of employment in their organization. This includes providing information about (a) the job opportunity and the workplace setting in which it occurs; (b) the vision and mission of the organization; (c) the functional performance levels needed to accomplish the outputs; (d) the working conditions: effort, responsibility, environment; (e) growth opportunities: educational support, promotions, compensation; and (f) accommodations the employer makes to meet special needs. This information can be provided by brochure, interview, video, or some combination of these modalities. It can be disseminated by advertisement (in a limited way), through outreach as in job fairs at schools, and through a PEQ administered in the offices of the organization. This open and forthcoming approach at first meeting lays a foundation for trust that becomes a vital element in future productivity.

Chapter 11

Selection—Testing Applicants

The last chapter noted that job seekers are empowered to self-select when the organization presents them with accurate and complete information through outreach recruiting or PEQs. Job seekers can then indicate their willingness to be considered for a job by filling out an application form that provides the employer with basic background information. Now it is the organization's turn to scrutinize the applicants. The goal of management is to ascertain whether the applicant has the both capacity and motivation to contribute what the organization wants and needs from its workers. The hiring manager needs to keep in mind that, consciously or subconsciously, applicants are seeking a situation where their skills have an outlet and where their efforts are adequately compensated. Tom Melohn (1994), the former owner of North American Tool & Die Company, said: "The definition of good people goes far beyond mere job competence. The basic values of your fellow employees are the real key to success—theirs and yours" (p. 106). In FJA terms, this means that people must be hired to fit both the content and context of the work being done.

Often testing takes place within an initial screening process whereby a relatively large number of job applicants is reduced to a short list of applicants who are then interviewed. Chapter 12 describes the use of FJA for developing structured interviews, which are especially useful for assessing applicants' qualifications. Together FJA-based testing and interviewing can provide a *thorough* means to identify the right people for the work available.

THOROUGHNESS OF THE SCREENING PROCESS

Employers vary greatly in the complexity and rigor of their screening systems. For some, screening means reading the application form and conducting an informal interview with a job applicant. The decision to hire—based on undocumented and often impressionistic criteria—is made on the spot by a manager. At the other extreme is a Japanese automobile manufacturer that puts applicants through a several-stage rigorous screening process (including reference checks, psychological testing, performance tests, and structured interview). Each stage is professionally developed and validated at considerable expense, for both lower level employees as well as for upper level employees. The second process, obviously more thorough than the first, is more likely to lead to good hiring decisions (satisfactory predictive validity). The many mistakes made by sending U.S. managers overseas to work in different cultures only to have them fail in situations unsuited to their adaptive skills also illustrates a lack of thoroughness in and the costs of poor selection (Briscoe, 1995).

The reasons for variability in screening practices may be due to variations in HR norms and customs across different industries. For example, the hospitality industry (hotels, motels, and restaurants) employs many people in jobs that are low in pay, learning opportunities, and status. These employment opportunities (sometimes called McJobs) suffer from very high turnover and are perpetually understaffed, especially in a growth economy. A prevalent belief in the hospitality industry is that investments in rigorous (and expensive) multiple-stage screening systems are a waste of money because the required job skills are minimal and a greater investment in selection is not recouped before the worker leaves the job. This attitude contrasts markedly with the view of the Japanese automobile manufacturer described earlier who invests heavily in screening new employees.

The belief that certain types of jobs are not worth an investment in high-quality screening assessments is antithetical to FJA. Employers using FJA show respect and care for their workers by developing and implementing a reasonably thorough screening system for all jobs, for the sake of both the applicant and the organization.

THE DEGREE OF SELECTIVITY IN CHOOSING AMONG JOB APPLICANTS

That jobs differ in their desirability in the eyes of job seekers is a basic fact of our economic system. As chapter 10 demonstrated, job seekers are especially interested in employment opportunities that have the following features:

- some level of status and respect,
- opportunities for learning and advancement, and

- a decent rate of pay.

These features are almost the same as those workers mention for leaving jobs: earnings, job challenge, opportunity for advancement, and geographic location (Mowday, Porter, & Steers, 1982). Individuals take jobs and switch to other jobs for similar reasons, although there are large differences in what these individuals look for in a job in the first place (one person may consider job challenge to be most important whereas a co-worker ranks pay as the number one reason for taking or leaving a job). Furthermore, not all of the features mentioned must be present for a job to be desirable and in demand for large numbers of potential workers. For example, Cronshaw consulted with a transit company where 10 people apply for each open position of transit operator and turnover is very low (2%–3% a year plus retirements). Management reported that most applicants were attracted to the job by the high level of compensation ($18 Canadian per hour plus generous benefits) rather than opportunities for growth/advancement or status, both of which were minimal. However, it is clear that where none of these features are present, employers have more difficulty attracting job candidates. Even where the job is desirable to many people, employers may still have difficulty attracting job applicants if employer demand for specialized skills exceeds labor market supply (e.g., tool-and-die makers who are constantly in heavy demand and short supply in the United States).

The attractiveness of a job and the availability of specialized labor have a direct bearing on how selective employers can be in the screening process. Where the job is attractive and applicants numerous, the employer can be choosy in the screening process. Where the job is unattractive or qualified applicants are in short supply, the employer must be less choosy. To some extent, employers can increase the numbers of applicants for a job by expanding their recruitment efforts, but there is a practical limit to this. Selectivity is discussed later in this chapter in conjunction with reliability and validity issues.

DECISION MAKING IN SELECTION—
THE SOURCES OF RIGHT AND WRONG DECISIONS
DURING APPLICANT SCREENING

Management makes the right decisions about who to hire more often than not when an applicant screening system is effective. Management makes these correct decisions by hiring people who perform up to or exceed expectations (correct hires) and rejecting those applicants who would have been less than satisfactory performers on the job (correct nonhires). Although management would prefer to be 100% accurate in these predictions such omniscience is impossible. Conversely, management can make two types of wrong decisions when hiring from a group of applicants. The first mistake is to hire someone who performs below expectations on the job. These people are the incorrect hires. Failure to hire people who would have been satisfactory performers but never got the chance to show their stuff is the second mistake. These people are the incorrect nonhires. Managers are sensitive to the first type of hiring mistake because an individual performing below expectation must be retrained or terminated. Hiring mistakes of this kind cause expense and inconvenience to the organization and are highly visible. On the other hand, managers are usually blissfully unaware of the cost of incorrect nonhires because this kind of hiring mistakes usually does not come back to haunt them. (One exception is the rejected applicant who becomes a star with another organization.) The 1996 All-Star Baseball Game shows how management can miss outstanding worker potential. In that game, catcher Mike Piazza led the National League to an easy 6–0 victory and earned the most valuable player (MVP) award. After the game, the media pointed out that Piazza was the 1,390th player taken in the 1988 draft. From those humble beginnings, he went on become rookie of the year and a four-time all-star. Many of us can point to other diamonds in the rough—incorrect nonhires—who overcame initial rejection to become outstanding contributors to their organizations and to society at large.

Management must make correct hiring decisions more often than incorrect decisions if applicants and workers are to gain trust in the hiring system. After a group has been hired, incorrect hires undermine the confidence in the hiring system because it becomes apparent to everyone that management hired the wrong person. Again, worker trust in the screening system is eroded. The effectiveness of the hiring system is improved by *predictive validity* of the assessments built into it. Confidence and trust is further built if, in addition to predictive validity, the selection assessments have the appearance of job relatedness (*face validity*).

In a situation where an employer has the option to take the cream of the crop from a group of people who have self-selected, the employer has to decide on an assessment device(s) and a system to make the best decisions based on these assessments. For example, the employer may decide to administer a psychological test to all applicants, then move only the top 10% of test takers to a structured interview where the final selection decision is made. This structured interview might include a number of preestablished questions asked of all job applicants with a special emphasis on assessing adaptive skills. But how is a decision made about which test to use and how to use it? FJA gives guidance on this as shown throughout the remainder of this chapter.

To better see where FJA leads in terms of selection applications, the basic themes of FJA are restated below in italics. How each of these principles translates into FJA-based selection follows each theme.

Applications reflect whole persons, does not partialize them.
Selection principle: Physical, mental, and interpersonal skills need to be assessed in a way that recognizes the relative occurrence of these skills on the job.

Workers are viewed in relation to both job content and job context.
Selection principle: Tests or other measures used in selection must assess applicants' KSA with the job context in mind (i.e., required level of effort, degree of responsibility, and adjustment to work conditions).

Interaction among worker, work, and work organization should be reflected in the application.
Selection principle: The selection process explicitly ties the work (as defined through task analysis) and the organization (defined through organization analysis) into the assessment of worker qualifications (capacities, experience, education, and training).

Job performance is realized from the interaction of specific content, functional, and adaptive skills.
Selection principle: Although the selection system directly assesses only functional and adaptive skills (specific content skills are usually acquired after hiring), functional and adaptive skills are recognized as important enablers to the acquisition of specific content skills later. Adaptive skills, determined by the job content and identified as a practical matter when the FJA task analysis is performed, are extrapolated from the task statements and performance standards. Melohn (1994) captured an example of a required adaptive skill in his statement, "we search for people who are willing to be good neighbors" (p. 92). These people, he goes on to say, "quietly and unobtrusively search out a new way—a better way—to do a job for the benefit of everyone." As shown earlier in Fig. 4.1, functional skills are exercised in response to the demands of job content and complement the need for adaptive skill.

Adaptations of the workers, once on the job, need to be matched by accommodations from the employer.
Selection principle: The selection process must recognize that jobs are not static. Employers make accommodations in the long run that change the job context to a greater or lesser extent. An employer's willingness to accommodate brings out the willingness of workers to adapt to the conditions present in the workplace. Because adaptation takes persistence and effort, a quid pro quo from management through accommodation helps to reinforce workers' perceptions of equity and show that man-

agement is holding up its side of the relationship. The selection system needs to reflect the accommodations employers are willing to put in place (e.g., an applicant may be told that he or she can choose to work either the day or night shift if that choice is available).

The two types of selection assessments used in many selection systems, standardized psychological testing and performance testing, are discussed next. (Employment interviewing for selection is covered in chap. 12.) FJA has found numerous applications to selection, but its assumptions are most sympathetic to the development of performance tests.

STANDARDIZED PSYCHOLOGICAL TESTING

In many organizations, an important part of management's attempts to be thorough in its selection process has included psychological testing—tests of broad human attributes and qualities such as intelligence and personality. These tests are always accompanied by instructions on how to administer them, including what to say to the examinee and often they must be administered under strict time limits. The test may be in either paper-and-pencil form or administered and scored by computer. The test should be supported by research reporting on its reliability and validity.

Wernimont and Campbell (1968), in their classic article, suggested a better way to understand what psychological tests measure and how they measure it. They draw a distinction between *signs* from which inferences are made about behavior and *samples*, which are simulations of the behavior. The results of standardized psychological tests, they asserted, are signs of future behavior. In other words, these tests measure a characteristic or attribute that the better applicants cum workers are assumed to possess. For example, job applicants with higher scores on a cognitive ability test at the hiring stage are assumed to become better accountants or lawyers than applicants with lower scores. The sign, in this case the score on a cognitive ability test used in the selection process, is assumed to measure a psychological attribute (here, intelligence) that in turn serves as a flag to identify those people who should perform better after they are on the job.

Standardized psychological tests have their place in selection, but as with all selection devices, they must be used advisedly with a full appreciation of their limitations. From the FJA perspective, the following limitations apply to psychological testing:

• These tests tend to partialize people in the selection process. Any single test is meant to measure physical skills *or* mental skills *or* interpersonal skills. In fact, one of the requirements of these instruments is that they be pure measures of one construct such as mechanical aptitude or sociability. The tests in and of themselves do not reflect the interrelatedness of these skills on the job. FJA, by contrast, recognizes the existence of three skill areas (specific content, functional, and adaptive), and emphasizes their interrelatedness in driving a holistic and complete task performance.

• Most standardized tests assess worker potential to master job content, rather than job context. To fully reflect job context, nontest predictors such as interviews and work samples must be used.

• Psychological tests are not broad enough to capture the interaction among worker, work, and work organization. These tests are designed as measures of personal qualities and attributes of the worker. The HR specialist must take additional steps to link the test to both the work and work organization.

• Because psychological tests are standardized, and often administered under strict time limits, they are not very accommodating of job applicants with special needs, especially those with disabilities. The opportunity for workers to demonstrate their adaptability once on the job can be severely constrained by psychological testing.

• Taking tests with the equanimity required to do one's best, is in itself an important adaptive skill.

If psychological tests are going to be used in an FJA-based system, some means need to be found to overcome these basic limitations.

Some types of psychological tests have adverse impact against members of certain racial groups, which means that proportionately fewer of them pass the test and are hired through the selection system. A *U.S. News & World Report* article written by Paul Glastris (1994) described a recent resurgence of this problem. Glastris reports a blizzard of criticism against a paper-and-pencil test developed by consulting firms at a cost of $5,000,000 to help the city of Chicago promote police officers to sergeants. Only 8% of Blacks and 4.4% of Hispanics achieved test scores high enough to win promotion, despite the fact that the city of Chicago is 39% African American and 19.6% Hispanic. Glastris points to performance tests, on which minorities score much closer to Whites, as an alternative to paper-and-pencil tests. We agree with Glastris in his concern about the adverse impact of paper-and-pencil tests and in the potential for performance testing. Performance testing, which has been the subject of some important FJA applications, is discussed later.

There is a class of tests which is not strictly psychological in nature and has many desirable FJA features. PEQs (described in chap. 10) belong in this class. The PEQ does double duty: it provides job seekers with information for self-selection and it serves as a selection instrument for the organization. How good are these types of experience questionnaires for sorting applicants during selection? One measure of the thoroughness (or more precisely, the accuracy) of a test for selecting the best people from a group of applicants is a statistical index called the *correlation*.

Quinones, Ford, and Teachout (1995) summarized the results of a number of previous studies looking at the correlation between work experience measures such as the PEQ and job performance. They found that the highest correlation between work experience and job performance could be expected when the experience measured was specific to individual tasks and when this experience was significant in amount. The correlation for these types of experience measures, which are similar in approach to the PEQ, was certainly high enough to make it a welcome addition to many selection systems. (In other words, use of these measures would result in selecting significantly better candidates for the job rather than relying on chance alone.)

Villanova, Bernardin, Johnson, and Dahmus (1994) developed a variation on experience ratings as a measure of job compatibility. These researchers developed a job choice questionnaire for theater personnel consisting of items organized into tetrads (four-choice questions). Each tetrad was comprised of either desirable or undesirable job characteristics (an undesirable job characteristic would be "having to deal with rude customers"). Applicants were asked to look at each tetrad and choose two of the four job characteristics most desirable or undesirable to them. These characteristics had been previously rated in a manner reminiscent of the PEQ as to whether they were relevant to the job. The sum of all the relevant items checked by the job applicants produced the total score used to predict a measure of job performance and turnover. Results of the job compatibility questionnaire indicated it would make a good selection device. Whether Villanova et al. used FJA in their research is not known; however, their approach is highly consistent with FJA and offers another FJA option for a nonpsychological test with good predictive abilities.

The last nonpsychological test to be considered is biographical data (*biodata*). A biodata questionnaire is a modified application form that obtains information about a variety of work and life experiences. The questionnaire is scored much the same as a standardized psychological test. Correlation of biodata with subsequent job performance generally has been good and a sophisticated technology has been built around constructing, validating, and using these instruments, especially in the life insurance industry (as evidenced in Stokes et al., 1994 *Biodata Handbook*). The use of FJA to provide a job analysis platform on which to build biodata instruments is described in some detail in Stokes et al. (1994).

PERFORMANCE TESTING

Earlier, reference was made to the work of Wernimont and Campbell. These researchers anticipated the current interest in performance testing by differentiating between tests as *signs* and *samples*. When tests are developed and used as samples of behavior, they are intended to elicit performance in a simulated situation; that is, the test consists of samples of the future behavior desired by the organization. A work simulation whereby job applicants are asked to perform a task required on the job provides a good example of a performance test. In performance testing, a person's responses are scored by trained observers against some preestablished criteria of effectiveness identified for that job. For example, the criteria for a salesperson in a work simulation would be to remain calm and polite in dealing with a rude and verbally abusive customer. The behavioral sample consists of an interaction between the prospective salesperson and a difficult customer—often a trained actor role playing the part—under conditions as closely approximating the job as possible. The evidence for the person's future job performance is direct and behavioral compared to a sign that is indirect and inferential. (A sign in this case might be a personality test providing a score on sociability as evidence that the salesperson would deal effectively or ineffectively with a difficult customer.) Many applicants prefer performance tests because they have more face validity and leave more room for people to demonstrate their adaptive skills. They also give applicants a real-life preview of the job and so further encourage self-selection.

Work samples can bring out both functional and adaptive skills. A work sample designed to assess the skills of an applicant for the job of airline flight attendant might have the applicant serving food to a difficult passenger (role-played by an actor) within a tightly confined area. In addition to observing and scoring the applicant on individual behavioral items, a work sample rater might score the individual on their flow in performing the task—that is, their ability to integrate the skills into a smooth, effortless, and holistic performance. (Csikczentmihalyi's concept of flow is discussed in chap. 13.) For the best workers, functionality and willingness work together in a natural way and in the work sample results in a relaxed and comfortable airline passenger. In fact, actors who role-play passengers in these work samples might be asked to provide subjective judgments on their experience of overall service quality—judgments reflecting their perception of flow inhering in the attendant's performance.

Performance testing allows the FJA principles of selection to come into play as follows:

- Physical, mental, and interpersonal skills are all brought into play. In the previous example of selecting salespersons, it becomes immediately apparent that the applicant must size up the interpersonal situation and make decisions about what to say to the difficult customer (mental skill). The applicant must manage important aspects of the interaction, including the affective tone of the exchange (interpersonal skill). Physical skill is reflected in body language. In the salesperson example, the applicant must maintain an appropriate physical distance between self and the difficult customer so as to neither antagonize the customer by standing too close nor alienate him or her by standing too far away. In scoring the performance test, all three skills need to be represented in proportion to their importance in the interaction and in a manner that reflects the interrelated way in which these skills are applied to achieve a smooth and well-integrated performance.

- Both job content and job context are incorporated in the assessment. The context factor most relevant to the salesperson example is degree of responsibility. That is to say, the applicant must assume responsibility for managing the interaction by remaining calm and objective rather than going tit-for-tat with the irate customer. The score given on the performance test reflects the applicant's success in adjusting to job context, in this case by accepting the appropriate degree of responsibility.

- The performance test recognizes the worker's involvement in the entire work system: worker, work, and work organization. The worker is assessed during the performance of specific tasks that resemble the actual requirements of the job as closely as possible and is evaluated by standards derived from the goals and objectives of the larger work organization.

- Performance testing requires applicants to draw on and integrate their functional and adaptive skills in achieving successful task performance. Specific content is also provided to the applicants where this is needed for successful task performance. For example, successful performance for a salesperson certainly draws on both functional skill and adaptive skill (a functional skill is getting along with others; an adaptive skill is willingness to deal with irate, abusive customers). The performance test is made even more valid if the applicant is provided with the employer specifications beforehand; that is, he or she is given the organization's customer relations policies and procedures to read before the performance test. Note that providing the relevant policy documents increases applicant trust in the selection system because they are not being tricked or forced to read the employer's mind about what is wanted. The performance test then captures applicants' ability to learn and use specific content skill as well as their levels of functional and adaptive skill.

- The performance test must allow for reasonable adaptations by the applicant and probable job changes in future. Referring again to the salesperson example, a person with a hearing impairment might adapt to the difficult customer by politely asking him or her to repeat the communication or to speak more slowly. This could very well have the beneficial collateral effect of reducing tension and making the customer more manageable. The advantages for assessment of the handicapped are obvious. The performance test can also be scored with some latitude for the "right" course of action. If the specific requirements and standards applying to the job are expected to change in the future, the assessment might focus on the quality of the physical, mental, or interpersonal performance brought to bear rather than adherence to any predetermined course of action.

An example of using FJA in selection involved the development of work sample tests for a national apprentice training program run by the International Union of Operating Engineers (Olson, Fine, Myers, & Jennings, 1981). The purpose of the work sample tests was to provide a job-related and legally defensible means for qualifying apprentice heavy equipment operators as journeymen. Conducting an FJA task analysis for 16 kinds of heavy construction equipment used by operating engineers (e.g., asphalt paver, bulldozer, grader) was the starting point in developing the work sample tests. Senior operating engineers served as participants in FJA focus groups and revalidated the resulting task banks. Using the task banks as a base, Fine and his project team developed performance standards for each of the 16 pieces of equipment. This development was undertaken in four steps:

- The job analyst (i.e., Fine) prepared a preliminary draft of the performance standards.
- This preliminary draft was reviewed in a 2-day meeting between Fine and a principal SME.
- The draft was revised, taking into account the input of the principal SME, and was resubmitted to him for review.
- The performance standards agreed on between Fine and the principal SME were given to equipment-specific task forces of four to six SME from across the United States. These task forces reviewed the performance standards over a 2-day period and revised the performance standards as they saw appropriate.

Significantly, in this project, members of the project team organized the detailed performance standards under several outputs for each piece of equipment. The performance standards were also classified as to whether they involved predominantly things, data, or people. These performance standards were then placed into checklist formats comprising the evaluation components for the work sample tests on the 16 pieces of equipment.

These performance tests were in effect work facsimiles in which an apprentice or trainee was required to perform a work activity under conditions resembling the final work site as closely as possible. The apprentice or trainee was closely watched by a trained operating engineer observer who carefully rated the individual's performance on the work sample checklist. The work sample checklist was designed to be as behaviorally specific as possible so that the observer needed to make only the minimum inference about whether the person being observed performed well or not. For example, apprentices being assessed on their operation of the asphalt paving equipment were required to operate that equipment to pave a stretch of roadbed. The work sample test for the asphalt paving machine assessed performance on a number of other tasks as well, including loading and unloading equipment from a trailer and operating a roller.

MEASUREMENT ISSUES IN SELECTION

Psychologists have spent many years refining technical concepts—notably, those of reliability and validity, important underpinnings to selection systems. As characteristics of an assessment, reliability and validity are highly relevant to FJA-based selection and greatly increase the likelihood that a selection system is sound in its treatment of job applicants. An assessment is reliable if consistent scores result from it. For example, scores on the work sample checklist for the operating engineers in the previous section were consistent—that is, reliable—to the extent that two trained observers independently gave the same (or nearly the same) ratings to a trainee. Different observers who watch the same person perform a work sample and who are consistent in their ratings provide a basis on which to claim that the assessment is thorough enough to justify certifying the applicant as an apprentice.

Validity is the sine qua non of selection testing. Showing that the behaviors and results identified in the task analysis correspond to the items in the test, questions in the employment interview, or behaviors asked for in the performance test demonstrates validity. Known as *content validation,* this approach is a primary means by which FJA-based selection instruments are validated. Showing that the scores on the assessment are related statistically to some criterion of interest to the organization provides a second means of validation. This is commonly referred to as *criterion-related validation.* For example, the job compatibility measure described earlier in this chapter was correlated by the researchers (Villanova et al., 1994) to both job performance and turnover. In both instances, the measure was found to be predictive of the respective criteria.

Construct-oriented validation, a third approach to validation, requires a number of empirical studies to establish that the test measures what it says it measures. For reasons of practicality and economy, it is uncommon for organizations to invest in this type of validation when FJA is used. For FJA selection, the reliance is heaviest on content validation, with some criterion-related validation where time and money allow.

Regardless of the validation strategy used, many practitioners have to rely on the assistance of measurement specialists to help design and conduct the necessary research. The same holds for assessment of reliability of FJA-based instruments. However, in addition to its technical merits, the selection device should have *face validity;* that is, it should look job-related to the applicants and engender the feeling that the organization knows what it is doing in selection and is giving all job candidates a fair chance to show their best.

SUMMARY OF SELECTION TESTING

In recent years employers have become more careful about hiring. As competition in the global marketplace intensifies, they seek hiring methods that are more valid for selecting the best performers. Add to this the need for nondiscriminatory selection and the promotion of a trusting relationship between applicant and employer and the substantial challenge to managers is manifest.

FJA takes a behavioral approach to addressing these challenges. It is highly suited to both structured interviewing and performance testing as well as types of paper-and-pencil testing that focus on past experience or task preference. When properly developed, these behavioral predictors have had the following advantages:

- good reliability
- good-to-excellent validity
- little or no adverse impact against minority groups
- good face validity to job applicants

Modern psychology tends to use selection predictors that partialize and label applicants into one or a few narrow categories of their capabilities (e.g., cognitive ability, mechanical aptitude, spatial ability). FJA works against this trend by preferring to relate functional capabilities to performance testing thereby allowing a fuller range of worker potential to be assessed in selection.

Chapter 12

Selection — Interviewing Applicants

The purpose of a selection interview is to identify the best person for a job from a short list of candidates. Although interviews are a very popular means of selection and promotion, they are often done poorly. The usual interview is an unstructured, rambling conversation with the interviewer asking the following types of questions:

- Why do you want this job?
- What can you do for our company?
- Tell me about yourself.

Unstructured interviews, because of their lack of focus and job-relevant questions, are poor at identifying the best candidates for a job or promotion. Structured interviews, on the other hand, ask job-relevant questions that can considerably improve an employer's ability to select the best candidate—a person whose skills are best matched to requirements. This section discusses how FJA can be used to structure an interview so employers have a better chance of selecting or promoting the right person. It also shows how to use FJA to present a realistic job preview during the interview, thus promoting applicant self-selection and contributing to a more satisfied worker.

THE PROBLEM WITH UNSTRUCTURED INTERVIEWS

The great strength of an interview is its one-on-one nature and its purposefulness. However, the problem with an unstructured interview is its lack of an objective screen to sort out dissimulation on the part of an interviewee eager to be hired. Although interviewers may be braced for and trained to see through dissimulation, what ensues in an unstructured interview is a game of who can come out a winner, obviously a very subjective process that calls into question the results of interviews.

Various means have been introduced to capitalize on the strengths of an interview and to control its subjectivity, including fixing the time, specifying the questions, devising scoring schemes for the interviewee's answers, and devising scales for evaluating the interviewee's behavior. On the whole, these attempts to structure an interview have had considerable success in improving the predictive efficiency of the selection interview by establishing a common context within which the interview takes place. Wiesner and Cronshaw (1988) obtained convincing empirical evidence of this. They combined the results of criterion-related validation studies from around the world into a single database and sought out previously published individual studies in the industrial psychology and HRM literature that examined the correlation between interview ratings and criteria of success on the job. Wiesner and Cronshaw quantitatively combined the results of these individual studies into a larger meta-analysis to determine whether there was an overall pattern to the correlations reported individually. Their results showed that structured interviews predict job success twice as well as unstructured interviews and that structured interviews rivaled, and even exceeded, the best prediction achieved by selection tests. Structured interviews made their best predictions when the interview questions were based on a formal job analysis such as FJA. Subsequent research to follow up on the Wiesner and Cronshaw study has closely borne out their conclusions about the predictive efficacy of structured interviews (Huffcutt & Arthur, 1994).

FJA, when combined with generally accepted rules for structuring interviews, helps increase interview validity. It provides for a greater degree of objectivity because questions are anchored in the task bank of the job for which applicants are applying. The particular focus of the questions is on the adaptive and functional skills required to do the job. The questions related to adaptive skills originate in (a) the known conditions—physical, social, and environmental—in which the job–worker situation occurs, and in (b) the level of effort and responsibility needed to achieve the performance standards. The questions related to functional skills originate directly from the information contained in the task statements describing functional performance and the associated performance standards.

OPENING THE FJA INTERVIEW

Many activities precede an FJA interview. Applicants have already been given information about the organization and the particular job for which they are applying. They have been shown a degree of openness and sharing that may be unusual to them. Where a PEQ is used, they have, in turn, shared a good deal of information about themselves in addition to the traditional application form. The interview thus becomes an occasion for affirmation and confirmation of the exchanged information.

A good way to open the interview, after the exchange of amenities and establishing rapport, is to simply ask: "Do you have any questions/comments about the information you have received concerning the job or the organization?" With this question, the interviewer comes down from a position of power (to say yes or no to hiring) and extends the sharing that was initiated earlier. The interviewer now listens carefully for the applicant's work needs, which express themselves through the questions he or she asks. Melohn (1994) explained this approach in the following way:

> After the first introductory five minutes, I ask each candidate if he or she has any questions about our company or job opening. Then I just listen. Sometimes the silence is deafening. But I keep quiet. Sooner or later, they'll speak up. And that's when I learn, really learn about the other person. (p. 97)

An applicant's questions are most likely directed to one or more of the growth areas—compensation, skill, and status—discussed in chapter 10. More alert applicants show an interest in the organization and some indication that they have checked it out. They may ask, "Where was the organization 5 years ago, and where does it hope to be 5 years from now? I would like to get an idea of how I can help the organization to get there." Applicants' preferred growth area(s) need to be noted for review when the final hiring decision is made.

USING FJA TO ASSESS ADAPTIVE SKILLS OF JOB APPLICANTS

Adaptive skills involve those competencies that come into play in the management of oneself in regard to conformity and change. Basically, adaptive skills' most obvious indicator is willingness. If workers are willing to engage in the work setting and remain on the job, they draw on their adaptive skills to bring their functional and specific content skills into high gear. (*Willingness* is a worker's heartfelt commitment to put forth the mental and physical effort, to persist in achieving results, and to accept responsibility as part and parcel of the job.) As the expression of this willingness, an adaptive skill usually surfaces across several tasks written into the task bank.

To ask a structured interview question assessing adaptive skill, an interviewer can invite the applicant to think of a prior situation that closely matches the environment he or she will work in after hire. Called a behavior description (BD) question, this interviewing method draws on work pioneered by Janz and colleagues (Janz, Hellervik, & Gilmore, 1986). For example, to assess the adaptive skill required of field engineers working for a large medical equipment manufacturing company, a structured interview question would be based on the field engineers' task bank: "Work in a team relationship, share expertise, and accommodate to other field engineers." The question, with probes, could be:

> Describe a time when you were working with others on a team. Think of a time when things were not going so well. What was the situation? Who were you working with? What happened in the team? What role did you play and what did you do? How did you feel at the time? What was the final outcome? What did the team produce as a final result?

Responses to such structured interview questions are best rated on a performance scale and the scores on the scales combined into an overall interview score. One method shown to be quite successful is to develop a 5-point rating scale for each interview question: 5 (*an outstanding response*) to 1 (*a poor response*). The 5, 3, and 1 are anchored on the rating scale with performance standards from the task bank or with information specially collected from job incumbents and supervisors. Table 12.1 illustrates a rating scale used to score applicant responses to the previous interview question for the job of field engineer.

TABLE 12.1
Example of Rating Scale for Scoring BD Interview Questions
Assessing Adaptive Skills

Score	According to Depth of Response
5	Remained open to inputs of all team members even if the situation was tense and difficult. Freely shared own expertise with all team members, as it was needed, even if not asked. Remained calm with a professional demeanor. Accommodated to working styles and needs of all members even if this was personally inconvenient or uncomfortable.
4	
3	Attempted to listen to other team members' concerns and input. Shared own expertise if it was asked for. Recognized needs of other group members and tried to work with them if it was not too difficult to do so. Felt frustrated but kept his or her "cool."
2	
1	Became frustrated and angry. Withheld information from team members to increase own power, placate others, or avoid having to take responsibility for making a mistake/offending others. Ignored the inputs and suggestions of others or told them to keep their ideas to themselves. Expected others to work strictly to his or her own style and needs.

The previous example is written as a BD question that follows through on the basis of actual experiences. That some applicants may not have this experience or, if they do, cannot remember the details of events some time ago limits this approach. The interviewer might then ask the same question in a different way. For example, if the applicant had no team experience, the interviewer might ask a previously prepared question based on a hypothetical scenario meant to tap into the same adaptive skill. Such a question for the field engineers (FE) could be:

> You are a field engineer who has just joined a team of four engineers repairing a large and expensive piece of diagnostic medical equipment for a large hospital. The repairs have already begun but the other engineers have serious differences of opinion among themselves about how the repair job should proceed. One of the other team members, who you recognize as the informal leader of the team, takes you aside and asks you to side with him in the disagreement. You are to support whatever he says so that the team can get on with doing the repairs his way and finish up before 9:00 a.m. the next day (failure to complete repairs by the deadline will probably result in the team losing the hospital account). Describe in detail what you should do in this situation and provide a rationale for your actions.

Responses to this question can be scored on the same rating scale as the BD by changing the stem to read, "*If the applicant's response shows that he or she would,*" for example, remain open to inputs (see Latham, Saari, Pursell, & Campion, 1980).

FJA interviews need to contain questions assessing candidates' willingness to use the mix of prescription and discretion demanded, exert the requisite effort, assume the level of responsibility required, and work under the environmental conditions prevalent in the work site. Additionally, questions assessing adaptive skills more or less specific to that job context are necessary. For the FEs, these adaptive skills include, "stay with a repair until the equipment is working reliably and satisfactorily," and, for a transit operator, "drive vehicle carefully and safely, especially when under pressure." Most of the questions formulated to probe for adaptive skills derive from the task statements and performance standards in the task bank. For example, the transit operator will have at least several task statements on driving the vehicle (starting, steering, stopping to pick passengers, and so on). Performance standards for these tasks may include turning corners without jostling passengers and coming to a complete stop before opening the doors to let out disembarking passengers. All of these tasks are done and the standards met under a tight, or even unrealistic, time schedule. Taken together, these tasks and performance standards support the inference of the adaptive skill "drive vehicle carefully and safely, especially when under pressure"—an adaptive skill described by participants in the original FJA focus group (see chap. 7 on conducting the FJA focus group).

USING FJA TO ASSESS FUNCTIONAL SKILLS

The interview can then proceed to applicants' work experience focusing on their functional skills. It is, of course, necessary to avoid querying about familiarity with specific content skills. Beyond what has been described in the announcement of the vacancy, applicants cannot be expected to know the specific content of the job for which they are applying. The FJA task bank however, provides a script for what the applicant can be queried about in the area of functional skills.

When using FJA in an interview to assess functional skills, every job–worker situation will have, in addition to the task bank, summary ratings containing the three highest functions and their accompanying orientation weights. For example, suppose the vacancy for which applicants are being interviewed is that of community development officer. The functions and weights for this job worker situation are:

Things:	1A	Handling	10
Data:	5A	Innovating	60
People:	4A	Consulting	30

This summary data tells the interviewer what needs to be looked for in the applicant: primarily, ability to *compile, analyze, and use data innovatively* as it relates to community development work and secondarily, ability to *source information and consult* with significant people both in and outside an organization in order to secure the information and develop ideas on how to use the information for useful social purposes. The emphasis is on the functional abilities in whatever context they may have occurred.

The task bank provides the actual tasks as a point of departure for the questions asked. In the case of the community development officer, a key task at the data functional level of Innovating (5A) is:

Review/rewrite refunding proposals for community programs, drawing on preexisting proposals, projected changes in the program, and funding service specifications, relying on writing skills and experience in preparing proposals *in order to* secure continued funding for the specified program.

This task converts to the following BD interview question:

Question 12.1
Describe an experience you have had that involved putting together a lot of information in response to a request for a proposal. How did you approach the task and decide which information to include and which to exclude? How was the proposal received? What was the final outcome?

TABLE 12.2
Example of Rating Scale for Scoring BD Interview Questions
Assessing Data Functional Skills

Score	According to Depth of Response
5	Drew on all relevant information, including preexisting proposals and funding requirements. Organized and presented data within (re)funding proposal in a highly effective manner. Was successful in obtaining all of the funding requested in the proposal.
4	
3	Drew on only relevant, although incomplete, information. Organized and presented data within (re)funding proposal in a satisfactory, but not outstanding manner. Obtained at least most of the funds requested.
2	
1	Drew on inaccurate, or otherwise inadequate, information. Data was poorly/ineffectively organized and presented within the (re)funding proposal. Funding was refused.

These questions are designed to show how the candidate deals with the analysis and workup of data. The scoring points, drawing on the performance standards corresponding to that task, would relate to (a) the apparent thoroughness of the data considered, (b) the way the data was organized and presented, and (c) the success of the proposal in getting funded. These performance standards can be summarized in the rating scale for Question 12.1 found in Table 12.2.

The questions that pertain to consulting (Level 4A—People scale) would be based on the FJA tasks that are assigned to that level. For example, consider the following task for the community development officer:

Present information about services offered by agency to a group (e.g., senior citizens, youth, persons in need of energy assistance) in response to direct requests or requests made to administrative heads of agency, by phone or letter, drawing on knowledge of the agency, its personnel and programs, assembled materials (brochures and the like), and assistance from supervisors or specialists of particular programs, and relying on communication and presentation skills *in order to* inform requesting group.

As indicated, the requirements of such a task are, "communication and presentation skills," which translates in this job to the ability to deal and communicate with diverse groups of people in an informed and sophisticated way. The interviewer needs to know if the candidate has had experience or proclivities along these lines. The questions that generate the desired information could be as follows:

Question 12.2

Tell me about a time when you went to authorities or gatekeepers in order to get the information necessary to do your work, for example, specialists and librarians. What were those sources? What was the information you needed? Did this involve personal interviews and/or simply arrangements with people to get at the data? Did you obtain the required information? How did you use this information later?

Question 12.3

Describe a time when you made a presentation to a group or consulted with peers. What was the nature of the material you presented or consulted about? What were the organizational or professional levels of the people you dealt with? What happened during the presentation? What was the final outcome?

These questions are designed to see how the candidate has adapted to and worked with people. The scoring points include (a) the preparation necessary to have an effective meeting with people, (b) the apparent challenge in making an impact on the audience, and (c) the success of the interpersonal contact. The rating scale for Question 12.2 based on these performance standards is found in Table 12.3.

As with the interview questions for adaptive skills, situational questions can be asked as alternatives to BD questions when the applicant cannot describe a past incident involving the behavior the interviewer is looking for.

TABLE 12.3
Example of Rating Scale for Scoring BD Interview Questions
Assessing People Functional Skills

Score	According to Depth of Response
5	Prepared thoroughly for upcoming meeting. Obtained all required information in a timely manner with full cooperation or presented/consulted in a highly effective way for the given audience. Completed work ahead of schedule or received highly positive feedback from audience or others on presentation/consulting assignment.
4	
3	Anticipated problems with authorities/gatekeepers or needs of audience beforehand. Obtained necessary information, made a satisfactory presentation, or had satisfactory consultation. Completed work within the deadline and received positive feedback from audience or others on presentation/consulting assignment.
2	
1	Did not prepare beforehand for meeting, presentation, or consulting assignment ("winged it"). Failed to persuade others or had an unsatisfactory presentation/ consulting assignment. Did not complete work on time or received complaints on communication and presentation skills.

These questions and corresponding rating scales are similar to the situational question illustrating adaptive skills in the previous section.

CLOSING THE INTERVIEW

After the questions assessing adaptive and functional skills are asked, the interview moves into its final phase with the interviewer asking the applicant if he or she has further questions. Applicants sometimes ask about the intention behind certain questions presented during the interview. In answering, the interviewer needs to explain that the questions originate in the work or in the training the new worker will receive. The interviewer, however, should avoid giving away the anchors on the interview rating scales (applicants may discuss the "right" answer among themselves, and so undermine the validity of the interview when subsequently used). After telling the applicant when and how he or she will be informed of the final hiring decision, the interviewer thanks the applicant and politely shares with him or her mutual good-byes.

MAKING THE FINAL HIRING DECISION

After the applicant leaves, the interviewer reads the interview notes and totals the ratings on the questions. The interviewer should look for consistency between the applicant's attitude at the opening of the interview and answers to the adaptive skill questions, for example, an applicant who asks about growth and challenge in the job is likely to do well on interview questions tapping into willingness to exercise discretion.

When tests are used to prescreen applicants for an interview shortlist, many employers rank applicants top-down in order of their total structured interview score. The first-ranked applicant is made the job offer with the second-ranked applicant held in reserve in case the top candidate refuses. Other employers set a minimum cut score on the interview and make an offer to those candidates above the cut.

TRAINING INTERVIEWERS

When used properly, the strength of the FJA interview is twofold:

- It avoids stereotyping the job applicant.
- It prevents intrusion of job-irrelevant information.

However, extensive interview training and experience is needed in order to use the FJA-based behavioral description interview properly. Training for the FJA interview focuses on acquiring the skills needed to meet the following seven interviewer responsibilities (these points are modified from an FJA interview-training program designed by Whelly and Cronshaw):

- Establish and maintain a positive, nonthreatening atmosphere for the interview.
- Question and probe effectively following the FJA interview questions.
- Use effective listening skills, focus especially on critical incidents indicating superior or poor performance.
- Display sensitivity toward the applicant, especially when discomfort is evident.
- Keep notes that are supportive of ratings.
- Understand the job as contained in the FJA task bank and the rationale for the FJA interview based on those job requirements.
- Maintain control over the interview, not relinquishing it to highly verbal and interview-wise candidates.

If two or more interviewers work as a panel, they need to discuss their individual ratings and reach consensus on them after the interview is complete. They also need training in discussing and reaching consensus on interview ratings. FJA interview training should always include a substantial practice component whereby interviewers administer the questions to each other and exchange constructive feedback to improve their interview style and technique.

SUMMARY OF SELECTION INTERVIEWING

The interview takes place after standardized psychological and performance testing is completed although in many smaller organizations the interview is the only assessment of the job applicant. The purpose of the FJA interview is to complete the holistic picture of the applicant that emerged with selection testing. Where the interview is the only selection predictor, it paints a picture of the applicant's capabilities in the areas of adaptive and functional skill. Its proper use requires considerable interviewer skill, but the FJA interview has the advantage of having the FJA task bank as a point of departure to keep both interviewer and applicant focused on the job requirements. The FJA interview can communicate a positive image about an organization. There is a no-nonsense, high quality, fudging-will-not-get-by aspect to this approach that is likely to lead to a greater frequency of job offer acceptances by those applicants the organization most wants to attract. Last, but certainly not least, interview structuring of the type proposed in this chapter is shown by research to increase the efficiency of the interview for predicting job success once the applicant is hired.

Chapter **13**

Training—
Improving Worker Skill

Some years ago, an automobile industry executive is reported to have said to his staff: "We are not in the business of building cars. We are in the transportation business!" Presumably, that statement was inspirational, designed to broaden the vision and aspirations of his workforce, and it seems to have had the desired effect. Over the past few years we have heard similar adjurations made to workers in the radio field ("you are in the communications business") and in the book field ("you are in the information business"). Granted, a motive behind these adjurations is to increase market share. It is also an appeal to see the big picture and involve workers beyond the immediate outputs of their jobs. Involving workers in this manner draws in the whole person and his or her full range of capabilities, not just the part of the person serving as an instrument of production.

As workers become more intensely involved on the job, their skills are challenged and management as well as workers must make a greater investment in training. By providing training, management can meet two fundamental objectives. The first objective is to bring the worker and manager into a healthy, productive relationship. This is not a choice. For good or bad, a relationship is on the line—either it will be cemented or sundered. Is this not as it should be if, as most organizations state, their human resources are indeed their most valuable asset? Ultimately, the combined efforts of management and the workforce satisfy customers and contribute to the total quality required to serve and please them. Management's fundamental role in the relationship needs to be overseeing, guiding, and facilitating this desirable outcome.

Once a worker is hired and a commitment made between the worker and management, a relationship is entered. Training provides the primary vehicle for the relationship to be affirmed or disconfirmed. Trust is on the line. If by its actions, management shows consideration for workers' job context as well as job-content needs, then competency and flexibility naturally follows. This is not to say it happens spontaneously, but if the relationship is positive—accommodating, caring, respectful, and professionally appropriate—workers naturally seek to achieve competence and flexibility because it is in their best self-interest to do so.

Thus the first objective of management in providing training is to be aware it is building a relationship, and this relationship can be regarded as the infrastructure within which all future problems can be dealt with constructively. Among other things, this means that although trainees and management are likely to make mistakes, they can be absorbed in the ongoing activity of the organization. It also means that from the very induction of the worker into the organization, sharing needs to occur. Through sharing and trust a positive relationship is created. This chapter shows how FJA can serve to facilitate this relationship.

The second objective of training is to help the worker come into *flow*. Csikzentmihalyi (1997), in his very insightful thinking and research, has described flow as a psychologically rewarding and productive state of total involvement in an activity, whether on or off the job. In FJA terms, flow occurs when the whole person becomes involved on the job, fully and optimally utilizing his or her TDP and adaptive potentials in achieving a desired result. When flow is achieved, the doubt of people is buffeted and jostled by organizational forces beyond their control and the awkwardness of self-concern melts away. The flow of a consciousness engaged in effortless action and comfortable task mastery replaces people's second-guessing of their adequacy for the task at hand. In Czikzentmihalyi's words, "Flow tends to occur when a person's skills are fully involved in overcoming a challenge that is just about manageable" (1997, p. 30). Flow is an optimal state happening all too infrequently in the average person's life. And flow is all too frequently frustrated, rather than facilitated, by the learning situations people are put into.

A few more words on flow are needed to fully demonstrate the usefulness of FJA in facilitating flow through training. Csikszentmihalyi (1997) pointed to the conditions that must exist before people can come into flow:

• *A clear and consistent set of goals.* In FJA, these goals are referred to as results and follow from the actions described in the task statements. Locke and Latham (1990) in their research on goal setting further specify that these goals should be challenging but not impossible if individual performance is to improve (or as Csikszentmihalyi says, if the person is to achieve flow).

• *Immediate feedback to individuals on how they are doing on the task.* FJA provides this information when workers compare themselves to the per-

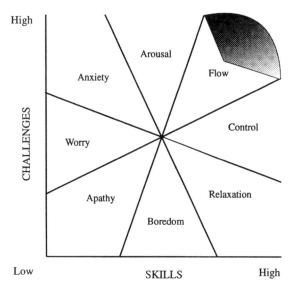

FIG. 13.1.   The quality of experience as function of the relationship between challenges and skills. (From M. Csikszentmihalyi, 1997, *Finding Flow: The Psychology of Engagement With Everyday Life* (p. 31). Copyright 1997. Reprinted with permission.

formance standards for the job while listening to the input of coworkers, supervisors, and subordinates.

• *Flow occurs when a person is working at the upper limits of his or her capabilities but is not overtaxed.* That is, a fine balance must be maintained between the challenge in the work and the skills a person can bring to bear in meeting the challenge. This principle is illustrated in Fig. 13.1, reproduced from Csikszentmihalyi's work. The optimal emotional state for the worker, and the state of greatest worker growth and productivity, is achieved in the area of the figure labeled "flow" where both challenge and skill are high. The greatest gains in worker skills from training occur for both the organization and the worker when the training of worker skills is stimulated by a high—but not excessive—level of challenge introduced into the workplace by management.

Relationship and flow are flip sides of the same coin. A management that sets up the right conditions for a trusting relationship and shared interpretation of experience has created conditions that can lead to flow. FJA provides a practical training tool for making the connection between the Worker and Work Organization, the skill and challenge essential to achieving and maintaining flow.

INITIAL ORIENTATION TO THE WORK PLACE

The worker has been hired. Management has determined the worker is qualified—he or she has the functional and adaptive skills to learn to do the work and fit into the culture of the organization—but flow has yet to occur. The worker has accepted management's vision of opportunity and is ready to give it a try. The first opportunity for management to initiate and cement a relationship and set the conditions for achieving flow comes at the worker's orientation to the workplace. What was presented as a vision of opportunity when worker and management first met, must now be related to the individual in the policies and procedures of the organization. Now it is the worker's turn to determine if this new situation will meet his or her needs.

The initial orientation takes as long as necessary to convey the organization's productivity mission, goals, and values. Although this is an ongoing activity, it initially calls for explicitness. Various media—print, audiovisual, video, or lecture/discussion—can be used for this purpose, usually in some felicitous combination. The mission and values can be stated explicitly in an organization manual issued to each new worker. They can also be printed on attractive charts, framed, and hung or posted throughout the organization's premises. An example of a clearly written mission statement is that of Starbucks Coffee Company given in Figure 13.2.

Benefits need to be described in relation to the organization's values. It is best if benefits flow from the organization's values rather than coercion from the government or contracts resolving labor-management relations. Many organizations insist their most valuable asset is their workforce. If this is so, how is it valued? For example, what is the pay system? (The market price for labor plays an important role in arriving at pay scales; this information needs to be shared.) What is the role of individual merit in achieving more pay? Does seniority play a part or, as seems to be the case today, is this less a factor? Does increasing experience in doing one's job— in effect becoming more valuable to the organization—play a role in receiving higher pay?

This is a good time to have a look at the organization's balance sheet over the past several years. Has its market penetration been increasing, decreasing, or is it static? What are the expectations in the short and long run? What plans have been made in connection with these expectations? What is the role of the workforce in these plans, particularly its growth and training? Do specific technological developments have a role in future expectations? What is the competition like, and how can workers best equip themselves to deal with the competition?

Establish Starbucks as the premier purveyor of the finest coffee in the world while maintaining our uncompromising principles as we grow. The following six guiding principles will help us measure the appropriateness of our decisions:

1. *Provide a great work environment and treat each other with respect and dignity.*
2. *Embrace diversity as an essential component in the way we do business.*
3. *Apply the highest standards of excellence to the purchasing, roasting and fresh delivery of our coffee.*
4. *Develop enthusiastically satisfied customers all of the time.*
5. *Contribute positively to our communities and our environment.*
6. *Recognize that profitability is essential to our future success.*

FIG. 13.2. Mission statement for Starbucks Coffee Company. From S. Balaban, C. Keita, D. Lunger, T. Lutz, & M. Wachiralapphaithoon (n.d.), *Starbucks Coffee Company* [Online]. Available at http://cpba.louisville.edu/bruce/cases/Starbucks/Starbucks.htm. Reprinted with permission.

Are there health care benefits? How are they paid for—by the organization, by the worker, or both? Are these benefits transportable or do health benefits cease if the worker is separated from the organization? What allowances are made for sickness? What about leave in case of family illness or emergency needs? Does the organization have or sponsor a day-care facility or make any allowance for day care? Are flexible hours a consideration? Are employee benefits one size fits all or is there flexibility for employees to choose "cafeteria style" among a range of benefit options?

What is the organization's policy with regard to disabilities? How does it accommodate persons with physical and/or emotional disabilities as required by law? Does it have a nonsmoking environment?

Does the organization give any support to growth and development relevant to the work assignment and pursued by the individual in educational institutions outside the organization? How are these opportunities for growth accessed in the organization?

Does it have a benefit policy with regard to temporary and part-time employment? Does part-time employment lead to full-time employment? Does the organization contract out work to independent entrepreneurs in competition with its workforce?

As far as being valued as a member of the organization's workforce, these and related questions are the bottom line. An organization's response to the previous considerations shows whether an organization is really interested in workers as whole persons and therefore willing to share their concerns. From this context stems the stimulus for the effort, responsibility, and resourcefulness that lead to effective performance and flexibility on the part of the worker.

TRAINING FOR COMPETENCY

The worker's ability to learn and follow SOP form his or her basis for competency. SOPs are the crystallization of the organization's experience in achieving its productivity. SOPs include specifications for the output that represent the standards to which the organization is working. They also include the methodologies (machines, tools, equipment, work aids) that can best help it achieve its objectives. Learning SOPs are at the heart of acquiring specific content skills, the skills necessary to achieve the performance standards that enable the organization to effectively compete in the market.

To one degree or another, the organization strives to be up to date in its SOPs so that it can be competitive in the market. SOPs develop from the interaction of management and workers on a daily basis in the process of dealing with problems of production and implementation of policy. Problems are inevitable. SOPs have never, and can never account for all the contingencies that arise in the normal course of production activity. In a sense, management and workers are in a constant state of mutual training and development. Thus, bringing new persons on board involves giving them a running start so they can more easily hop on an already-moving vehicle. How can this best be done?

One way is to assign trainees to an experienced worker who serves as a coach or sponsor. (In the past supervisors have undertaken this role; in today's labor force this role is frequently assigned to experienced workers and is seen as a way to enhance their jobs.) Such coaching must be made an integral part of the experienced worker's job along with the expectation that their productivity will be slowed down. The coach becomes the active element in building a relationship. Essentially the relationship is of the journeyperson/apprentice form and an example of learning by doing. In addition to instructing and guiding the trainee, the coach encourages the trainee to ask for help and clarification in order to avoid costly errors. Learning to do the job right is often a collaboration.

The trainee/coach relationship can begin by using the FJA task bank as a basic reference for the work to be done and the challenges to be met. From the task bank, trainees obtain an idea of outputs, knowledges and resources involved, tasks performed, functional skills that come into play, and the results of the activity. The focus of the training provided by the coach is the FJA task paradigm: "To do this task to these standards you need this training." Especially important for the coach is to point out to the trainees how the prescriptive elements of the tasks contribute to the standards of the outputs. These are the more objective aspects of the SOPs. It is equally important for the coach to call attention to the use of discretion in situations that cannot be completely prescribed. This is often overlooked. The need to use discretion is especially challenging and allows a worker in flow to function more as a whole person, bringing experience and resourcefulness into play.

For a limited period of time, the trainees are observers, asking the inevitable questions that come up during observation of an actual performance. Gradually, the coach allows trainees to try their hand in performing the tasks, helping them to stay focused on results, providing continuous and immediate feedback, accommodating awkwardness and failure, and allowing practice to refine performance. In this way, the relationship is cemented and the worker moves toward flow.

There is no precise way to prescribe the trainee–coach relationship other than having the coach serve as a resource, support, and positive reinforcer of the trainee. Possibly, the coach's own initiation into the organization can serve as a model for the role he or she is asked to perform. Training to become a coach and additional compensation are reasonable incentives for an individual to take on the work of coaching.

Another approach to the induction of the trainee into the organization is assignment to a team engaged in carrying out a specific objective. The trainee can come under the wing of a single team member acting as a coach or can be rotated systematically among the team members—a matter for the team to decide. In either case, the trainee once again is required to learn by doing—a demystification process whereby the trainee gradually sees how all the pieces in the puzzle (all the tasks in the task bank) are put together to produce the outputs that achieve the organizational objectives. As a part of this process, the trainee gets a clearer picture of the results he or she is to achieve and learns where to look and to ask for the feedback needed to stay on target. Here again the emphasis is on collaboration—on relationship—and the possibility of achieving flow as a member of a team performing a challenging assignment.

ONGOING TRAINING AND DEVELOPMENT

After a brief period of "getting their feet wet," doing some things well and others not so well, new workers may need additional training in specific content skills that neither a coach nor a team can handle in the normal course of operations. The worker may need additional knowledge and skill practice to be fully functional and to move toward flow in a challenging situation. Use of the FJA task bank can pinpoint this need. Workers can check off the particular knowledges and skills for which they need more training—either on the job or in an off-the-job classroom. Figure 13.3 shows such a checklist by field service engineers working in medical electronics. (The numbers in this table represent the responses of a focus group of six job incumbent to each item in the needs analysis checklist.) The training need is identified not only as a subject area but also in relation to the particular tasks in which those subjects are involved. In this situation the task bank serves a dual purpose: (a) as a needs analysis for subjects that need to be taught, and (b) as an index of tasks the subjects must carry out. During training realistic practice exercises can take the form of the tasks that incorporate the requisite knowledge and skills.

WHICH SKILLS CAN BE LEARNED THROUGH TRAINING?

Not all skills are acquired in the same way and not all skills are amenable to training. This must be understood in order to most efficiently and effectively use training and educational resources. Training alone will not produce the sought-after flow—some of the necessary skills must be present at the time a person is hired. Unfortunately, the welter of terminology relating to skills has only added to the confusion over skill acquisition. It is no wonder that educators are confused when confronted with terminology such as cross-functional skills, global objectives, global competencies, transferable skills, broad goals, general goals, basic skills, generic skills, enablers, Work Keys, and SCANS outcomes. Surely a sharper focus on what is meant by skills can lead to an understanding of which skills can best be taught and when, where, and how.

FJA calls attention to three types of skills as simultaneously involved in holistic performance (total quality performance): functional skills, specific content skills, and adaptive skills. If flow is to be achieved, these skills (which represent the gamut of skills required on the job) must be combined smoothly, holistically, and competently in response to some substantial work challenge. Recognition that these skills are learned/acquired under different circumstances is crucial for facilitating the training conditions leading to flow.

> *Functional skills* (cross-functional skills, generic skills, basic skills, core abilities, global competencies) are those competencies performed on levels from simple to complex in relation to the TDP in our environment. They are acquired from birth in the natural course of events and

Please review the **Knowledge** and **Skills/Abilities** lists on this and the next page(s) and check (✓) appropriate spaces according to where you are with each item expressed at the top of each column. If for any item you would like additional training, indicate whether your preference would be for formal, on-the-job training, or both.

	Feel adequate/ competent in the subject	Like more training nevertheless	Formal (workshop)	Informal (on-the job) Job self-study
1. Electronics: Theory		3*	1	2
2. X-Ray Equipment: Imaging Expertise		3	1	2
3. Mechanics, Optics, Physics: as they relate to Imaging Equipment		4	2	1
4. Electricity: Power systems linkage with Imaging Systems		4	2	3
5. Clinical applications (capabilities of equipment) as they relate to anatomy and physiology; understanding limitations of equipment		2	2	

	Feel adequate/ competent in the subject	Like more training nevertheless	Formal (workshop)	Informal (on-the job) Job self-study
1. Zeroing in on technical problems: drawing on technical sophistication to deal with unknown: assessing and locating problems in X-Ray equipment		4	2	
2. Troubleshoot familiar equipment; follow through on alternative paths; skilled use of test equipment		1	1	1
3. Organizing work situation; set priorities; arrange/schedule time; keep things organized, systematic		1	2	
4. Deal with several things (elements of a problem or more than one output) at the same time; parallel processing		1	1	1
5. Communication Skills: Oral (speaking); writing: Adapt communications to situations and persons addressed		2	1	2

FIG. 13.3.   Sample page of needs analysis checklist for field service engineers.

147

later developed through schooling in basic, general subjects such as language and math and activities such as sports

Specific content skills (specific skills, specific competencies, specific objectives) are those competencies acquired to master specific subjects and/ or work procedures in order to meet/fulfill the standards of the disciplines and/or organizations that people propose to serve. Specific content skills involve the application of functional and adaptive skills and are acquired in specific practice or job–worker situations, or frequently, in technical education courses.

Adaptive skills (transferable skills, getting along skills) are those competencies that enable people to manage themselves in relation to conformity and change and are elicited as responses to persons and environments. They reflect temperament and personality as represented by a willingness to engage with, react to, and accommodate contextual situations and are expressed as behavioral styles. They are acquired subconsciously during all forms of life experience and are extremely difficult to teach or train in a cognitive manner.

Many employers feel they should not have to train employees except in specific content skills. These employers would like to believe their hiring procedures are perceptive enough to select persons with the appropriate functional and adaptive skills, persons able to learn what employers have to teach and who can adapt to the conditions provided. The educational system—the schools—face the same problem at earlier stages in people's lives. Schools too expect students to have the level of functional skills appropriate to their age and stage of development plus the adaptive skills usually acquired in the home environment—willingness to be punctual, listen, pay attention, respect authority, practice courtesy, exercise impulse control, perform assignments—so they can acquire the functional and specific subject skills being taught.

This is probably what the report of an independent research and educational organization was referring to when it asserted, "schools transmit important messages about what is and is not acceptable behavior through an 'invisible curriculum'" (Committee for Economic Development [CED], 1985, p. 20). The committee argued: "Schools that develop and reinforce good habits, shared values, and high standards of behavior are most likely to produce graduates who succeed in higher education and work." They urged schools and teachers "to institute policies and practices that are specifically designed to encourage self-discipline, reliability, perseverance, and other positive traits" (p. 20).

The skills Butler (author of CED report) mentions are adaptive skills, and he is correct in calling them "an invisible curriculum." They are as invisible as water is to the fish that swim in it. Before schools can teach their subject matter, they must have an environment, an infrastructure, in which students are willing to learn. Schools must create an ambience in which self-discipline, responsibility, and self-reliance are natural. School curricula must be embedded in contextual situations that require these traits, and faculty behavior must provide positive reinforcement for their appropriate expression. This means that school faculty must meet the children halfway, be nurturing not punitive, caring not harsh. Schools cannot teach these traits; they can only make students aware of their importance, draw them out of their everyday behavior, and reinforce them.

In an FJA focus group, adaptive skills do not come up directly. They almost always come up indirectly in response to the last question, "What performance standards do you work to achieve, both your own and those of the organization?" Probably the reason they come up in this discussion is that meeting standards is a matter of willingness. The kinds of adjustments and adaptations people grudgingly or willingly make in the job–worker situation help define people's personal style.

Adaptive skills are deep-seated in the personality of the individual. More than any other skills they are integral and reflect behavioral styles. More than any other skills they move with the individual and are represented in the worker's lifestyle and adjustment to a work situation. Often an individual will make fundamental decisions, for example, to stay on or leave a job, on the basis of adaptive skills. It behooves management to avoid being overoptimistic about the possibility of training adaptive skills. Adaptive skills develop over a long time period and in response to general life experiences in which the organization can, and should, play only its limited part. When examined from the perspective of flow, it is clear that the essential adaptive skills must be in place for a worker to achieve the flow state talked about by Csikszentmihalyi (1975, 1997). Without these essential adaptive skills, workers lack the basic willingness needed to tackle challenging goals and to stretch their skill set into new domains. An appreciation of the role of adaptive skills can help the organization be more realistic about what it can and cannot expect as returns for a given amount of time and money it puts into training.

TRAINING AND EXPERIENCE

Training in a particular discipline is the beginning of experience. Experience has two aspects. The first aspect is the application of tried-and-true procedures to deal with everyday problems occurring as part of a discipline. The first aspect gives workers the opportunity to build up a database, which can be shared with other workers in the field. The second aspect deals with individual solutions to problems not covered by existing organizational procedures. These are situations in which workers have to use discretion in place of, or to modify, SOP. In these instances, workers may have another ally to support their personal judgment, namely peers or supervisors.

Through experience in a supportive training environment with challenging goals, workers build self-confidence, a feeling of mastery, and self-esteem—and they move toward flow. A supportive environment embraces an openness, a tolerance for failure and its role in the learning process, particularly in the early stages of job learning. It also provides a clear picture of the results required on the job and constant feedback as to how the trainee is doing. Training provides the knowledge and skill to perform assignments using the appropriate mix of prescription and discretion. Experience provides the added confidence to use personal judgment in moving beyond SOPs to deal with unique events in the workplace for which generalized rules have not yet been developed.

INTERPRETING PERFORMANCE STANDARDS
FOR TRAINING DESIGN

Setting clear and unambiguous goals (called *results* at the worker level) is crucial if the worker is to get the most out of training and have a chance of achieving flow on the job. The task bank is a basic tool to which workers and coaches can refer for the desired results. The basic question they must always keep in mind when using the task bank is, "What training is needed to perform this task to these standards?" If total quality and individual worker flow is to result, everyone involved must focus on and understand with unwavering clarity the performance standards associated with the tasks in the task bank. Some organizations monitor workers on a continuous basis (e.g., supervisors listen in to operators handling telephone inquiries). They can best use the resulting performance information by providing nonpunitive feedback and by coaching workers to help them do their jobs better. The overriding principle is that when workers know the standards, they can judge for themselves the adequacy of their performance and make necessary adjustments.

Through its training and supervisory structure, the work-doing system —organization or agency—can ensure that the results of the tasks performed are in fact contributing to its objectives and goals. Theoretically, all tasks performed in an organization should be clearly understood and contribute to the organization's objectives. However, unless the expected results of the tasks and their respective performance standards are specified during training or at the time they are assigned, workers will have a difficult time giving the organization what it wants. Clarification of results and standards is made easier if the employer helps the workers distinguish between the prescriptive and discretionary elements of their tasks during training.

Performance standards are of two types: *descriptive* and *quantifiable*. Descriptive standards are generally nonspecific and subjective; for example, "please type this letter as quickly as possible," "be reasonably accurate in checking these figures," "be as complete as possible in collecting the information," "don't spend too much time in compiling this report." They are in effect discretionary instructions. They tell the worker in general terms what is to be achieved, but the worker must provide his or her own interpretation of what the manager means by "as quickly as possible," "reasonably accurate," "don't spend too much time."

New workers in training could be quite uncomfortable with such standards. With experience, workers in this situation become familiar with the standards expected, and, in fact, become confident enough in their abilities to impose their own discretionary judgments. Unfortunately, workers are too often called to account when their personal judgment calls are unsatisfactory while, at the same time, they go unrecognized and unacknowledged when they do precisely what was expected. This is bound to undermine both self-esteem and self-confidence and workers will be unwilling to take risks or undertake higher levels of challenge due to the anticipation of negative consequences for failure. If workers are unwilling to take risks or tackle work challenges, they will exercise only the minimum of worker discretion and total quality will be impossible.

Quantifiable standards are prescriptive performance criteria that require little if any interpretation. They usually take the form of numerical or categorical statements, e.g., "please have this letter typed by 5 p.m." "please double-check these figures to ensure there are no errors," "have this report compiled by next Monday at noon." Because they are objective, they explicitly communicate the standards by which the worker's performance will be assessed on the job. Presumably the standards have been derived directly from the objectives and desired ambience for the organization.

Task statements prepared by using the FJA technique provide a basis for determining the standards of successful performance. For example, take the task statement used previously:

> Ask client questions, listen to responses, and write answers on standard intake form, following a SOP with some leeway in the order in which questions are asked, drawing on the organization's procedures and training and relying on skill in conducting a structured interview in order to record basic identifying information.

The performance standards to serve as targets for training on this task (as well as criteria for evaluating their performance on the job) might be:

Descriptive Standards

Writes answers legibly.

Listens carefully to client's answers and records responses accurately.

Flexible in changing sequence of questions to meet unique situations or problems.

Quantifiable Standards

Asks all required questions of client (form 100% complete).

On average completes X number of forms per day.

No more than X complaints from clients per month about manner during the interview.

Note that the standards are essentially a commonsense conversion of the explicit content of the task statement and the worker function levels assigned earlier. In addition, the performance standards reflect the orientation measure. Recall that the task under consideration was oriented toward Data: copying at 50%, and People: exchanging information at 40%. Involvement with Things was minimal: handling at 10%. These orientation measures indicate there should be an emphasis on the standards associated with data functioning and only slightly less emphasis on standards associated with the worker's involvement with people. The Things function is not important enough in this task to warrant specific standards.

The coach and worker trainee must then ask: What does this worker need to know, and what skills does he or she need to have to perform the tasks of their assignments according to the standards indicated? How, where, and under what conditions are those knowledges and skills acquired? Often existing job descriptions are grossly inadequate to answer the first question making it very difficult to provide satisfactory solutions to the second question. In a very fundamental sense, the task statements of FJA are uniquely designed to answer that question for workers and their trainers. Functional levels and orientation; reasoning, math and language levels; prescribed and discretionary levels; and performance standards provide the information necessary to describe both the functional and specific content training needed to perform the task.

WHAT DO FUNCTIONAL AND SPECIFIC CONTENT SKILL TRAINING MEAN?

Functional skills refer to those competencies that enable an individual to relate to TDP (orientation) in some combination according to their personal preferences and to some degree of complexity appropriate to their abilities (level). They include skills like tending or operating machines; comparing compiling, or analyzing data; and exchanging information, consulting, or negotiating with people. These skills are normally acquired in educational, training, and avocational pursuits and reinforced in specific activity situations such as schooling, work, and/or play.

Specific content skills refer to those competencies that enable an individual to perform a specific job according to the standards required to satisfy the market. These skills are normally acquired in an advanced technical training school or institute, in extensive on-the-job experience, or on a specific job. These skills are as numerous as the specific products or services that they produce or the standards and conditions established by employers under which they are exercised.

The reason for the distinction between the two types of skills becomes apparent from their definitions. They are acquired at different times and under different conditions, and too often the appropriate time and place for providing one or the other is confused. The confusion begins with the simple fact that functional skill training in schools must have some specific content, and specific content training in job situations must draw on functional potential. Functional skills have a broader application than specific content skills and are more likely to be transferable from one job situation to another.

Using the example task, functional and specific content skills can be identified as follows:

Functional skill content is:

How to copy responses of client in answer to questions.

How to ask questions and listen to responses of client in a noninvestigatory manner.

When, how, and why to vary the sequence of questions to meet specific problems, for example, hostility, reticence.

Specific skill content is:

Meeting the performance standard for the task result and relating it to the agency objective.

Fulfilling agency guidelines for interviewing clients.

Using the agency's standard intake form.

The previous derivations of functional and specific content skills for the task under consideration follow quite naturally from the content of the task statement.

With the task bank in hand, including performance standards and training content, workers and their coaches can together plan training experiences in the most effective order and at the most auspicious times. As one task is mastered, it can be linked through training with other related tasks with the goal of acquiring a seamless and skilled performance of the whole task sequence. As the larger and larger pieces of the job fall into place through learning and practice, the trainee's growing feelings of competency and esteem are validated and the relationship between worker and organization is strengthened and affirmed. If all goes well, the worker may eventually achieve the flow state with the highest possible levels of work involvement, satisfaction, and productivity.

FITTING IT ALL TOGETHER

More and more in our complex society, individuals are advised to take charge of their own fate, whether it be health maintenance, security for old age, or the education of their children. Part of the reason for such advice stems from the loss of independence and responsibility people experience when these functions are delegated to specialists. These specialists cannot see the whole person and how different aspects of a whole person interact with one another and affect decisions that need to be made. People need practical tools to be able to sort through their skill sets and tailor self-development programs to meet the challenges of a more competitive job market. In addition, many people seek and expect the satisfaction and meaning in their work that is represented by the flow experience.

Training thus presents a challenge both to the individual and to management. For the HR manager the question is: How can I best use my training resources to continuously improve productivity and attain total quality? For the worker the questions are: How can I tell what training I need to make maximum use of my personal resources to contribute to total quality? How does the training contribute to my overall personal growth? Within the work organization context these are questions concerning the dynamic relationship between the Work, Worker, and Work Organization in a work-doing system. Within the social context these questions are holistic in nature, concerned with the total involvement of the individual. Only if managers and workers establish and maintain a relationship to act in concert to address these questions while setting the conditions that facilitate flow can the needs of both be fully met. FJA helps in the training effort on all counts.

SUMMARY OF TRAINING

Training is much more than a technical exercise to impart knowledge and skill to the worker. It is first and foremost a point of contact among a worker's need to grow, to feel capable, to be respected for what he or she can do, and management's need for productivity. If the FJA task bank is present at that point of contact, it can provide a shared interpretation and understanding of what training is required as well as how and when that training can be best delivered. The organization then makes the investment in training required for worker competency. In return, the worker brings the flexibility and willingness to apply these newly acquired competencies to the inevitable problems and challenges on the job. A partnership develops that, if nurtured through the words and deeds of management, further reinforces the trust that is required for a quality product or service.

Performance Appraisal— Acknowledging Worker Contributions

Acknowledgment and evaluation of performance is the quintessential HR operation. All the prior operations—recruitment, selection, hiring, assignment, training—come together to be appraised for their results and efficacy. For this to be effective, both worker and manager need to be open to one another and to be in relationship—trusting of one another and mutually concerned for the work and the organization. Performance appraisal is less a time for making judgments and more a time for workers and managers to be a source of information to each other about the specifics of performance. Ideally, it is also a time to mutually set the conditions workers need to achieve flow.

Deming (1986) and other advocates of total quality have downplayed the importance of performance appraisal or even recommended discontinuing it in the interests of pursuing total quality. They point to the many downsides of traditional performance appraisal and stress that systems factors, rather than differences in skill or individual worker's efforts, are mostly responsible for outstanding quality and productivity. We believe that performance appraisal, used properly, has a valuable role to play in total quality organizations. However, it must be treated as an opportunity to open dialogue between workers and managers as to what is working and is not working to produce quality performance. Partlow (1996), in his descriptive study of human resources practices at TQM hotels, described the approach used by The Worthington Hotel:

> At the Worthington, managers and employees each complete separate evaluations of an employee's quality-related accomplishments. The two parties

then get together to discuss areas of agreement and difference. The emphasis is on sharing information, understanding the other person's expectations, and setting performance goals for the future. (p. 74)

This is the recommended approach to performance appraisal and is supported by an ample research base which shows that timely, accurate feedback has a marked positive effect on worker productivity and motivation, especially when the worker is committed to achieving challenging goals (Locke & Latham, 1990). On the other side of the quality coin, managers must be fully open to feedback from workers pointing to system improvements needed for total quality, including changes in management.

A PRIME OPPORTUNITY

Few activities in the employment system offer an opportunity to do as much good—or as much harm—as performance appraisal. It is a high wire act. Nowhere in a manager's relations with his or her employees are skill and patience put to a greater test, and nowhere else can trust and openness be displayed more clearly and convincingly. When performance appraisal is done right, trust is reinforced, creativity encouraged, partnerships forged, work problems resolved, and productivity enhanced. When it is done wrong, when both worker and manager find themselves on trial, not only are positive results forsaken, but the negative ones—especially distrust and loss of confidence in the organization—take their place.

What can be expected from performance appraisal when it is done right? It is the opportunity to:

acknowledge and reward good work (behavior, performance, quality output) through growth and promotion opportunities,

determine whether the organization and the workers are working well together to achieve production objectives, and

learn what can be improved to advance the competitive position of the organization, which involves taking a hard look at an organization's resource capabilities.

WHAT IS REQUIRED TO MEET THE EXPECTATIONS OF A PERFORMANCE APPRAISAL?

To realize performance appraisal expectations, the worker–manager relationship should be cognizant of the following:

1. The worker needs reassurance that he or she is on the same wavelength as management in meeting the mission objectives of the

organization. This reassurance establishes a well of trust for the worker and manager to draw on and to achieve a meeting of minds and spirit.

2. The worker needs a clear statement of what is expected—the tasks that need to be performed, the results that need to be achieved, and how both contribute to objectives.

3. The worker and manager need to feel confident that all necessary resources of the work-doing system are available and accessible to deal with work problems as they occur.

4. The worker and manager need to have an ongoing, open relationship so that continuous feedback can occur concerning work and any problems that arise.

THE ROLE OF FJA

FJA provides the fundamental tool—the FJA task bank—for the performance appraisal expectations to be realized. The task bank is an objective basis for locating and diagnosing failures when things go wrong, for assigning and fixing responsibility for problems. It is the ultimate bedrock for a shared interpretation of experience underlying a trusting relationship. How is the shared interpretation of experience effected? Through *feedback.*

Workers receive and use feedback on a continuous basis whether or not formal performance appraisal is in place. This feedback comes from various sources—the work itself; from machine dials or readouts; from the comments of customers, peers, and supervisors. Often immediate, sometimes minute by minute, feedback is constantly monitored and used by workers to make fine adjustments to personal and system performance in real time. An expert teacher who watches student classroom reactions (especially nonverbal ones) for signs of boredom or disinterest at one extreme or confusion and anxiety at the other provides immediate, routine feedback by adjusting his or her teaching style. He or she draws on humor to capture the attention of wandering minds or slows down a presentation to allow struggling students to catch up. Csikszentmihalyi (1975) quoting surgeons' comments described the use of immediate feedback by surgeons undertaking operations:

> Each movement results in changes that are clear to interpret. This visual feedback can be judged either at a raw sensory level or at a very intellectual and technical one: "I know what is right not on an intellectual level, but I sense the correctness by the way things look." Thankfully, yes—it is usually clear what is the right thing to do. You get a feeling about it when things aren't going well. There will be supply problems and the tissues will not be

rejoined properly. You rely entirely on precise, immediate visual feedback. . . . When you look down the microscope to do an operation, it's like coming home. You have precise visual feedback. (p. 134)

Feedback through the formal performance appraisal system is much less frequent than the routine and sometimes continuous feedback workers get in the course of a normal day. Where organizations use formal appraisals they do so once, or at most twice, a year. Nevertheless, feedback has a crucial role to play. Formal performance appraisal feedback provides a frame of reference for the worker, encompassing the entire job and extending into the relevant aspects of the Work Organization. Judged at an "intellectual and technical level" (Csikszentmihalyi, 1975), performance appraisal data is an extended but highly focused conversation between worker and manager. It provides a holistic and comprehensive context within which the worker can weigh and interpret immediate feedback received from various sources when back on the job. Performance appraisal is a mutual creative exercise of pulling together bits and pieces from the jumbled stream of the preceding months' performance feedback and putting them into the larger context of a job's performance standards (expectations) and the objectives, goals, and purpose of the work-doing system. Performance appraisal is the time for the worker and manager to see the whole as greater than the sum of the parts, to integrate ideas and information, to make full sense of the work enterprise they share. It offers an opportunity to fashion a joint understanding of the work situation that is intellectually and aesthetically pleasing to both.

People work best when they feel in control of an activity, when their skills match the challenge of the work they are performing, when goals and feedback are clear and unambiguous, and when there is an organized set of opportunities for action (Csikszentmihalyi, 1975). A formal performance appraisal identifies whether workers experience these conditions that lead to flow. When these conditions *are* present, workers can invest themselves fully in the job without having to second-guess management. They can work with full confidence in their ability to get the job done to the standards expected. When these conditions are *not* present, workers are tentative and uncertain about investing effort or taking responsibility. This tentativeness works to the detriment of both worker growth and organizational productivity.

THE ROLE OF THE TASK BANK
IN PERFORMANCE APPRAISAL

When people receive feedback that they have fallen short of expectations (their own or management's), they tend to defend their integrity and their

positive view of themselves by blaming others or factors in their environment. Conversely, people tend to grab at credit for success when they feel
their efforts are being overlooked. These ways of thinking often play themselves out in performance appraisal where workers feel on trial. Without a
fair and impartial frame of reference to work from (i.e., the FJA task bank),
workers who must explain poor results to a manager tend to cite factors beyond their control such as equipment breakdown, material shortage, or
unpredictable problems. Managers who identify with and defend the work
organization tend to see the system as deserving accolades for good work
accomplished and the worker as being at fault for poor work. Theory X assumptions—workers are basically unmotivated to do a good job and are
essentially holding back from giving their all—also reinforce managers'
view of seeing workers as responsible for poor performance. This kind of
climate clearly breaks down trust and positive relationships between
workers and management.

Consider how the performance appraisal proceeds when the FJA task
bank is available. The following task statement from the job of X-ray support engineer (SE) in medical equipment servicing provides an example:

> Give on-the-job training to field engineers (FE) depending on support
> needed or requested by them, guiding the FE through a troubleshooting or
> adjustment procedure, using explanation, demonstration, and graphics ap-
> propriate to level of FE, drawing on references in manual or to schematics
> and relying on experience and interpersonal skills to coach and model ap-
> propriate approach to customer *in order to* enrich/enhance knowledge and
> skill of FE, both technical and personal.

The performance standards, which are basically descriptive, applying to
this task are:

> *Standard 1.* FEs are satisfied with both the short- and long-term effect of
> the support received by them from SE in terms of (a) the knowledge and
> understanding imparted, (b) the references given, and (c) the graphics
> referred to.
>
> *Standard 2.* FEs are satisfied with the manner in which the support was
> given and their ability to replicate the modeling shown, in their ap-
> proach to the customer.

Essentially, answers to three questions about the performance provided in
this instance need to be known:

> Does the performance meet requirements?
> Was the performance inadequate, that is, Needs Help?
> Did it go beyond requirements, that is, was Outstanding.

These judgments can be expressed on a 5-point scale as follows:

Needs Help		Meets Requirements		Outstanding
1	2	3	4	5

The range for Meets Requirements is quite broad, from 2 to 4, to accommodate the considerable distance between meeting minimal standards of performance and performing up to a level that falls just short of outstanding. With respect to on-the-job training, a rating of 2 given by an FE might indicate that he or she is only minimally satisfied with the training received but is not yet ready to complain to management about the SE's performance. A rating of 4 might mean that the FE is well satisfied with the training but not quite enough to nominate the SE to management as outstanding and deserving of a bonus or other additional reward. The purpose of the outstanding rating is to discover higher levels of excellence and to reward those who contribute to them.

Who makes the performance judgment in this example? Obviously, the FEs. FE satisfaction with the assistance given is expressed directly on the report of the event. Ratings of 1 (SE *Needs Help* or FE is dissatisfied) requires the FE to write a critical incident describing a specific example of the poor performance. For example, an FE who rated an SE as 1 on the performance scale for Standard 2 might write the following critical incident to anchor that rating:

> A week after receiving the training from the SE, I attempted repairs on a customer's X-ray machine using the procedure taught to me by the SE. It didn't work and several patient appointments were canceled while I called the field office for additional help. I later found out that the SE who demonstrated the repair for me forgot to mention a critical step in the repair cycle. We may lose a large customer account as a result of this mistake.

Similarly a rating of 5 (SE is *Outstanding* or FE is highly satisfied) requires the FE to write a critical incident to describe a specific example of outstanding performance; for example, a critical incident for SE Standard 2 is:

> I was called in on a crucial repair of X-ray equipment in the emergency ward of an inner-city hospital. The physician in charge was very impatient to the point where he stood over me while I was getting the repair done. Luckily, I was able to remember Ms. _____'s training demonstration to the letter, and the repair was done right and completed faster than anyone expected. To make it even better, the physician wrote me a commendation letter and sent it to my supervisor! I owe much of the credit for that to my training from Ms. _____.

Although critical incidents are written from the point of view of the FE, the recipient of the assistance, they provide concrete material for performance appraisal discussion between the worker (SE) and the manager.

Critical incidents along with the task bank provide the information needed by a worker and manager to sort out whether inherent causes (attributable to the Work Organization) or assignable causes (attributable to the Worker) are responsible for the poor performance illustrated in the first critical incident. Together the critical incident and the task bank provided a basis to test a series of hypotheses about the source of the poor performance. The least contentious place to start (at least from a worker's point of view) is inherent cause. The task states that the SE draws on references in manuals or to schematics when providing on-the-job training to the FE. The worker and manager read over the manual and other training materials to make sure they are complete and accurate in the area where the FE experienced the repair problem. If they are not, a systems explanation for the poor SE training performance can be identified and management must correct the technical material provided to the SEs. If no inherent cause is present, the worker and manager can then consider the possibility of an assignable cause. To this end, FJA (which recognizes the smooth interaction of the three kinds of skills—specific content, functional, and adaptive—as a basis for competency) enables the pinpointing of assignable cause to diagnose what can be done about improving poor worker performance. The worker and manager could pursue the following additional questions, after having assured themselves that the manuals and schematics are complete and accurate:

1. *Are Specific Content Skills Adequate?* The manager asks the SE whether he or she is familiar with the sequence of repair steps in the manual. If not, the remedy to poor performance might be as simple as having the SE review the repair manual for the specific make of equipment.

2. *Are Functional Skills Adequate?* To perform the training task, the SE must function at Level 4B on the People scale (Instructing). Together the worker and manager can review how the training is conducted, its pace and content, and the use of demonstrations and other training aids. If the performance problem is attributable to lack of People functional skills, the manager may be able to provide advice on how to conduct more effective on-the-job training or work with the SE for a short time to assist him or her in providing training to individual FEs.

3. *Are Adaptive Skills Adequate?* Even if the previous two questions are answered in the affirmative, the SE may not have the *willingness* to devote the necessary attention and effort to provide on-the-job training to FEs. The SE may have the wrong temperament to instruct others (e.g., is a perfectionist and impatient) in which case another SE should probably take over the training duties. Or the SE may believe that he or she is not rewarded for the time and effort put into training. If so, this brings the worker and manager back to inherent cause. Management may have to modify its bonus or

incentive reward system to adequately compensate SEs for their on-the-job training efforts. (Chap. 16, Rewarding Worker Performance and Growth, addresses system rewards for worker contributions.)

If the manager and worker agree that requirements of the indicated standards have been met, then FJA can be used to focus the discussion on improving the performance of the entire system.

Where both worker and manager agree that the worker is performing beyond requirements, and the critical incidents support this fact, then the worker is in a position to advise the manager on how that level of performance has been achieved. The manager can then add this knowledge to his or her discussions with other workers in order to achieve a higher level of excellence.

> *Example:* During a brainstorming session, maids of the Bergstrom Hotels suggested they carry screwdrivers on their housekeeping carts along with the usual sheets, towels, cleaners, and such. Now when they run into a problem like a loose toilet seat, they fix it on the spot, and they do not have to go through the complex routine of calling maintenance and slowing up customer service. The same initiative is granted to doormen. Doormen have been provided with a snow shovel to clear snow from the entryway, thus making guest reception easier. This approach follows from the Bergstrom principles: Employees come first, give where you get, and repeat business will pay the bills. These principles lead to the following policies: Anyone working more than 20 hours a week gets health insurance, a 401(k) plan, paid vacations, and holiday pay. In an industry where turnover is typically near 100%, the Bergstroms report theirs is less than half that. The Bergstrom chain won the 1996 Wisconsin Service Business of the Year Grand Prize. (Sharma-Jensen, 1997, p. 1)

TWO KINDS OF PERFORMANCE STANDARDS

The FJA task bank and underlying concepts together provide an infrastructure of insightful and penetrating questions in the pursuit of quality. But that is not enough; questions must have answers. And the answers must be as hard-nosed and specific as possible. Wherever possible they need to have numbers attached to them. And when numbers are not available the qualities of product or service must be vividly described and clearly communicable to be understood. Thus, FJA makes use of numerical and descriptive standards.

Table 14.1 shows how these standards are best written to communicate what management and workers want from the performance of a task or a job. Performance standards must be carefully written. The meaning of a descriptive standard will revolve around a single, or at most two, adverbs

TABLE 14.1
Two Kinds of Performance Standards
as Applied to Worker Action and Task Output

Standards	Worker Action	Task Output
Descriptive Can apply to whole situation or to a specific action. Broad, allows leeway in interpretation. Consists of descriptive phrases, the subject of which may be understood.	Adverb or adverbial phrase. *Example:* as soon as possible, politely, sympathetically.	Adjective or phrase. *Example:* neat, correct, includes all available data.
Numerical Specific, objective, prescriptive, limited. Allows little leeway in interpretation.	Speed, errors, commendations, and complaints. Too costly to monitor on the job; therefore, standards frequently set up on entry under simulated conditions with assumption that behavior will carry over to output.	Measured by how much output contributes to objective (time, money, geography, manpower). Number of rejects, performance specifications, dimensions of accuracy.

or adjectives. The meaning of a numerical standard is more self-evident. In the case of numerical standards, it is easier to indicate different performance expectations by raising or lowering the numerical criteria contained in the numerical standards. For example, consider the following possible task performance standards in the job of high school teacher.

> *Task:* Lecture/talk to students, answering questions and guiding class discussions, drawing on knowledge of course curriculum, content area, experience, and training and relying on communication, presentation, and interpersonal skills, *in order to* facilitate the learning of course content by students.

Descriptive standard for worker action:
Speaks loudly *or* speaks distinctly.

Descriptive standard for task output:
Covers greater part of required curriculum.

Numerical standard for worker action:
Number of written complaints from students about lectures *or* number of complaints from students about lectures.

Numerical standard for task output:
95% of students pass final examination *or* 75% of students pass final examination.

These are samples of possible standards that may be available to give the teacher the guidance needed to get the work done.

BASIC FJA THEMES APPLIED
TO PERFORMANCE APPRAISAL

The FJA process of performance appraisal plays out against a backdrop of trust as basic to a productive and wholesome work:

> Northwest Airlines says that the only issue in the week-old strike by its 6,200 pilots is pay. The pilots counter that job security as well as money are the two big hurdles standing in the way of a settlement. But the real issue that has divided the two sides—leading to the longest airline strike since maintenance workers shut down Eastern Airlines in 1989—seems to be trust.
>
> "Even though there are some significant issues between them," said Kit Darby, a longtime United Airlines pilot who is also president of Air Inc., a company that helps place commercial pilots in jobs, "they are not significant enough to cause a strike. The two sides really don't trust each other. And in an atmosphere of total distrust, you really can't sell anything." (Zuckerman, 1998)

Contrast this atmosphere with that extant at Midwest Express Airlines (developed 11 years ago out of the corporate aviation division of its parent company, Kimberly-Clark Corp., formerly headquarted in Neenah, Wisconsin, and now based in Dallas). Tim Hoeksema, president and CEO of Midwest Express, which *Consumer Reports* and the *Zagat Airline Survey* rate as the best airline in the United States, has the following to say regarding trust.

> There is a myth that anybody who's going to get ahead at a big company has to be shady or bend the rules. That's not true at Kimberly Clark, where there's a very strong commitment to values and integrity. If you treat people in a straightforward, honest, ethical way; you don't cut corners; you don't cheat; you don't promise that you'll deliver something you can't, then you'll build positive long-term business relationships. ("Airline chief," 1995, p. 15D)

However, for many the concept of trust is considered laughable and is illustrated by a recent Dilbert cartoon strip. (Dilbert, a hugely popular serialized cartoon in major daily newspapers, lampoons management foibles and hypocrisies.) In the first panel of the strip the pointy-haired manager informs Alice, an employee, that her performance meets expectations and she will get a 2% raise. Alice protests that she has worked 80 hours every week. The manager responds, "I expected that." Alice points out that this year she has earned three patents that will make the company millions. After initially being caught off guard ("Really? Wow!"), the manager says he expected that, too. Alice then attempts to sway the manager by reminding him that she donated bone marrow to their biggest customer—twice. To which the manager responds that he noted this under "attendance problem." The last panel has Alice—her head buried in her arms—commiserating with two cynical and burned out employees who regularly inhabit the cartoon strip.

It would be putting one's head in the sand to deny that the crassness represented by the cartoon is a common occurrence. Workers are vulnerable and managers can exert their power to exploit the performance appraisal to their advantage. Fortunately, however, the research literature suggests it is possible for workers and managers to work together in a fair and constructive manner in testing hypotheses about the sources of performance problems. However, without trust, the performance appraisal becomes a mechanical exercise without spirit or the excitement of mutual sharing and resolving of work problems together. The opportunity for achieving a shared interpretation of experience is lost, and with it, probably the long-term health of the organization.

When trust is established, five basic FJA themes are operative in the performance appraisal process. These themes are expressed as follows.

Performance Appraisal Theme 1: Performance Feedback Must Reflect the Worker as a Whole Person

Many labor economists view workers as bundles of utilities—capabilities, experience, education, training—that are sold to the employer at the going rate in the labor market. Others try to measure the human capital that people build up as they become trained and educated to take their part in the labor market. Although these views are not necessarily wrong, they paint an incomplete picture of people at work. Workers are much more than interchangeable bundles of utilities that can be simply and routinely removed and replaced like worn parts in a car. Each worker has a constellation of strengths and limitations. If weak in one area, a worker nevertheless will attempt to compensate through adaptive strategies to meet the performance standards expected by management. (A car part does not modify itself to better fit the mechanical system it is placed in.) People are volitional; they make their own choices. They draw on and combine their physical, mental, and interpersonal potentials holistically, in varying degrees, and in inventive ways to adjust to the work system and get the job done. If a manager conducting a performance appraisal understands this, the worker will less likely be treated as another pair of hands for getting the work done. It is also more likely the manager will be prepared to draw out a worker's potential and capabilities, assisting and supporting them in the process of integration.

Performance Appraisal Theme 2: Worker Performance Must Be Seen as a Function of Both Job Content and Job Context

FJA-based performance appraisal begins with the task bank and its performance standards along with critical incidents used to describe when the worker needs help or is outstanding. These information sources emphasize job content (knowledge, functional skills, and ability). However, the worker and manager must also draw on the FJA model to generate hypotheses about the effect of job context on the worker's performance. Questions that could be raised about job context include:

With Regard to Effort. Do work conditions require an undue amount of physical exertion or psychological stress imposed over a long period of time, thus negatively affecting worker performance? Does the worker need to concentrate on a continuous monitoring task over an extended period thus causing fatigue and errors in performance? Are there system constraints that block worker performance no matter how much effort is expended?

With Regard to Responsibility. Do the worker and manager agree on the discretionary and prescriptive standards for the tasks comprising the job? Is management ready to back the worker if he or she makes a mistake when exercising discretion? Is added responsibility balanced by accommodations from management?

With Regard to Work Conditions. Is management fully aware of physical conditions present on the job (e.g., excessive heat or humidity) incompatible with the best worker performance? Does management appreciate the differences in supervisory styles across the unit that are more or less motivating for workers?

Performance Appraisal Theme 3: Performance Appraisal Must Acknowledge the Interaction Among Worker, Work, and Work Organization

In one sense, FJA is a method for differentiating and assigning responsibility. It has already been pointed out that it takes a smooth dynamic among Worker, Work, and the Work Organization to get work done. Each of these components involves its own primary responsibilities:

the *Worker* for integrating and perfecting TDP functional skills, and applying them effectively to specific work content and in adapting to the work environment.

the *Work Organization* for providing the necessary resources and environmental adaptations so that work can get done efficiently and with a minimum of stress.

Work so designed and structured that the Worker and Work Organization potential can come together in the most productive way possible for both.

In performance appraisal the difficult task for the worker and manager is to sort out those aspects of performance determined by the worker's efforts and those aspects over which only management has control. Worker's efforts are largely represented in Themes 1 and 2. The manager's efforts lie in representing the purpose, goals, objectives, and resources/constraints of the organization. When this division of responsibility is clear, the worker can better see his or her contribution to the overall work system. Workers and managers are intricately and unavoidably interdependent. They must work together if the job is to be done right.

Performance Appraisal Theme 4: Worker Performance Results From the Interaction of the Three Kinds of Skills

Earlier in this chapter, the questions a manager could ask of a field SE to identify skills needing additional help were presented. The example showed that all three kinds of skills (functional, specific content, and adaptive) interact to achieve a holistic and smooth performance. The SE might be perfectly adequate in the People functional skill of Instructing, but if he or she does not have the specific content knowledge for repairing particular models of medical equipment, then the task cannot be performed properly. Even with the specific content and functional skills in place, a deficit in adaptive skill—a basic willingness to put the other two types of skill to the test in on-the-job training—will degrade worker performance. The different skills mutually support or erode worker performance.

Csikszentmihalyi (1975) described the operation of this fourth principle in his study of surgeons:

> Skill means not only technical competence but emotional, managerial, and cognitive abilities required to structure the stimulus field of surgery into a flow activity and to operate within it. It is probable that dropouts from surgery are technically competent but unable to avoid anxiety or boredom. (p. 128)

A worker's skills must be online and combined at the right time and in the right measure if he or she is to perform well and find satisfaction in the work.

Performance Appraisal Theme 5: The Employer Must Make Accommodations for the Effect of Systems on Worker Performance

Management has an obligation to honestly evaluate its own contribution to worker performance problems and to cooperate with workers to make the accommodations needed to release their full potential. To do less blames workers for poor performance by default, without bothering to invest the time and effort to establish objectively where the responsibility lies. Blaming by default can only lead to finger pointing, blame laying, and mistrust between workers and management. Of course, accommodation is not a new idea—legislation, including the ADA, requires employers to accommodate the mentally and physically disabled.

A SUGGESTED PROCEDURE
FOR FJA PERFORMANCE APPRAISAL

To do justice to these FJA themes, performance evaluation needs to be objective and fair; that is, everyone needs to be evaluated according to relevant criteria, with consistency, avoidance of bias, open and honest diagnosis of performance problems, and maintenance of self-esteem. To do this involves a number of elements:

Job analysis to specify what is to be evaluated and keep it consistent for all incumbents of a particular job.

Prepared evaluation scales that specify the particulars of the evaluations to be made. (The best of these scales have behavioral anchors—examples of behaviors that describe particular performance levels.)

Evaluators (managers or their surrogates) trained in the instruments used during the evaluation and in the methods of sorting out nondefensively inherent and assignable cause.

Keeping records of critical incidents and their retrieval for use in the evaluation.

Interviewing for a performance evaluation.

Each of these elements is discussed in detail, noting the influence of FJA theory.

JOB ANALYSIS

The fundamental challenge of job analysis is to describe and define the dimensions of the work activity being evaluated. FJA has a very comprehensive approach to this challenge (described in chaps. 1–6). An FJA task analysis describes the behaviors the workers indicate are necessary to produce the desired results. It opens up to examination the assumptions workers and managers have with regard to each other. The behaviors can be evaluated in terms of functional skill levels, orientation to knowledge resources, the performance standards workers seek to fulfill (their own and management's), and the adaptations workers make to achieve those standards and overcome obstacles. The task analysis is the informational base. It represents the interaction of worker, work organization, and work to achieve productivity and contains within it the standards necessary to maintain competitive advantage in the marketplace.

THE EVALUATION RATINGS

What do management and workers want to know at the time of the performance review? Workers want feedback on whether they are meeting requirements, falling behind, or are performing beyond requirements. These three ratings serve the psychological needs of the incumbent and the developmental needs of the organization.

People want to know whether they are doing their part, getting their assigned job done, and meeting the objectives of the organization. They need to know this in order to maintain their self-esteem and integrity among their fellow workers. Management also needs to know this in order to determine whether it is communicating its objectives correctly and effectively, whether it is providing the necessary training to achieve those objectives and to identify outstanding work for special rewards—bonuses, transfers, promotions. For both the worker and the organization, a performance evaluation takes stock and provides a breather from which to go on with revitalized energy.

Each task, because it is structured around a behavior and a result, posits obvious questions, Has the result been achieved, and has it been achieved according to the required standard? Has the behavior been appropriate? Furthermore, because each task contains data concerning the KSAs and system enablers, the data is immediately available to analyze possible sources of difficulty if standards are not being achieved. If they are, or if the achievement is beyond expectations, the tasks provide a basis for evaluating training and understanding individual accomplishment.

Also in using the task analysis, workers evaluate themselves drawing on the performance record for the stated period. Evaluating work accomplishments on a task basis serves a diagnostic purpose for management and workers to discover particular strengths and/or weaknesses. Work can also be evaluated output-by-output to obtain an overview of performance with reference to the primary objectives of the organizational unit.

In pursuit of total quality, organizations have sought performance appraisal feedback from customers and peers in addition to supervisors who are the traditional and usual source of performance appraisal ratings. Bergstrom Hotels takes this approach: "To help managers develop a more complete picture of each employee's contributions, Bergstrom routinely considers peer reviews as part of performance evaluations, as well as information from both internal and external customers" (Sharma-Jensen, 1997, p. 1).

When performance appraisal feedback comes from several directions (supervisor, self, peer, subordinate, customer) it is sometimes called 360-degree feedback and is used increasingly in business, industry, and government. Such comprehensive feedback in a formal performance appraisal can be helpful to worker coaching efforts, but it must be balanced by greater skill, training, and preparation by both worker and manager in performance appraisal.

TRAINING EVALUATORS

It is possible to see two levels of respect playing out through the performance evaluation:

> the listening/querying level—the evaluator is able to ask the right questions and listen to what the worker has to say about getting the work done.
>
> the corrective/coaching level—the evaluator may be able to propose options, alternatives, and corrections with regard to technique and behavior.

Conceivably the evaluator need not go beyond the first level if the performance review is carried out with interest and appropriate acknowledgment for things done correctly and well. Often systematic querying and attentive listening provides just what the worker needs to open up and be self-critical, particularly if the querying pursues some of the *whys* things are being done the way they are. For this purpose the evaluator needs to have a thorough understanding of FJA in order to follow through on the line of questioning described later.

As noted earlier, the task bank can serve as a behavioral inventory. A first line of questioning can be, "Does the task bank satisfactorily cover 95% of the job as it purports to do?" If it does not and things have changed since it was developed, it is essential to ask and take note of changes that have occurred and the reasons for those changes. This in itself can lead to an understanding of adaptations that have or have not been made by the worker and the organization. Questioning at this point would be, Are the new tasks associated with an existing output, and if so are they the result of new technology or reengineering of the process? Are they the result of worker input and the natural process of continuous job redesign? Are the new tasks associated with a new output? What has been the effect on the performance of the existing tasks? Have any of them changed or been dropped, and if so how has it affected the work of others?

Assuming that the task bank is still accurate, the evaluator can inquire whether the enablers are sufficient for the incumbent to meet requirements or whether there is anything more that the organization can do to improve the process.

The second level of respect depends on who the evaluators are. Have they done the work, been in the position of the incumbent and therefore possess an intimate knowledge of the job? Or does their knowledge derive from having been in a design relationship to the work, or is it the result of extensive experience in managing incumbents in the particular jobs? In any of these cases, evaluators need to understand the appropriateness of particular worker actions to achieve particular results. This understanding best depends on the querying and listening pursued earlier, which bring the evaluator up to date on the current situation. Once managers have shared with the incumbents their understanding of the interaction among instructions, KSA, and the adaptations that workers make to achieve results, they are in a much stronger position for their proposals to be accepted

Beyond their knowledge of the technology of the work and FJA methodology, raters need to have a point of view about the performance evaluation situation. They need to understand its purpose is not to make judgments and obtain scale values for the workers but to review, and where necessary adjust or correct the working relationship between the incumbent and the organization. The essential idea to be conveyed during the review process is that both management and the worker are working toward the same goals, namely improved productivity and worker growth.

KEEPING RECORDS

Because the performance review is behavior-oriented, records that focus on specific behaviors need to be kept. Generalities and unsubstantiated observations are not helpful and even harmful. The most effective types of observations are critical incidents noted as having contributed to effective or ineffective performance. Such incidents can be recorded by both the incumbent and management. They call for specifics that describe what happened, why it happened, what the particulars were that led up to the incident, and what the outcome was. They focus on actions and thus can provide substance to any discussion of performance. It is best to discuss critical incidents close to the time that they occur and give immediate feedback. They can also be stored until the scheduled performance review at which time they can be viewed in perspective and have, perhaps, a somewhat different significance.

If the context in which these incidents occur is one of hostility and distrust—one in which the game being played is "I gotcha!"—it would be easy to haul out a dossier of complaints or accusations during a perform-ance review. Such action would negate the entire spirit of FJA and the cli-mate it seeks to create, namely one of mutual trust between management and the worker. It would also be counterproductive because it is unlikely to contribute to improved productivity and worker growth. Such a nega-tive approach would fragment rather than unify relationships within the organization.

One possibility for avoiding this negative contingency is to have work-ers in a production unit function as a team for performance review pur-poses. They could meet ad hoc frequently (at least once a week) to evaluate how things have gone, where any glitches occurred, who was responsible, and how they might have been overcome by the efforts of the individual or by the concerted efforts of the team. The value of such meetings depends in large measure on the specific critical incident data that would be forth-coming during the exchange. The HR office can play a useful role in help-ing workers formulate critical incidents and document them in an easy-to-read format. When drawn on by the worker and the manager during a per-formance review, these critical incidents provide a ready source of data for coaching, feedback, and problem solving.

Renfrew (1997) described the use of critical incidents in anaesthetic de-partments of hospitals in the United Kingdom:

> At the beginning of the reporting period all members of the department are informed of what incidents are to be reported. Forms are made available in all theatres and a receptacle for the forms is placed in an agreed upon place. The forms are then reviewed on a weekly basis by a senior staff member who decides if any incident requires early action. Otherwise a report is given at a monthly meeting where specific cases can be discussed and action decided upon.

Renfrew points to hesitancy of people to own up to mistakes made by the anesthesia teams by apportioning blame to themselves when writing criti-cal incidents. Again, an ethic of trust and fair play has to prevail if critical incidents are to be used to their full potential for improving the function-ing of the work-doing system. Nevertheless, critical incident reporting may identify problems not otherwise covered by case or peer reviews and can complement quality assurance programs (Renfrew, 1997).

THE PERFORMANCE EVALUATION INTERVIEW

No HR function touches an individual as closely as performance appraisal yet it is a pretty good bet that no HR function is handled as awkwardly and ineffectively. On the whole, workers feel they have given a job their best shot. They need to have this acknowledged. On the whole they know where they could have done better if . . . . The *if* usually has to do with circumstances that seemed overwhelming or beyond their control at the time. They do not appreciate being reminded of what they feel they already know particularly when the good things they did are not likely to be mentioned. Actually the evaluator, usually a supervisor, does not especially relish being in the position of making judgments, of "playing God" as some have said. Sensitive supervisors are awkward and do not come across as effective. Insensitive supervisors botch the appraisal by being unprepared; they do not bother to collect detailed specific information about the so-called inefficiencies or satisfactory remedial proposals. All either succeeds in doing is to erode the worker's self-esteem or embarrass the supervisor.

The purpose of the performance interview is to give the supervisor an opportunity to review the worker's performance with him or her, diagnose causes of inadequate performance, and set in motion initiatives to improve performance in future. How can FJA make performance interviews more meaningful and productive?

The FJA task bank with its wealth of descriptive information providing a framework within which to present and discuss performance standards offers an advantage over most other performance rating systems. It makes possible a dialogue on two fundamental questions around which the performance evaluation interview should revolve: (a) How can we bring out that the work system itself is being evaluated through the worker's input? and (b) How can we create a situation where workers can indicate how and why they need help? For example, a worker may point out that a standard was not met because the necessary enablers were not present (e.g., management did not provide the necessary training or instructions or that the instructions were discretionary when they could have been prescriptive). The supervisor and worker can then use the task bank to diagnose the causes of poor performance within the context of the entire organizational system, jointly establish responsibility for taking corrective measures, and set the stage for lasting performance improvements in future.

The FJA performance interview is at least 1 hour long and held away from the work site in a quiet, private office. Beforehand, the supervisor and worker review the FJA task bank, an objective source of information, and the supervisor's ratings. That way, they both come to the meeting prepared. At the start of the performance interview, the supervisor and worker review the ratings on all the performance standards. Then they devote at least half their time to discuss the performance standards on which the worker needs help. To the extent a balanced treatment is given of both system and worker causes, these standards will be less contentious. The supervisor reviews the critical incident supporting the rating, providing additional clarification as needed. The supervisor and worker may also review the task(s) from the task bank corresponding to that performance standard.

The interview can begin with the evaluator observing: "The purpose of our discussion is to review how we have worked together so far and to see where we might improve on things, one way or another." Essentially this observation is a lead-in to create rapport and open up the discussion. The evaluator can take the initiative to comment on how things went from management's point of view thereby emphasizing that the interview is a two-way street. At this point almost anything can come up. Whatever can be directly referred to the task bank should be. For example, if what comes up has to do with tools, machines, equipment, or measuring devices, the tasks that involve them should be referred to. Similarly, if the item raised concerns a knowledge or a skill level, the appropriate task should become the text for the discussion. At any time during the discussion of task performance, it is appropriate to ask the incumbent if he or she is having any problem achieving the stated standards for the results. It is important to ascertain if problems have something to do with the technology available to achieve the results, a matter of training, or a matter of adapting to the job–worker situation. This last situation could involve the instructions, other workers, or perhaps the environmental conditions. If the worker is a member of a team, the performance review is a good time to inquire how well the team is working.

If the evaluator is the worker's manager, the issue the incumbent is most likely to bring up as an opening gambit may have to do with worker growth—that is, pay, training, transfer, or promotion. The importance of these matters needs to be acknowledged. However, if the supervisor feels a direct response to these inquiries would get the interview off on the wrong foot, he or she must acknowledge the query and indicate that the issue will be taken up after the detailed performance review. The detailed task review may very well be relevant to these issues and a good reason to delay the discussion.

For the performance interview to succeed, the supervisor must present and discuss the performance results with the worker in a nonprejudicial way: He or she has made a judgement about the worker's performance on a specific standard, but he or she will not and cannot make a judgment about the worker's worthiness as a human being. The fact that the worker has not met one or another of the performance standards does not mean that the worker is any less a person or less deserving of management's respect and consideration. Therefore, the supervisor's demeanor should always be one of respect, attentiveness, and openness to the worker regardless of how well or poorly the person has performed. Where the supervisor has made a mistake in assessing the worker's performance, there should be openness to that possibility and a willingness to correct the rating. Where the rating is accurate but the worker still disagrees, the supervisor must al-low the right to disagree but still respectfully insist on a change in behav-ior so that performance is up to expectation the next time around. Such a stance requires much maturity on the part of the supervisor and the worker, but it is the only way that FJA can achieve its full potential.

Again note that the performance interview does not replace regular communication about performance issues on a day-to-day basis. The in-formation in the performance interview should summarize and recap what the supervisor has shared with the worker over a period of several months. If the information in the performance interview comes as a surprise to an employee, the supervisor must work to improve everyday communication with that employee.

Ultimately, trust is the most important consideration in performance appraisal. FJA works best when workers and managers are willing to meet in the middle to establish responsibility for performance problems and to work together to find solutions. Thereby performance appraisal is a meet-ing of partners in a common endeavor to achieve positive goals and to build a relationship. This notion of trust is of course quite different from what usually happens in industry but nevertheless it does occur and, when it does, it pays off.

SUMMARY OF PERFORMANCE APPRAISAL

Performance appraisal is a hands-on test of trust. It is the juncture at which the interpersonal skills, patience, and goodwill of managers and workers are tested to the maximum. There are countless ways a performance ap-praisal can go wrong, but only one way it can go right and live up to its promise as a means for increasing productivity and promoting worker growth. This right strategy requires that workers and managers build an environment of mutual trust and work in concert with unflinching hon-esty as scientists of commonsense to test hypotheses about the causes of worker performance. Only by engaging in open dialogue and striving for a shared interpretation of experience can this be done. After isolating performance causes, and pinpointing the causes of substandard and out-standing performance and their corrective or supportive conditions, per-formance appraisal becomes part and parcel of the ongoing working re-lationship between workers and managers. Sometimes managers must accept the responsibility for correcting system constraints on worker per-formance and growth; sometimes workers will have to make adjustments within their sphere of responsibility to get the desired results. In helping to set and strengthen these basic conditions for effective performance ap-praisal, FJA comes into its own as an HRM tool.

Chapter **15**

Career Development and Coaching — Encouraging Worker Growth

PURSUING A CAREER IN TODAY'S WORLD

People pursue careers to achieve stability, security, relationship with others, personal growth, and ultimately status, prioritizing these goals according to their personal value system. For much of the past century, when the drive for careers matured as a goal in offers of employment and in vocational development, this was a very tenable and fulfilling pursuit. Careers provided opportunities for individuals with potential and determination to aspire toward goals that enabled them to achieve comfortable economic status. It provided employers with dedicated employees.

Times have changed. As the new millennium approaches, the pursuit of careers appears to be in a state of flux. The turmoil in industry brought about by global competition and industrial consolidation has shaken the concept of stability and the idea of lifelong employment in a single occupation for a single employer. Employers are less able to offer lifelong employment in a clearly defined occupational niche. Technological change and the enormous expansion of knowledge have blurred the lines of career content. Today, it appears, nothing less than lifelong training and education are necessary to stay current let alone get ahead in a career field.

It is not that the idea of pursuing a career is no longer feasible. Rather, a *career*—in the sense of achieving stability, security and personal growth—must be pursued differently. The primary locus of these goals has moved from the employer, industry, or profession, to the individual. An individual can no longer rely on a career label, even a licensed one, to provide the niche of security, stability, and status. Instead an individual must be able to deliver high performance in highly changing situations. The focus appears to be more on adaptability than achieved status.

AN EXAMPLE OF CURRENT CORPORATE CAREER COUNSELING

Sears Credit undertook a major restructuring that resulted in the creation of many new jobs and redesign of existing ones. A career development process was designed to address these new social perspectives (O'Herron & Simonsen, 1995):

> The group . . . established that Sears Credit needed to help its associates and managers reframe their mindset—from "the company will take care of me" to a proactive attitude that redefined success in terms of what's important to the individual rather than how fast one moves up the ladder. People would need to understand, not just hear, that career development wouldn't be limited to promotions.
>
> The company also needed to redefine responsibility. Not only would associates have to take on new responsibility for managing their own careers, but managers also would need to recognize their role as coaches in supporting associate development. The organization, too, represented by HR practitioners and senior management, had responsibility to provide information and resources so associates could take the initiative. In short, Sears Credit needed a partnership to ensure that individuals at all levels could continually add value to the company. (p. 104)

How can organizations assist their workers in career development at a time when company resources are tighter than ever? Sears Credit addressed this need by making career information as widely and freely available as possible (O'Herron & Simonsen, 1995):

> Since the old, known ways had changed, Sears Credit had to adopt a more open philosophy about opportunities and company information. We needed HR systems such as position descriptions, organizational competencies and a new compensation structure to support career-development efforts and reinforce the overall message of development to meet company needs. This prompted us to write position summaries of the many new jobs that the organizational restructuring created and make them available to all associates via e-mail. In the past, Sears had treated this information as confidential. HR managers safeguarded it, and it wasn't available to associates.
>
> We also created a data bank of associates' desired career goals to be used for organizational planning and staffing decisions. The associate and his or her manager develop the information for the data bank. The input includes details such as, "job next aspired to," "preferred location," or "education needed." This information is available to match against specific jobs in specific locations and to assist in planning training for a particular population. (p. 106)

In the old economy, *knowledge was power*, so HR managers held on to job description information, tucking it away in locked file cabinets, relinquishing it only with a signed authorization from a superior. Today, *knowledge is empowerment*. For workers to take responsibility for their career development they need extensive job information resources—readily accessible and in easily readable form. When combined with the accessibility and speed offered by modern computer technology, FJA fills this bill.

CAREER DEVELOPMENT
IS WHOLE-PERSON DEVELOPMENT

A healthy personality grows in parallel with the 40 or so years that many people spend in their careers. In fact, work impacts on and helps to shape an individual's personality in many ways, for better or for worse. Erikson, the great humanist psychologist, believed that human beings go through a series of stages from infancy to old age in the development of their personalities. The general direction of this development is toward a more complete, unified whole—a person who has dealt successfully with the challenges laid before him or her and has moved on to the next level of personality development. These stages of change in the human personality are in response to a person's inner potential as well as the demands of the environment at critical points in his or her life. Throughout much of this growth and development, a person's work life plays an insistent and ongoing role. Two themes developed in earlier chapters of this book, *trust* and *wholeness* of an individual in the work situation, are integral to the development process.

According to Erikson, a healthy personality faces its earliest challenge in the first year of life. Whether an infant develops a sense of basic trust or basic mistrust depends on whether it finds reciprocity (resulting in trust) or duress (resulting in mistrust) from the primary caregiver. Positive resolution of this stage toward trust sets the stage for an individual to move through subsequent stages in the development of a healthy personality from early childhood through adulthood. By the time a person enters early adulthood and is ready to begin a career, several stages of development have come and gone and set an irrevocable stamp on the individual's style of relating to others and the larger environment. (FJA conceptualizes this aspect of personality development in terms of adaptive skills.) During the period of adulthood when careers are trained for, established, lived out, and eventually given up for retirement, an individual (according to Erikson) must resolve the conflicts inherent in three additional growth stages: Intimacy versus Self-Absorption, Generativity versus Stagnation, and Integrity versus Despair. Successful resolution of each of these stages in turn results in personal growth and greater integration of the human personality (becoming more a whole person in the FJA sense) and movement to the next stage of life. The last stage, that of integrity, is reached only by surmounting the challenges presented in the seven earlier stages of life. As Erikson (1980) so succinctly and powerfully explained in *Identity and the life cycle:*

> Only he who in some way has taken care of things and people and has adapted himself to the triumphs and disappointments of being, by necessity, the originator of others and generator of things and ideas—only he may gradually grow the fruit of the seven stages. I know no better word for it than integrity. (p. 104)

In FJA terms, this could be stated: integrity is achieved by those who have acquired insight into their TDP potentials, developed them to their optimum, and effectively adapted to managing conformance and change to the environment. Inasmuch as a career is a vital aspect of the larger life cycle (and most people believe this to be the case), FJA has a lot to say about career development and the means necessary to coach career seekers toward personal outcomes that are not only beneficial for them but also for their organizations.

INFLUENCE OF FJA ON CAREER COUNSELING AND JOB HUNTING

No one has perceived the usefulness of FJA better than Bolles in his enormously popular book, *What color is your parachute?* Since 1970, this book has been the "bible" for job hunters and career changers, and to date, more than six million copies have been sold all over the world, in English and seven other languages. It is written and illustrated to have a universal appeal, and no doubt its success has been its accessibility to people from all kinds of backgrounds.

Over a quarter of a century ago Bolles demonstrated some remarkable insights for the time; two of these are:

The pursuit of a career is a matter of lifelong learning.

In pursuing a career, people need to be empowered to do as much as possible themselves.

To help individuals visualize their potential as well as likes and dislikes in the world of work, and to empower them in seeing themselves as whole persons, Bolles conceptualized a flower with seven petals surrounding a central stem. The central idea of this flower is Bolles' adaptation of the TDP concept of skills and his elaboration of functional, specific content, and adaptive skills and their role in the world of work. Each petal of the flower and the stem calls for an inventory/listing of facts and options that an individual fills in. The completed flower reveals the whole person and serves to empower individuals with self-knowledge in their pursuit of a career. The categories of information represented by the stem and the petals are listed here. (*Note: For the sake of consistency, the terminology used is the terminology used throughout this book and is not intended as a critique of Bolles' creative interpretation of these terms.*)

Bolles Self-Empowerment Flower
The central stem—
 Transferable skills, essentially those of the functional system: TDP
The three bottom petals—
 Kinds of Things I like to use these skills with . . .
 Kinds of Data I like to use these skills with . . .
 Kinds of People I like to use these skills with . . .
The two upper petals—
 Physical setting I like to work in
 Spiritual or emotional setting I like to work in
The right and left petals—
 Salary and level I want and need
 Outcomes: immediate product or service and long-range goals

Generation of this information by an individual serves to answer the "what" of the three fundamental career-search questions: what, where, and how.

If the use of Bolles' book by millions of apparently satisfied career searchers is any indication of validity, then the functional framework is a practical way for people to evaluate and understand their skills.

THE PERVASIVENESS OF THE TDP CONCEPT

In FJA job analysts training sessions, participants routinely perform two exercises to explore their relationship to TDP. Figure 15.1 shows the format used for the first exercise. The results have been consistent from one workshop to another. Disliked jobs have been very different from ideal jobs, whereas liked jobs were very close or the same as the ideal job. A participant's present job could have the pattern of either the liked or disliked job. A liked-job pattern suggests the participant is on the right track; a disliked-job pattern suggests the participant needs to start at square one in his or her career search. Participants rarely have a problem completing this exer-

In this exercise, rate jobs that you have held in terms of *how you see the jobs now.* (If you have held few jobs or only one job, rate tasks of a job and change the item " Job" to " Task" in the first heading of the left column of the table.) Think what demands the job made and the standards you had to meet.

For each category (liked most, liked least, etc.), rate in percentages the emphasis on Things, Data, People, making the total percentage of each category add up to 100; e.g., Things, 25%; Data, 25%; People, 50%. Do the percentages in multiples of 5.

		(in percent)		
JOB	**THINGS**	**DATA**	**PEOPLE**	**TOTAL**
(describe briefly)				
Liked most				**100%**
Liked least				**100%**
Present				**100%**
Ideal				**100%**

FIG. 15.1.   TDP and job preferences.

cise and have almost always reacted with delight that it could reveal so much about their preferences and job adjustment.

Figure 15.2 is also illuminating to participants because it tends to tell them something important about their own evolution in terms of preferences. A common insight is that in their adolescence they tended to prefer physical involvement and as they matured, their preference changed to Data or People as far as work was concerned. In the discussion following the exercise, this too proved to be illuminating to participants. At no time was the response to these exercises thought trivial.

Thus, it is evident that FJA core concepts regarding whole-person functioning and orientation to TDP and functional skills are in harmony with Erikson's developmental model. They are also in harmony with Holland's vocational choice model. Here again Bolles has quite brilliantly married the TDP approach to Holland's Realistic, Investigative, Artistic, Social, Enterprising, and Conventional (RIASEC) characterization of people in the world of work, a characterization that also carries over to the jobs they work in. Perusal of the jobs in the various RIASEC categories suggests that: Conventional and Investigative jobs are primarily oriented to Data, with the Investigative jobs on a higher functional level; Enterprising jobs are primarily People- and Data-oriented; Social jobs are primarily oriented to People; Realistic jobs are Things- and Data-oriented; and Artistic jobs oriented to a mixture of TDP.

FJA helps in understanding the career concept and what has been going on in two major ways: (a) The orientation (interests, preferences) that people have tends to correspond to the TDP components. People with a strong orientation and capability in the data area, for example, pursue careers that are high in data demands, and (b) Although individuals choose to focus on one or another functional area, they tend toward whole-person involvement in their work and private lives. Individuals engaged in highly cerebral work frequently have hobbies or spare time activities where they work with their hands or become involved with social service activities.

In this exercise, indicate how you saw yourself in the past and how you see yourself today with regard to your physical, mental, and interpersonal makeup. Think of the kind of person you were at the ages indicated and the kind of person you are now — how you functioned then and how you function now. Think of the things that you enjoyed (now enjoy) most and least; the things from which you got (now get) your kicks; and how you preferred (now prefer) to spend your time.

Do your ratings in percentages, making the total percentage for each age category add up to 100; e.g., physical, 25%; mental, 25%; interpersonal, 50%. Do the percentages in multiples of 5.

	(in percent)			
AGE	PHYSICAL	MENTAL	INTERPERSONAL	TOTAL
15 years old (entering high school)				100%
22 years old (college graduating class)				100%
Today				100%

FIG. 15.2.   TDP and personal growth.

Individuals pursuing a career are more likely to achieve personal goals by:

- getting to know themselves in terms of their interests, inclinations, and personal talents in the course of their schooling, everyday living, reading, and focused activities, such as odd jobs.
- exploring various fields—retail, computers, machining, office administration, medicine, and engineering—for the types of situations that suit what they have discovered about themselves.
- being ready and available to work in any of the job–worker situations that come up, both in their field of choice and other fields as well.

This exploration is of course a lifelong activity. Individuals get to know themselves through doing things. Most of the likes and dislikes, preferences, and displeasures experienced in carrying out particular activities are registered on a subconscious level. People tend to become aware of them only when questioning certain choices and decisions. To some extent determinations about who we are and how we got that way may be a theory that we test from time to time by trying new things, undertaking new experiences, pushing ourselves to extremes, and in the process affirming or disconfirming theories about ourselves.

In the course of growing up, people focus on particular interests and content areas. But perhaps more importantly, they develop behavioral styles, preferred ways of functioning, and preferred environments to be in. Erikson points to these same factors in terms of the development sequence in which they occur and the challenges that impel individuals toward adopting a particular behavioral style. Included among these behavioral styles are preferences for:

- instructions—prescriptive or discretionary
- leadership—authoritarian or participatory
- physical environment—inside or outside, office or construction site
- social environment—homogeneous or diverse
- relations with people—moving toward, away, or against
- ambience—calm versus dynamic, cooperative versus competitive, teamwork versus individualistic.

People learn to make numerous other adaptations to such matters as punctuality, dress, impulse control, cordiality, and the like. Some of these adaptations come naturally, perhaps because of what people have grown accustomed to in their families or among their friends (they have passed through the appropriate development stage). Other adaptations take discipline and self-control and become part of a skilled performance and assumption of responsibility (because people are still grappling with specific developmental issues).

FJA AND CURRENT CAREER DEVELOPMENT

An FJA task bank can provide a variety of career information. Cronshaw conducted an FJA job analysis in a software development laboratory of a major computer company. Actually, there were no individual jobs to be analyzed. Instead individuals involved in the development of an advanced software product destined for worldwide distribution were organized into a team, which included not only staff members from the computer company but experts from the user and vendor groups that would eventually use or sell the product. This was a project-based team that would be disbanded after the software was developed and unveiled by the head office. Team members came from various technical areas with different specialized vocabularies, represented different vested interests, functioned as equals, and delivered the final product to a "product owner" who represented their interests to upper-level management.

In this instance, the FJA job analysis identified team functions that held the group together and focused it on common goals, rather than on specialized tasks performed by single team members. The four outputs identified by the software development team were:

Project management/task coordination. The team was required to develop a project plan, update it as necessary, monitor the progress of the project, compare progress to initial projections taking necessary corrective action to stay on schedule, and revise group processes as needed to continually improve internal management of the team.

Setting goals. The team listened to the product owner's expectations, made a project proposal to the owner, discussed/evaluated project targets with the owner, and declared in writing the team's commitment to the project.

Team member selection. The team identified its staffing needs, searched for and recruited qualified personnel, and interviewed/hired service vendors (formerly known as "employees").

Team evaluation. The team identified and developed the specific criteria to be used in team evaluation and conducted the team evaluation.

Suppose you are an experienced programmer in this company but have always worked under the close supervision of your line manager. You see an internal posting seeking applications to the work team, and, in thinking about whether to request a transfer to the work team, you have to decide whether your skills are adequate to the new situation. Whereas management currently plans, sets goals, hires, and evaluates your coworkers, those activities will be assigned to you as an equal member if you decide to transfer to the software development team. You will be accountable directly to the project owner rather than fall under the protective wing of your supervisor in the chain of command. An examination of the task bank for the software development team shows you must operate at the People negotiating level in dealings with the product owner and the other team members. You will have to be tactful, tolerate others, listen to their concerns, share ideas with team members in an acceptable manner, and deal constructively with conflict. When dealing with Data, you will have to anticipate and objectively analyze problems facing the team in order to determine causes and come up with solutions. In the area of Adaptive Skill, you will have to show personal initiative; demonstrate self-discipline, personal maturity and professionalism; and effectively manage the stress of tight deadlines and long working hours (including relinquishing your personal life to some extent.)

On reflection, you may decide this work situation is not right for you and stay where you are (see self-selection in chap. 10—Recruitment). If you are interested in the position but need additional training (e.g., conflict management skills) to give yourself a reasonable chance to get on to the team and succeed once there, you should discuss your plans with the HR manager responsible for career development and counseling.

ENTER THE PROFESSIONAL COUNSELOR: THE FJA CAREER DEVELOPMENT AND COACHING INTERVIEW

As noted earlier in the comments about Bolles' approach to career counseling, much of what is called career development will become even more self-directed than it has been. Organizations are not likely to be willing to invest in lengthy and expensive career development for their transitory workforces. However, help can be sought from counselors in organizations that have them and in the private sector.

In these instances the counselor will function best when serving as a resource for counselees in the exploration of their personal and career potential along the lines of the Bolles model. Counselees need to be encouraged to recall and describe their previous work-related experiences and personal achievements including those in the current organization if they are employed. The counselor should then summarize and give back these thoughts in a way that helps individuals to gain insight into their behavior and suitability for various work situations. Using the FJA model as a guide, the counselor asks questions about what individuals have done in previous jobs as well as how and why they got to their present job. By encouraging individuals to describe those peak periods when they were stretching their potential beyond present circumstances, the counselor can also uncover intriguing and productive possibilities for future growth (i.e., worker potential). In this context, FJA is used as the guide to prompt workers to tell their unique story in their own way. FJA provides the counselor with the depth of understanding needed to hear that story—the *manifest content* of actual experience and the *latent content*, which consists of feelings about experience, interests, and aspirations generated by education and other exposure to the real world.

Consider the example of a young woman newly graduated from high school who has not yet resolved the challenge of establishing a personal identity (career and otherwise). Still attached to her parents' beliefs and values, she seeks the career direction that will satisfy her parents' aspirations for her. The *manifest content* presented to the counselor probably is centered around a few temporary or summer jobs at relatively low levels of functional skill and worker instructions. The adaptive skills that inhere in that kind of work will reflect her stage of personal development: seeking to do the "right thing" by carefully following SOPs and garnering the approval of the supervisor (as substitute parent). In listening to the manifest content, the counselor hears about only low-level functioning and perhaps very low potential for higher skill levels. The latent content of this interview probably tells a different story about the individual's career potential. If she is to continue on the path of development to a fully integrated self, she must come to a realistic assessment of her skills and skill potential including how she felt/reacted to her early work experiences. With the help of the counselor, she can inventory her past work accomplishments and nonwork achievements and explore her goals, values, and interests in a protected, nonjudgmental interaction. On hearing her future hopes and aspirations reflected back from the counselor—independent of her parents wishes for her future—she is empowered to take further steps that capitalize on her interests and potentials in her career exploration.

The best way to conduct an FJA interview for career development and coaching is to prompt an individual to give a personal work history. After rapport has been established (essential to any interviewing situation), the counselor begins by asking the individual about his or her most recent job, which is often the one presently held. (In the case of a young person who has not held a job, the counselor needs to focus on tasks performed at home, in school, or in the pursuit of hobbies.) The counselor continues by asking the individual to describe the basic duties he or she performs (outputs) and making note of these. After listing the outputs, the counselor goes over them one at a time with the individual to get the details needed to rate the highest level task in the outputs with respect to TDP complexity, and perhaps also to rate them with respect to TDP orientation. This will require discussion at key points and asking the individual to describe in some detail the behaviors involved (e.g., in the case of an ambulance attendant, "Lead me through the things you do when you arrive at an accident scene."). The objective is to identify the highest level of task complexity in the job in an efficient and focused manner that does not bog down the interview or take too much time. As the interview proceeds, the individual will need to identify the key performance standards that he or she must meet in producing the outputs and what must be done to achieve them. This will prompt the emergence of adaptive skills that are also noted.

In proceeding through the individual's previous jobs in this way, definite patterns—behavioral preferences—should emerge, especially with respect to adaptive skills (which are the most transferable of the three skill types). For example, difficulties with accepting close supervision or distaste for routine (boring) tasks will become apparent as the individual describes reactions to different bosses or to the more distasteful aspects of work across successive employers. With respect to functional skills, the counselor may notice an upward movement through employers from less-skilled to more-skilled work or that the individual has been at the same skill level for a period of years. One clue that the individual is at an impasse is a *stuckness* at a low level of Worker Instructions across time and employers. This may cause considerable concern or no concern at all on the part of the individual, depending on whether he or she values the growth possibilities inherent in paid work.

As the interview proceeds from most recent jobs to as far back as the individual can reliably report, the counselor will begin to see a unique career and life trajectory—a trajectory that the individual may already be partially aware or blissfully unaware of. This could be good place to have the individual complete the exercises in Figs. 15.1 and 15.2. These exercises might help the individual clue in on the significance of the trajectories already pursued. Discussion of the results of the exercises and the substance of the interview can assist the individual to achieve self-insight into whatever twists and turns have been followed in his or her career life. The counselor's responsibility is not to identify the individual's career trajectory but to ask the necessary questions and reflect the manifest content that is needed for the individual to personally piece this together. Rather than have the counselor write an assessment report *for* the individual (a usual practice), it is far better for the individual to write this up for himself or herself, summarizing the key learning and understanding emerging from the FJA interview. This self-assessment could be read by the counselor in preparation for a second interview session in which the insights from the first session are reviewed and enriched.

If the counselor is a coworker or manager and the FJA task banks can be accessed on the computer from the company's database, all the better. The task banks in the hands of job-knowledgeable helpers serve as a rich source of information to ground the self-assessment coming out of the FJA career development and coaching interview. Workers will be better helped to see any gaps between their present skills—functional or adaptive—and those required in the contemplated employment situation. If they wish to grow beyond their present employment situation, task banks for more highly skilled jobs, roles, or teams in the organization will be of great help in pointing the way to necessary additional training or experience.

SUMMARY OF CAREER DEVELOPMENT AND COACHING

As the end of the 20th century nears, the notion of career is changing. What was once seen as a long, steady progression up an organization's ladder or professional hierarchy to positions of higher pay and responsibility has become unrealistic for most people. The career pattern of the future will more likely resemble a web, an interconnected series of lateral moves within and among employers by workers taking responsibility for themselves as they move between employers. In such an environment, workers require the personal flexibility and self-insight that can be honed by career development coaching. The reality is that fewer and fewer employers are likely to be of a mind to give it. Workers more and more need to look to self-help alternatives such as those offered by Bolles in his book, *What Color Is Your Parachute?* The FJA approach provides an effective and low-cost alternative to traditional career assessment that relies on a lot of testing as well as extensive interviewing and report writing by professionals. Without categorically ruling out the helpfulness of psychological tests in the hands of qualified professionals, it is important to note that FJA allows career counselors to devote more of their very limited time to direct contact with workers and counselees. The goal is to empower workers to navigate their own way to career integrity through a process that helps build initiative and confidence in taking control of their own career and life course.

Chapter **16**

Pay — Rewarding Worker Performance and Growth*

Pay is, of course, the payoff for work done. Pay directly affects what individuals can do off the job, their family's standard of living, the extent to which they can travel, and the leisure time activities in which they can indulge. Pay indirectly conveys to workers the value an organization places on them and the status they have achieved. When workers are paid less than they think they are worth, they are likely to reduce their efforts in order to restore a sense of equity in their relationship with the employer, a fact well demonstrated by psychologists in their studies of equity theory (Walster, Walster, & Berscheid, 1978). Conversely, there is evidence that paying workers bonuses based on organizational performance can markedly increase their effort and performance (Lawler, 1990). Pay can thus be a powerful motivator in encouraging many workers to higher performance and greater growth. Nevertheless, effective pay systems—satisfactory for the worker as well as productive for the employer—are more the exception than the rule.

Pay is the result of a dynamic between worker and employer. The employer, motivated to produce a good product or service at a high profit, is driven by competition and greed to keep costs down, especially pay. To maintain an efficient and productive operation the employer must go to the marketplace and pay workers market rates for the jobs that need to be filled. Market rates depend in large measure on the availability of workers with the particular KSAs the employer needs.

Workers want to be paid enough to provide a decent living for themselves and their families. At a minimum this includes health care, provi-

---

*This chapter is adapted from Appendix E (Application of FJA to Job Evaluation) Fine and Getkate (1995).

190

sion for disability, and retirement. Because all jobs are not the same and some jobs are harder to fill than others, employers pay for what they consider of value; that is, employers pay for the characteristics necessary to fulfill the requirements of the job. These characteristics include *skill, knowledge, effort, responsibility, and adaptability to physical demands and working conditions*—characteristics workers acquire through education, experience, and training. Workers learn to value the acquisition of these characteristics because these characteristics are what employers value and are the basis for establishing whether they—the workers—are being paid *fairly and equitably*. Both fairness and equitability transcend the economic need of making a decent living but are nevertheless intertwined with it. They are derived from workers' comparison of their pay with that of relevant others inside the organization—internal equity—and others outside the organization, known as external equity. These comparisons are hardly objective or scientific, nor are they always conditioned by market factors. Nevertheless they have a great deal to do with an individual's sense of self-worth, identity, and status in the community

Up to this point, pay has been discussed as though it is simply a matter of matching what the employer needs with the characteristics possessed by the worker. This is an oversimplification. Employers want highly motivated workers who will provide the extra effort that contributes to the success of the enterprise. Workers want to be paid for their extra effort and excellence of performance (performance beyond expectations), which adds to the profit and value of the enterprise. Again this needs to be done *equitably and fairly*. To achieve this end, objective measurement to the maximum degree possible must occur.

TWO MAIN WAYS OF PAYING WORKERS

There are two main ways to pay workers fairly and equitably. They can be paid on the basis of the job, ranked for level of difficulty or complexity of its requirements in relation to other jobs. Or workers can be paid on the basis of their personal skills, the more skills they bring to a job–worker situation, the more they will be worth. Both methods are influenced by the worth of the job and/or the skills in the marketplace.

Both methods have advantages and disadvantages. Paying on the basis of the job is by far the most common, perhaps because it is the oldest. It has the advantage of being, or at least appearing to be, the most objective. It is based on job descriptions. These job descriptions are typically quite brief and written so they can be compared with similar brief descriptions contained in market surveys of jobs in other organizations within the same industry. These job comparisons and the pay rates for the jobs help establish

the so-called market rates of pay. Brief as these job descriptions are, estimates are made as to their requirements for education; training; experience; verbal, numerical, and spatial relations abilities; and physical demands. The more (higher levels) of these factors that are required, the more
the jobs are valued. The disadvantage of this approach is that workers put
forth far more skill and effort in their jobs than is rated in the job description. What is more, this approach tends to limit workers to their job description when the natural tendency of many workers is to grow in their
job, go beyond its boundaries, and meet the challenges of the moment.

The latter method, paying the person, is not very common, although
depending on how it is defined, surveys find this method in use in from
5% to 40% of large corporations for some segment of their workforce
(Lawler, 1990). It is especially associated with research and development
endeavors, teamwork, participative management, and high technology organizations. A major disadvantage of this method is that it presents significant problems in definition of relevant skills to be paid for and in administration.

FJA lends itself equally well to either approach. It combines the main elements of both approaches in its concept of a job–worker situation, and the
integrated combination of job requirements and worker characteristics. In
FJA, all jobs are considered as job–worker situations and are rated for the
same factors. These ratings can all be assigned point values that establish
their relative difficulty or complexity.

Willingness to accept the idea that more complex jobs are by and large
worth more money has more or less been ingrained in the U.S. value system and appears to be widely accepted—as long as other contingent factors are also taken into consideration. Contingent factors that can receive
special pay allowances but are not included in the ranking of the complexity of the job–worker situation include: hazards, extreme working conditions (heat, cold, fumes), seniority, allowances for cost of living, family
size, child care, general education, nonspecific training, and performance
excellence (paid by bonus). Payment for these contingent factors is by no
means universal and is frequently a matter determined by the social culture, sometimes by legislation, and at other times as the result of collective
bargaining.

FJA APPROACH TO SKILL EVALUATION:
OVERALL RATIONALE

FJA considers that a job–worker situation, whatever its level of complexity,
involves the whole person and therefore all aspects of a worker's involvement in the job should be considered in the compensation.

Four components contribute to this whole-person involvement: Functional, Holistic, Organizational, and Premium or Special Adaptation. The first three components are intrinsic to the skill requirements of jobs and reflect qualifications that are necessary to perform adequately in the job. These qualifications include an individual's capacities, investment in self, and willingness to assume responsibility. The Premium component represents special adaptations individuals make to the environment in which job–worker situations occur and reflect ways in which workers are willing to extend themselves to adapt to the work situation.

Close examination of these four components reveals they include the effort, training, responsibility, and working conditions covered in traditional compensation plans but do so more comprehensively and in greater detail. The information required by the FJA job evaluation system is obtained by using the 10 measures already described in Chapter 5 (three measures for skill level; three for orientation; three for Reasoning, Math, and Language; and one for Worker Instructions, WI) and several additional scales that are very simple to use. Among these additional scales is a Strength Scale with values already supplied. A few of these additional scales, for example, "Consequences of Error," require the organizations using this approach to establish their own scale of values.

At first glance the amount of information used in FJA job evaluation might seem daunting. However, the information needed for the evaluation is readily at hand via the ratings of the summary description of the task bank. Thereupon it is a matter of transposing the information into the job evaluation form in a logical step-by-step process. Once performed, the process becomes quite simple.

The ratings are made from summary descriptions of the task bank designed to reflect the highest functional levels in each of the functional scales. For the present purpose, the summary of a field service engineer (FSE) X-ray, which occurs in the medical systems industry is used to illustrate the FJA method of calculating point values for job-worker situations.

Summary Description of FSE X-Ray

Repair and/or service (e.g., preventive maintenance) x-ray equipment in response to calls for help (phone or pager, from headquarters or customer) or according to maintenance schedule, observing problem on site if possible, drawing on knowledge of equipment, training, and information elicited from x-ray technician or radiologist and relying on experience and skill in asking questions *in order to* correct problem by phone fix or on site, bring equipment to peak performance and ensure customer is happy with result; apply/use test equipment (oscilloscope, multi-meter, h.v. bleeder, radiation meters) as necessary to particular points in x-ray equipment, verifying location of problem, explaining to customer results of troubleshooting, indicating on-spot repairs possible or delays that might occur if special parts are to be ordered, drawing on knowledge of parts carried in vehicle, parts available through computer access (FSE has portable computer) and relying on diagnostic and computer skills; attend to paperwork to report on service calls, parts replaced, time spent, etc., drawing on company procedures to keep detailed and complete records and relying on skill in processing data *in order to* establish a basis for billing; exchange information with management and other FSEs by phone, voice, or e-mail concerning schedules, itineraries, customer relations, status of equipment with ongoing service calls, responding to calls on pager, drawing on own prepared itineraries and priorities *in order to* keep management and other FSEs informed of whereabouts and personal availability to help if needed; attends to equipment maintenance schedules, coaches new employees on the job, reviews primary accounts checking fulfillment of obligations, and participates in self-development activities (reading technical material and attending seminars) drawing on understanding of organizational objectives and personal adaptability *in order to* meet needs for growth.

The ten basic FJA ratings for this job-worker situation plus strength are shown in Fig. 16.1. These ratings are derived from the FJA task bank and represent the following analysis of the summary description of the FSE job–worker situation. The ratings are used as values for completing the FJA Job Evaluation Form.

The functional levels show this job–worker situation involves Setting-Up (4B) as it relates to tools and equipment; Analyzing (4) as it relates to all of the variables that need to be considered in arriving at a diagnosis, and Coaching, Sourcing Information and Persuading (3a, b, and c) as they relate to the several ways the FSE needs to deal with People.

The Orientation ratings show this is primarily a Things job–worker situation (a rating of 40) almost equal to the secondary involvement of Data (35) with the People (25) involvement substantial but still in third place. A

Functional Level			Functional Orientation			Worker Instruc- tion	Enablers			Strength
							General Educational Development			
Things	Data	People	Things	Data	People		Reason	Math	Lang	
4B	4	3A,B,C	40(3)	35(2)	25(1)	4	4	3	4	7

FIG. 16.1. Summary ratings for FSE—X-ray.

close look at the orientation ratings also shows that all three are relatively important although they rank 3, 2, 1 (as shown in parentheses) and the performance standards for each merit close attention.

The Enabler abilities include WI, General Educational Development (GED), and Strength (Str). The Worker Instructions include the ability to follow instructions in both verbal and schematic form, figuring out his or her own way of getting a job done including selection of tools, test equipment, parts, and sequence of operations (tasks), and obtaining essential information from handbooks and resources in the computer. May set up procedures for others to do the work.

The Level 4 for reasoning ability indicates knowledge of a system of interrelated procedures in this instance relating to the electronics of X-ray equipment and the ability to access optional solutions to ordinary problems. Level 4 also indicates the ability to apply principles to everyday problems and deal with a variety of concrete variables in situations where only limited standardization exists. Level 3 for mathematical ability requires making calculations involving fractions, decimals, and percentages. Language ability, Level 4, involves reading and comprehending technical manuals and written instructions, as well as the verbal fluency necessary to communicate with professional customers, colleagues, and management. The strength rating, Level 3, reflects the need to transport test equipment and parts from the transportation vehicle to the work site.

The next step in the FJA job evaluation process is completion of the job evaluation form; the format is shown in Table 16.1. As noted earlier, the values to be entered are in most instances the number representing the rating. However, in the case of Orientation, the ratings are converted to rankings ranging from high to low with 3 being the highest.

FUNCTIONAL SKILL

This column has four sections, one each for Physical (Things), Mental (Data), and Interpersonal (People). The fourth section involving an executive decision concerning organizational values is discussed following a description of the calculations relating to the first three sections,

Each of the first three sections has a place for the values for the FSEs. Thus, under Physical, Things Level takes a 4 for Setting Up/Precision Working (only the numbers are used in the calculations); Strength (the Enabler) takes a 3; Orientation takes a 3 (the rank of the percentage). The formula for combining these values to obtain a subtotal is as follows: Level plus (+) Enabler times (×) Orientation = Subtotal. Substituting the figures in this formula yields $4 + 3 = 7, \times 4 = 28$.

Before continuing, it is necessary to explain the rationale for adding the Enabler value to the Level value and multiplying by the Orientation value.

TABLE 16.1
FJA Job Evaluation Rating Form

Functional Skills	Holistic Factors	Organizational Factors	Premium Factors
Physical Factors	Consequences of Error	Number of programs managed	Extreme work conditions
Things level		Value of programs managed	Shift work
+			Hazards
Strength			
×			
Orientation			
=			
Subtotal:		Number of clients served	Overtime
Mental Factors			
Data level	Responsibility (Prescription/ discretion)	Level of persons contacted	Isolated location
+		Internal	
Reason/math		External	Labor market
×			Shortage
Orientation			Surplus
=			
Subtotal:		Number of persons directly supervised	Seniority
Interpersonal Factors			Merit performance
People level		Number of persons indirectly supervised	Cost of living
+	Specific vocational preparation (SVP)		
Language			
×			
Orientation			
=			
Subtotal:			
Relative value management places on:			
Things _____			
Data _____			
People _____			
Skill Subtotal:	Holistic Subtotal:	Organizational Subtotal:	Premium Subtotal:

GRAND TOTAL:

Rationale for Adding Enabler Values to Level

Skill levels have as *Enablers*—physical, mental, and interpersonal factors appropriate to TDP. Enablers are added to the functional level because they are complementary to the level and integral with the behavior.

The enabler for Things is the active strength required to do the job as rated on the 5-point scale in Table 16.2. The ratings on this scale, which range from Sedentary to Very Heavy, reflect different degrees of physical involvement where the worker draws on physical effort in lifting. The appropriate scale value is added to the skill level value before the effort multiplier is applied.

The Enabler for Data is obtained from the Reasoning and/or Math scales. The higher of the two ratings is added to the functional level. The rationale for applying this factor to the Data value is that data require mental activity to apply knowledge, and both reasoning and math are the appropriate mental activities for this component. Again the Reasoning and/or Math are integral with the behavior. In most jobs, other than certain selected academic or scientific jobs, Reasoning has the highest rating and will be the one applied.

The Enabler for Interpersonal function is obtained from the Language scale and the rating for language is its value. In the job–worker situation the most common form of interpersonal activity is spoken language (accompanied, of course, by body language). Written job orders may also be enlarged on through the spoken word. The Language scale provides speaking and reading illustrations. (When interpersonal activity occurs mainly through writing, it is considered a data function and would be rated for the reasoning involved.)

Rationale for Using Orientation Value as a Multiplier

The orientation component is the source of the effort multiplier. It is not integral with function as is the enabler. Instead it is a function of the demands of the work and the quality of the worker. The effort contributed to

TABLE 16.2
Strength Scale

Physical Effort (lifting):	Weight
Very Heavy: Over 75 pounds	5
Heavy: 50–75 pounds	4
Medium: 25–50 pounds	3
Light: 5–25 pounds (on feet)	2
Sedentary	1

the function and enabler can increase productivity enormously, far beyond mere addition.

The rationale is as follows: effort applied for each task is total effort or 100%. However, a skilled worker gives each of the three functional components—TDP—the proportion of 100% that is warranted by the nature of the task in order to achieve the desired standards. An individual does this more or less unconsciously as a result of training and experience. (It is not unlike the feeling and tonal value that a concert violinist or pianist learns to give each note and phrase of a musical composition drawing on training and personal experience.)

Functional job analysts assign such proportional values on the basis of their understanding of the standards that need to be achieved in a given task. The three proportions must add to 100 but must be supported by data in the task statement and be acceptable to the incumbent. Although the proportions are estimates, there usually is not any problem in arriving at consensus as to what these proportions should be. Differences among a group of incumbents are resolved by summoning up additional data on which agreement can be reached. The main purpose of the estimates is to arrive at their relative importance.

Although the rationale has been described in terms of tasks, the basic units of job–worker situations, the same rationale applies to the evaluation of the job summary. The summary is written to reflect the highest functional levels of the job's tasks and the appropriate Orientation.

The proportional values are translated to multipliers of 3, 2, and 1 according to their rank order by orientation. These multipliers can be adjusted to higher numbers, for example, 30, 20, or 10, to obtain a greater spread of skill values. These larger numbers do not have any effect on the relative rank order of the skill subtotal for the particular job.

Following through for Mental in the same manner as for Physical, the following numbers are used in the formula: Level 4 for Analyzing, Enabler (Reasoning or Math, whichever is higher)—4, Orientation—2. Combining these numbers as in the formula results in a subtotal of 16 ($4 + 4 \times 2$).

In the case of Interpersonal, the numbers are: Level—3 for Sourcing Information (or Coaching or Persuading), Enabler (Language)—4, Orientation—1. Combining these numbers in the formula results in a subtotal of 7 ($3 + 4 \times 1$).

Relative Value of TDP Skills

The final item in the Functional Factors column, Relative Value Management Places on TDP, deals with an important management decision that needs to be made at the outset of the job evaluation process. Management must ask the following questions: What is most important in the given organization? What does it value most? Whatever it decides, it must apply the values arrived at to all the jobs in the plant. It cannot, in all fairness, shift its decision for the convenience or favor of a particular group of workers. If management decides that what it values most is Things, then Data, and then People, on the order of 7, 5, 3, and uses these weights to add to the component subtotals, it must stay with these weights for all the jobs in the organization. The addition of these weights is a way of bringing underlying beliefs to the fore and accounting for them by adding points to the basic skill total.

The organization employing the FSEs is a corporate manufacturing giant serving the health care industry. Prompt servicing of equipment when something goes wrong is critical—lives may depend on it. The organization prides itself on the excellence of its equipment and stands by the equipment's reputation for reliability. Keeping the equipment in good repair is critical, hence the organization places the highest value on Things— 7. Nevertheless, because of the advanced technology of the equipment and the considerable skill required in its maintenance, the organization also places a high value on Data—5. Finally, the organization values People last (but not insubstantially)—3. Thus, TDP are valued in relation to each other 7, 5, 3.

These numbers say that to this organization, people's ability to work with Things is worth a little more than twice as much as their ability to work with People, and their ability to work with Data is almost as important as their ability to work with Things. (The numbers are arrived at by consensus to reflect the dominant feelings expressed by the organization's leaders.)

HOLISTIC FACTORS

Holistic factors are so named because they relate to the whole job. They underlie or overlay the whole person's functioning in the job. The three holistic factors are: Consequences of Error, Responsibility (as reflected in the execution of the prescriptive and discretionary aspects of instructions), and Specific Vocational Preparation (SVP). They cannot be expressed in terms of the analytic factors TDP.

Consequences of Error

Error results in losses. Losses can occur in materials, money, staff time, morale, and organizational image. Losses occur because of ignorance (lack of training); failures in judgment, courtesy, and cooperation; and lack of discipline in following the social and work rules relating to work behavior and time. The extent of the losses (expressed for the subject organization) can be:

High   Affect the whole organization—give the organization a black eye and have a ripple effect in the community or marketplace. Can lead to bankruptcy or a tremendous uphill struggle to overcome the negative effects.

Medium High   Affect the organization in loss of significant financial support—for example, loss of a major account, funding, grant, and/or database, or disaffection of a segment of population served (loss of market share).

Medium   Affect a program in loss of materials, money, or staff time or harms client.

Medium Low   Affect a department or work unit in loss of material, money, or staff time or harms client.

Low   Affect an immediate work process in loss of personal and/or supervisory time needed to correct error.

These five scale levels are simply indicative. They can be extended to as many as 10 levels with assignments of dollar value (see Table 16.3). In defining values for this scale the issues are: Is information available to make the judgment, and can the judgments be applied consistently?

Needless to say, the organization needs to be aware of where and how losses can occur, know which tasks in which jobs are vulnerable, and take appropriate precautions in safeguarding against these losses. Such precautions can occur in hiring, training, design of the workplace, design of procedures, for example, traffic, safety and security education, and signing of documents. Sometimes losses can reveal significant management neglect and point to remedial measures. As part of each worker's training and induction into the organization, it is essential that he or she be alerted to the potential consequences of error inherent in failure to perform according to training and orientation.

TABLE 16.3
Dollar Value Consequences of Error

Level	Description	Amount
5	High	$50,000+
4	Medium High	$20,000–$50,000
3	Medium	$5,000–$20,000
2	Medium Low	$1,000–$5,000
1	Low	$0–$1,000

There is a medium consequence of error for the FSE x-ray, one that can result in a loss of material, staff time, harm to client, and cancellation of repair and maintenance contracts. This is a Level 3 with a weight of 12.

Responsibility

In the view of FJA, responsibility ultimately is a matter of following instructions, being accountable for that what is prescribed and what is discretionary. Every job, from highest to lowest, has a set of instructions. As noted earlier, in higher-level jobs the instructions are heavily weighted in the direction of discretion or judgment. The lower the level of the job the more it involves prescription, following SOP. It must not be overlooked that even on the simplest level there are discretionary aspects to the job and that even on the highest level there are prescriptive aspects.

Responsibility is a matter for the worker to effectively and efficiently mix the prescriptive and discretionary aspects of the job as they relate to the culture (values and traditions) of the organization in order to achieve the required standards. It is easier to evaluate responsibility for following prescriptive instructions because they are specific and often involve numerical (quantifiable) elements. (These quantifiable elements represent the distillation of much experience.) It is much more difficulty to evaluate discretionary instructions because they have not yet been reduced to SOP. Nevertheless, judgments will be made. A caution to be observed is to treat errors and successes in the uses of discretion equally. A discretionary failure may be as much the fault of the person issuing the discretionary instruction as the person executing it.

The rating for worker instructions as defined in the WI Scale provides the basis for the value assigned (see Table 16.4). For the FSE, the WI Level is 4 with a value of 20.

> Output (product or service) is specified in the assignment, which may be in the form or a memorandum or schematic (sketch or blueprint). The worker must work out his or her own way of getting the job done, including the selection and use of tools and/or equipment, sequence of operations (tasks), and obtaining important information (handbooks, databases). Worker may either do the work or set up standards and procedures for others to do it.

SVP

This factor places a value on the relevant preparation in experience and training that an individual needs to reach normal production (RNP) for a given job. (It is not intended to characterize the individual who may have more or less training than is needed for the job.) The scale for SVP is shown in Table 16.5.

TABLE 16.4
WI Scale

Range	Weight
8*	
7*	
6*	
5	30
4	20
3	12
2	7
1	3

*Weights for Levels 6, 7, and 8 of the WI Scale need to be arrived at by executive decision where these exceptional jobs occur.

TABLE 16.5
SVP Experience and Training

Level	Description	Weight
9	10 Years +	50
8	4–10 Years	45
7	2–4 Years	35
6	1–2 Years	30
5	6 Months–1 Year	25
4	3 Months–6 Months	20
3	30 Days–3 Months	15
2	Up to 30 Days	10
1	Short Demo	5

Certain conventions have been adopted in evaluating an individual's qualifications.

A 4-year college education is valued at 2 years of vocational preparation whether in English or engineering.

A 2-year associate degree with vocational orientation is valued at 1 year of vocational preparation.

A specific 6-month business (e.g., secretarial) or vocational course (e.g., electronic technician) is given full value as 6 months of vocational preparation.

A fully served apprenticeship to achieve journeyman status is valued as 3 years of vocational preparation.

Internships are given full value for time involved, year for year.

Experience background needs to be evaluated for relevance—on functional, specific content, and adaptive skill levels—and judgment calls made as to the time value assigned.

In general, Level 7, 2 to 4 years, is the level required to perform in a craft such as carpenter or plumber or enter a professional occupation, such as teacher, accountant, nurse.

The SVP for the FSE is judged to require 1 to 2 years or Level 6, which yields a weight of 30. The addition of the three scores for this column, 12, 20, and 30 yields a subtotal of 62.

ORGANIZATIONAL FACTORS

These factors are a further elaboration of responsibility as they largely and specifically apply to the management functions in the organization. About the only item among these factors that applies to workers generally is Level of Persons Contacted unless the workers have assigned functions in participative management.

These factors deal quite specifically with the management of money, plant and equipment, and persons. Each of the items can have its own scale and may require some definition in terms of dollar ranges or programs. Programs can also be understood as departments.

Judgment calls need to be made as to the number of points assigned to persons supervised directly versus person managed indirectly. Typically supervision is a more direct relationship with people.

Level of Persons Contacted and
Number of Clients Served

The assumption made is that the higher the level of person contacted the greater the responsibility and possibility of error. Thus a major difference between a low-level secretary and executive secretary may be chiefly in this factor. This assumption can be extended to all jobs but is probably more evident in managerial jobs. For the FSE, a scale constructed for a social service agency serves as an example. However, a similar scale should be constructed for each organization using this methodology.

A typical scale for people contacted is shown in Table 16.6. The assumption here is that the higher the level of the person contacted the greater the responsibility and cost of making an error.

The Number of Clients Served factor (Table 16.7) is intended to reflect client load for those jobs having contact with clients of the organization.

The factors in this column that apply to the FSE are the Level of Persons Contacted and the Number of Clients Served. The former involves contact

TABLE 16.6
Scale of Values for Level of Persons Contacted

Weight	Level
	External
5	Service providers, line to line, vendors
7	Clients
10	Program directors, department heads
15	Agency heads
20	Legislators
25	Power brokers
	Internal
3	Program or project directors
6	Interdepartmental
9	Executive staff
12	Agency board members
15	Board of directors

TABLE 16.7
Scale of Values for Number of Clients Served

Number of Clients	Weight
1	1
2–3	2
4–5	3
6+	5

with the Program director internally, which has a value of 3, and with Clients externally, which has a value of 7. The two values, 3 and 7 add up to a total score of 10. The latter involves contact with 6+ clients of the organization, therefore yields a weight of 5. The total score in this column for the FSE is 15.

BASE POINT JOB EVALUATION SCORE

The addition of the three component scores, Functional, Holistic, and Organizational—62, 10, and 15—for the FSE yields the basic job evaluation score. The score compares this job–worker situation to all other job–worker situations within the organization on the basis of the same kinds of data. It does not include additional values that might be assigned following the consideration of Premium factors.

PREMIUM FACTORS

As noted earlier, Premium factors are *not* appropriately woven into the job evaluation point scores. The reason is these factors call for special adaptations on the part of individual workers or organizations to contextual factors of jobs that are not necessarily associated with skill acquisition. Premium factors are of roughly three types:

Worker adaptation to extreme or hazardous working conditions calling for the particular willingness of the worker to adapt to the conditions. This category includes shift work, overtime work, or work in isolated situations.

Employer adaptation to workers unique needs and labor market conditions causing shortages or surpluses for particular specific content skills or employee willingness to adapt to very special conditions.

Employer adaptations to loyalty and meritorious performance that contributes to the employer's stability, profitability, and growth potential.

These factors need to be compensated for by bonuses or premiums tacked on to the base pay of a particular job. In this manner the comparative status of the jobs based on skill can be maintained and compensation for special circumstances can be seen for what it is.

SUMMARY OF FJA AND PAY

Pay, the basic and most immediate reward for work, presents employers with a tremendous challenge. They need to be fair and equitable in two vital ways: (a) how they compensate workers for qualities the workers bring to the workplace—KSAs, effort, and adaptability and (b) how they treat workers in comparison to each other within the organization and also to workers in comparable work in the community at large.

Workers need to feel they are being paid fairly and equitably not only to meet their personal needs but also to maintain their self-esteem and sense of self-worth. When these conditions are met, workers are best able to contribute effectively and efficiently to the profitability and excellence of the organization and its competitive position in the marketplace. When this dynamic between employer and worker is working well, it is a win–win situation for both.

FJA is a comprehensive and effective tool for establishing the value of a job–worker situation, taking into consideration functional skill requirements, holistic factors (consequences of error, responsibility, and SVP) and organizational factors relating to management and contact with people. FJA focuses on both the job requirements that establish the level of the job and on the worker characteristics that meet those requirements—characteristics that indicate the human potential involved and available for growth. It also provides for a fourth component, Premium factors. Premium factors call for special values to be placed on adaptations to particular working conditions, shortage of qualified workers for the job, and performance beyond expectations (meritorious performance). Should the employer wish to compensate for unique skill potential, this too can be accommodated by the FJA job evaluation approach through the Premium factor component.

The FJA job evaluation method, although detailed, involves a simple transposition of values to a job evaluation form developed for this purpose. The values have mostly already been determined during the FJA phase of the process. There is considerable advantage in the four component approach of FJA because it reveals to workers and the employer exactly what is valued and what is being paid for. It permits flexibility in arriving at a final score by allowing for the assignment of specific weights to one or another component in a uniform manner. Determination of such weights needs to be arrived at through a shared interpretation of experience to ensure continued trust between the employer and workers.

Chapter **17**

Job Design—
Building Better Work

Workers experience their jobs in depth and with an intimacy rarely appreciated by their managers. After all, jobs are a significant part of workers' lives, providing not only a livelihood for them and their families but often also providing the basis for the expression of their potential. Job descriptions can only faintly reflect the richness and meaning in any work experience, although FJA comes closer than many job analysis methods by working within the experience of incumbents and writing the task bank in their language. As a worker makes sense of the work and grows in the work situation, he or she modifies the work in ways both large and small to suit personal style and growth needs and to make the work-doing system more productive—most often without the awareness of management. To expect workers to do any less is to deny their need to express their sense of self and their competency.

Fields (1998), in an Associated Press article about Harley-Davidson's newest assembly plant in Kansas City, Missouri, illustrates what can happen when workers are given free rein to express their potential in the workplace:

> Three dozen employee-designed carts that swivel 360 degrees and can be lowered or raised to suit each worker, carry components among stations. For welding, frames are mounted on special wheels so that welders don't have to contort themselves to reach each corner. For greater consistency in Harley's hallmark striping, traditionally painted by hand, the workers designed a device to guide the brush. (Fields, 1998)

We have seen innumerable instances of this type of personal initiative and adaptability in their many years of conducting FJA focus groups. Invariably, workers' efforts have positive effects on product or service quality and on productivity. In fact, this is one of the central facts of work life that emerges during an FJA focus group, regardless of job, organization level, or country.

Unfortunately, worker efforts to improve the workplace often go unrecognized and unappreciated by management. Even worse, management frequently censures workers when they redesign their work in ways management has not foreseen. This is not to say that managers should not be involved in job design. Managers who leave workers entirely to their own devices abdicate their responsibility to add value to job design—value contributed through the synergy of joint problem solving. Without this mutuality, workers' job design efforts, however well intentioned, sometimes come off as improvised, especially because workers do not have the "bird's eye view" of operations afforded to the manager. The need for cooperative effort in job design has been known for a long time. Taylor (1911), who, at the beginning of this century, started the scientific management movement that revolutionized management practices in U.S. industry, was harshly critical of managers who abandon workers to their own devices. In *The principles of Scientific Management* he said:

> The body of this paper will make it clear that, to work according to scientific laws, the management must take over and perform much of the work which is now left to the men [sic]; almost every act of the workman should be preceded by one or more preparatory acts of the management which enable him to do his work better and quicker than he otherwise could. And each man should daily be taught by and receive the most friendly help from those who are over him, instead of being, at the one extreme, driven or coerced by his bosses, and at the other left to his own unaided devices. This close, intimate, personal cooperation between the management and the men is of the essence of modern scientific or task management. (p. 26)

JOB DESIGN—SYNERGY
BETWEEN MANAGER AND WORKER

So what exactly *is* management's role in job design? It is a cooperative and supportive one. Managers have perspective on the goals and purpose of the work-doing system (the big picture). They should clearly articulate the objectives and goals for the work unit or team and inform workers of systems factors that can impede or facilitate the workers' efforts that need to be accounted for in job redesign. For example, if an old machine is to be phased out in a few months and replaced with a new one having up-to-date technology, the manager needs to inform the workers of the upcoming replacement before they undertake extensive work to modify the old machine. Managers also need to provide technical or other data that can contribute to more effective job design; for example, engineering specifications, designs, and advice may be very helpful to workers making modifications to increase the production of a machine. Additionally, management should give workers access to the vital resources, including money, required to effect the improvements; for example, an anticipated work redesign may require a training program to familiarize workers with a new technology. Finally, management should provide support and encouragement when workers willingly take on self-initiated job design. In short, the manager is the catalyst for job design. A catalyst provokes change, induces the system to move to a place where it would not otherwise go, but the energy driving the reaction (change) is provided by the workers.

It must be recognized that work varies to the degree that workers have the latitude to redesign their jobs. In tasks and jobs having lower levels of discretion and relatively more prescription, opportunities for worker initiative is more limited than in high discretion jobs. In jobs at the lower levels of discretion, workers are constrained to a greater extent by the technology used and/or by managerial prescriptions about how materials are to be processed or worked, or how customers are to be served. Transit operators on urban bus routes, for example, must do much of their work from a fixed position (drivers seat) within a moving metal platform (the bus) that they control on a moment-by-moment basis but within a time and route schedule set by management. To the extent that he or she can, the operator tailors the work within the prescribed parameters. But the physical layout of the work situation and necessity to work within a time- and route-sensitive system (e.g., Passenger A must be at a specific transfer point before the next scheduled bus leaves) constrains—sometimes severely—what the operator can do. Nevertheless, as operators strive for work satisfaction and service quality, they express individuality and adaptation even under these restrictive conditions. One may pull especially close to the curb to facilitate exit of an older or physically handicapped person while another carries a personal copy of a city map to better instruct out-of-town passengers in how to get to their desired destinations. As jobs allow more discretion, the tendency of workers to express themselves through job redesign becomes more pronounced. The only limit is the degree of prescription management decides to overlay on the work.

People design their own work to the extent possible whether management knows this or not. Csikszentmihalyi (1997), in his work on flow, predicted this. Work without sufficient challenge produces boredom after the worker has mastered the requirements of the job. Boredom is a noxious state and many workers take it on themselves to raise the bar—to challenge their languishing skills—by adding additional value to their work. *They will do this with or without explicit endorsement by management and often without its knowledge.* Examples of worker-initiated job design includes the teacher who sets up extra tutoring sessions for students after regular classroom hours, the service person who delivers a badly needed appliance to an elderly shut-in's home on his or her own time, the press operator who does extra maintenance on a machine outside of SOP in order to increase the life of the equipment and avoid breakdowns during busy periods. These workers strive for continuous improvement, sometimes in otherwise sterile work environments, as a natural reaction to their need to learn and grow, to feel competent and in control of their fate, and to avoid the spirit-crushing weight of interminable boredom. Workers like these are more the rule than the exception. Management does not need worker motivation programs to bring out this tendency. Managers who set the necessary conditions of trust and adopt a listening stance can be motivated to participate in the natural process of job design and add value to it.

A PRECONDITION FOR SUCCESSFUL
COOPERATIVE JOB DESIGN:
SHARED INTERPRETATION OF EXPERIENCE

A listening stance by management sets the stage for the shared interpretation of experience (Shapiro & Carr, 1991) between workers and management that is the sine qua non for a healthy and maximally productive work system. Management must understand where workers are coming from with their informal job design efforts and trust them to have the best interests of the organization at heart. Then the communication can flow between workers and management—they can work together to get the most out of job design and serve the interests of worker growth as well.

The Japanese management model of *kaizen* (continuous improvement, CI) requires a shared interpretation of experience between workers and management to be successful. Imai (1997) described it as follows:

> Most "uniquely Japanese" management practices, such as total quality management or company wide quality control, quality circles, and our style of labor relations, can be reduced to one word: *kaizen*. Using the term *kaizen* in place of such buzzwords as productivity, total quality control (TQC), zero defects (ZD), just-in-time (JIT), and the suggestion system paints a clearer picture of what has been going on in Japanese industry. *Kaizen* is an umbrella concept for all these practices. (p. 2)

Kaizen has apparently served the Japanese very well in helping increase their competitiveness over the past few decades. Imai (1997) provided a vivid example of how this shared interpretation works in kaizen:

> Eric Machiels, who came to Japan from Europe as a young student to learn about Japanese management practices, was placed in a Japanese automotive

assembly plant as an operator: Comparing his experience there with his pre-vious experience in European *gemba* [workplaces], Machiels observed much more intense communication between management and operators in Japan, resulting in a much more effective two-way information flow between them. Workers had a much clearer understanding of management expectations and of their own responsibilities in the whole *kaizen* process. The resulting constructive tension on the work floor made the work much more challeng-ing in terms of meeting management expectations and giving the workers a higher sense of pride in their work. (pp. 15–16)

Japan's highly cooperative culture expresses itself strongly in Japanese workplaces (Hofstede, 1984). In this light, the ability of Japanese workers and managers to achieve a shared interpretation of experience is not so surprising. In the highly individualistic United States and other Western societies, workplace competition and lone effort are the norm and shared interpretation of experience between workers and management is harder to achieve. On the other hand, it is being achieved in more and more work-places. Entrepreneurs seeking to move in the direction of shared interpre-tation will find FJA a useful tool for this purpose.

CHOICES IN FJA JOB DESIGN: SHOULD MANAGEMENT STRIVE FOR TOP-DOWN RADICAL CHANGE OR BOTTOM-UP CI?

Hammer and Champy (1993) proposed a reengineering approach to job design and organization change. Reengineering seeks to have corporations "reinvent" themselves:

At the heart of business reengineering lies the notion of *discontinuous think-ing*—identifying and abandoning the outdated rules and fundamental as-sumptions that underlie current business operations. Every company is re-plete with implicit rules left over from earlier decades: "Customers don't repair their own equipment." "Local warehouses are necessary for good service." "Merchandising decisions are made at headquarters." These rules are based on assumptions about technology, people, and organizational goals that no longer hold. Unless companies change these rules, any super-ficial reorganizations they perform will be no more effective than dusting the furniture in Pompeii. (p. 3)

This is the heroic or cowboy-in-the-white-hat approach to job design and organizational change. The reengineering approach is exemplified by a company that, after years of management neglect in the face of foreign competition, is reengineered and turned around from near bankruptcy to a world-class manufacturer by a small cadre of elite consultants and senior managers. By taking a "blank sheet of paper" and with a bold and imaginative reconceptualization of the company's core processes, they set in motion a top-down change process to revitalize the organization. Reengineered organizations literally *reinvent* themselves or, to be more precise, are reinvented by senior-level decision makers. This model is consistent with belief in the efficacy of command and control management from the top of the organization.

In contrast to the reengineering approach that seeks very large gains in productivity at a single throw, the Japanese have taken the incremental approach of kaizen. Rather than "discontinuous thinking," they exercise the discipline and patience of the *continuous thinking* needed to engage in incremental, gradual, evolutionary improvements to work systems and processes over long periods of time. To quote Imai (1997), a major proponent of kaizen:

> In Japanese, *kaizen* means continuous improvement. The word implies improvement that involves everyone—both managers and workers—and entails relatively little expense. The *kaizen* philosophy assumes that our way of life—be it our working life, our social life, or our home life should focus on constant-improvement efforts. (p. 1)

The preface to this book noted that FJA requires its practitioners to walk in, and experience first-hand the real world where work gets done. Kaizen requires this as well. Imai (1997) used the Japanese word *gemba* to refer to this real world—the shop floor, the service counter, the classroom—where frontline workers add value to the product or service. All other activities in the organization—project and engineering management, finance, and marketing—must be in support of frontline activity; otherwise, the work-doing system will eventually fail in today's competitive, quality- and cost-conscious world. This place where the critical activity occurs, where value is added, must be respected and lived in constantly by both workers and managers. FJA owes its existence and draws its strength from its ability to capture in words the vitality that exists in the workplace. FJA finds its home in organizations that take worker involvement to heart and direct their managers to partner with workers where the real action happens.

Whatever the relative long-term economic and productivity benefits of reengineering or CI, each of these approaches has a markedly different impact on workers. People who endure wrenching change, including that introduced by top-down reengineering (often accompanied by severe downsizing) have their sense of personal control and self-worth—and their belief in a stable and essentially benign environment—shattered. Trust and a shared interpretation of experience vanish along with the familiar landmarks of everyday experience built up through years in the same job and workplace. People become helpless victims of circumstances and, even if they keep their employment in a reengineered workplace, have to start over in making sense of their new work situation and mapping a way through it. CI, on the other hand, allows time for workers to adjust and adapt to the incremental changes in the workplace often introduced at their initiative. The shared interpretation of experience between workers and management is negotiated and renegotiated on an ongoing basis, resolving small differences before they become large ones and giving workers a stable, if evolving, set of management expectations to work toward. Clearly, CI is in sync with what behavioral scientists know about human adaptability and the maintenance of minimum-stress, psychologically healthy organizations. It is therefore safe to assume that organizations using FJA to embark on job design have a CI process in mind in partnership with the workers.

FJA: A FLEXIBLE TOOL FOR JOB DESIGN

FJA is sometimes misunderstood as being a static tool for HRM planning. Some managers have come to believe that FJA is a one-time process: a focus group is convened, a task bank collected; then some "key" top-down management decision such as development of a new training program or performance appraisal system is made; and finally, the task bank is filed away. Several years down the line when another major management HRM initiative is in the works the task bank is dusted off, revived, and updated. In this view, the FJA task bank is like a mummy, enshrining a job or at least a good part of it. *Nothing could be further from the truth.* The potential of FJA can best be realized if it is used daily and revised frequently as jobs evolve. A task bank represents an ongoing conversation between workers and managers because it captures a realistic picture of work as it is actually done *here and now* and in the gritty reality of the workplace where value is added to any product or service. It should be used liberally in combination with other continuous improvement tools such as cause-and-effect diagrams and control charts, and as job design needs evolve in the normal course of events. FJA should be front and center to assist and support workers and their managers as they tackle the challenges of continuous improvement.

Choi, Rungtusanatham, and Kim (1997) captured the essence of this idea in their study of seven companies which initiated continuous improvement:

> For this concept [flexible task routines in continuous improvement or CI] to take root, companies must reconsider their routines. Traditionally, work routines are viewed as unvarying elements of an organization. They constitute the best ways of performing a task, and they are something workers must abide by whenever they do their work. However, routines do not have

to be maintained faithfully; instead, they can become dynamic and be constantly updated and upgraded. For instance, rather than telling a worker to set up and run a machine in a certain way, the line leader would encourage the worker to constantly try to think of new and better ways to set it up. From this perspective, the outputs are viewed not as a function of static production routines but as a function of dynamic production routines that encompass CI activities. (p. 45)

Translating the above into FJA terms, the task bank represents the cumulative expertise of both workers and the work organization for achieving productivity. This is why the task bank needs to be constantly available to workers and managers for daily use and updating. If ongoing job changes nudge worker skill to higher levels of complexity or significantly change the mix of TDP orientations on tasks, the constantly evolving task bank immediately signals managers and workers that new HR requirements are appearing in the work site. These new requirements can be dealt with proactively through additional training or other means before they become a serious impediment to operations. *FJA offers a means to sensitively calibrate and match HR requirements to ongoing technological and organizational changes within CI.* FJA data, including ratings, can be used to their best effect if they are tracked over time and periodically reviewed by HR staff in partnership with workers and line managers, in order to assure that HR efforts are keeping pace with CI of process and enlargement of expertise.

BASIC FJA THEMES APPLIED TO JOB DESIGN

FJA provides an objective framework to ask the right questions during ongoing job design. Questions workers and management should address during CI efforts include:

- What is the likely impact on us—the workers—of introducing new technology (added stress, workload)? Will time be allotted from normal productive activities to allow us to ease into the new technology?
- At what point will management need to change the selection, performance assessment, and reward processes to better accommodate ongoing job change?
- How and where have worker skill requirements changed? What types of skills are involved? What are the implications for training and development of workers?
- With all this change, are workers and managers as accountable for

results in their respective spheres of activity as they were under the previous system?

- Given that performance standards are a moving target in a CI system, what are those standards at present?

If the initial investment in the focus group is to pay off, FJA must be viewed as a flexible tool for job design and an integral part of CI efforts. The overall FJA themes relevant to job design are now reviewed to underscore the type of diagnostic thinking workers and managers can use to make the most of FJA information.

Job Design Anticipates Whole-Person Involvement

The literature of industrial and organizational psychology is replete with examples and studies of the consequences of treating workers as adjuncts of machines. One of the most famous of these studies, a study of automobile assembly line jobs was reported in *Man on the assembly line*, by Walker and Guest (1952). All of these studies made the point that although the jobs were designed from the standpoint of efficiency, they were essentially inhuman. The jobs were designed to use people in limited physical ways to perform tasks repetitively according to the speed of an assembly line or the productive capacity of a machine. Many jobs in meat packing plants and insurance companies were similarly designed. All of these jobs were based on the idea that incumbents could be trained quickly to become expert and therefore highly productive in the few operations involved in the particular work station to which they were assigned. Worker initiative was designed out of these jobs in the further belief that such initiative would disturb the procedures and result in a lowering of efficiency and productivity. During the 1950s, Fine directed a study of 4,000 jobs, approximately 18% of all the jobs defined in the *Dictionary of occupational titles*, and found that most of the so-called low end, semi-skilled jobs were characterized as involving "repetitive, short-cycle tasks."

The engineered use of people as adjuncts of technology often resulted in poor quality and high percentages of waste. Workers were bored with this kind of work and dissatisfaction was rife. Within industrial organizational psychology this finding led to the movement of designing jobs to include variety and enrichment. Management began to recognize that workers were whole persons and functioned best if there were challenges to their potential in their jobs. Managers further recognized that workers were human resources and could contribute far more value to their work than a few limited physical operations. FJA builds on this recognition that workers are whole persons and jobs need to be designed to allow for the expression of workers' potential rather than suppress it.

Job Design Changes Draw on Both Job Content and Job Context

Many job design efforts focus on changing job content as shown in the quote from Lawler (1986), who is a leading expert in the introduction of job design into high involvement work systems:

> Job enrichment does not necessarily involve changing multiple systems within the organization. That is, most job-enrichment projects focus only on changing the content of the job itself and do little to change the management information system and training programs. In fact, all the other systems in the organization, including the pay and selection systems, the overall organization structure, and the nature of supervision are usually ignored. (p. 91)

The FJA model recognizes and attends to Lawler's observation. *Job content* in FJA is a combination of *what the worker does* and *what gets done* drawing on the worker's functional and specific content skills (see Fig. 7.1). *Job context* on the other hand is comprised of the environment a worker must adjust to in performing the job content to a given standard and draws on the worker's adaptive skills. Typically, job content is the focus of attention in job design or redesign efforts; and again typically, job context is a secondary consideration, if considered at all. Nevertheless, the context cannot be escaped. One needs only to be reminded of the problems associated with getting animals to reproduce when removed from their natural habitat to a zoo (e.g., pandas), even when attempts are made to simulate the original environment. Redesigning jobs to increase their orientation to people, as in shifting to teamwork production, at a minimum requires training workers in people interactions within the context of the work system. Furthermore, redesigning jobs adds to the variety and level of skill required and perhaps also requires some changes in the reward system. For example, equipping FSE with portable computers provides direct access to material, design, and troubleshooting resources and reduces their need to contact other engineers either on peer or consultant level. There is an enriched involvement with Data, a lesser involvement with People in the organization, and an added physical skill—computer proficiency. There is also a challenge to the workers' adaptive skills. Can the worker adapt to the greater independence now required of an FSE—an independence approximating that of an independent contractor? Clearly, this involves reconsideration of the reward system if the organization is going to retain the services of such key personnel.

Job Design Incorporates the Interaction of Worker, Work, and Work Organization

The FJA task statement provides a module of the work system. In describing the work, each task statement incorporates worker functioning, what workers do in order to get the work done (results). The result reflects the values added to fulfill the objectives, goals, and purpose of the organization. Insofar as the objectives, goals, and purposes of an organization are communicated to workers, they have a better understanding of what the results of their work mean to the organization. Workers can see themselves as part of the flow of the system.

This sharing of information about goals and objectives is an irreducible minimum for the shared interpretation of experience that has been reiterated throughout this book as a precondition for trust. Trust is essential if resources and constraints to getting work done are to be dealt with creatively by workers and supervisors. There is little point in talking about workers having opportunities for experiencing their potential unless they are party to the resources and constraints that are integral to the work organization achieving its goals and purpose.

Management has come to recognize the benefits of sharing information with workers. In recent years it has implemented this recognition with workers through quality circles, self-managing work teams, management–worker committees, and similar devices to boost productivity, often with salutary results. These efforts fit under the umbrella of kaizen. However, there are numerous reports of situations not measuring up to expectations. One possible explanation is that they were undertaken on a piecemeal basis without fully exploring the system-wide implications of their introduction. The fact remains that work, worker, and work organization are inextricably meshed. Changes in one area require follow-through in the entire system.

Job Design Looks for the Interaction of Functional, Specific Content, and Adaptive Skills

The interrelatedness of the three types of skills (functional, specific content, and adaptive) must be taken into account in job design. Consider the example of a production worker in the pulp-and-paper industry who previously performed the hourly task of compiling production and quality control figures (e.g., paper thickness, water content of pulp) by reading dials and gauges fixed on large paper-making machines. The worker recorded these data on the prescribed forms that were filed with the production control supervisor at the end of the shift. Any large discrepancies from standard were reported to the supervisor immediately for appropriate action (e.g., stopping the line, asking operators to adjust machine settings, etc.). All this changed when a computerized control system was networked into the control systems built into the paper making machines. This computer was located in the middle of the production floor and the production worker's job became largely sedentary in that one location. The worker now also had the responsibility for immediate action in response to any discrepancies in the control readings. For example, the worker would now decide on the likely source of a problem and call on maintenance staff to deal with the problem or even make minor machine adjustments. The obvious impact of this job change is on the Functional skill of Data: The work has moved up from Level 3B (Compiling) to Level 4 (Analyzing). What may be less obvious (but should be thoroughly explored jointly by the worker and manager) is the impact of the change on specific content and adaptive skills. The worker must now learn to use the particular computer keyboard and terminal as well as read the output of computer software specifically designed for production monitoring on paper-making machines (a specific content skill). The worker also has to exercise greater discretion by making the decisions about how to deal with production discrepancies picked up from the computer screen. Reference to the WI Scale shows that the assignment has moved from a Level 1 (almost everything the worker needs to know is contained in the assignment) to a Level 3 (the worker has some leeway in the procedures and methods used to get the job done). The effects of the job design ripple out to affect all three categories of skill the worker must exercise on the job.

Job Design Requires Employer Accommodations as well as Worker Adaptations

Whether or not employers should be expected to make accommodations to workers to facilitate their job performance is now a moot point. It has been legislated as a requirement for physically and mentally disabled individuals by the ADA. The recognition that accommodations should be made in extreme situations has made it all the more de jure and de rigeur to make those accommodations wherever they are needed for everyone. These accommodations include adaptations and alterations to buildings and streets (ramps), machines and equipment (lifting and slowing devices), jigs and fixtures for those with visual problems, climate control for persons with allergies, time and pace of production adjustments for persons with emotional difficulties, and so on. More recent adaptations have included job sharing, flextime, working at home, and provision of day care for young children. All of these adaptations and alterations can become part of the design of job–worker situations. As is evident, some of these design changes deal with functional level and specific content. Others deal with job environment and challenge workers' adaptive skill.

Although some worker complaints can be attributed to malingering, others may be the tip of the iceberg of real problems. Workers need to feel free to report when they are experiencing stress in their job–worker situations although sometimes the work situation is not the source of the stress. Merely being listened to can often result in a correction of the situation. Negative, dismissive attitudes of managers (usually with Theory X presumptions) that "times are rough" and workers "need to do more with less" are no longer as tenable as they once were. One consultant of similar point of view, proposes "new work habits for a radically changing world," advocates such nostrums as "become a quick-change artist," "commit fully to your job," "speed up," and "accept ambiguity and uncertainty" (Pritchett, 1994). Such approaches are less and less likely to work where real stress is being experienced. Employers must meet workers halfway if for no other reason than efficiency, effectiveness , and productivity of the work-doing system.

The most fundamental accommodation that management can make is to adopt a genuine listening stance to workers. This listening stance, which aspires to a shared interpretation of experience, is intended to contribute to an ambience of nondependent trust. In this type of relationship, job design through CI can flourish and become an ongoing shared activity in response to technological change and outside competitive pressures. The resulting job changes then anticipate the adaptive needs of employees as well as the business needs of the employer.

SUMMARY OF JOB DESIGN

The success of so much else in HRM starts with sound, realistic, and well-informed job design. Well-designed jobs in harmony with competitive marketplace demands through CI are the firm foundation on which other HRM activities rest. Good job design, undertaken in an incremental manner by the workers themselves with management in the supporting role, channels human effort and capability in a coordinated way and in the direction of high productivity. With the rapid frequency and pace of change today, the challenge of job design is greater than ever before. It must become more responsive as job requirements shift constantly in response to new technologies and competitive demands in the global marketplace. But, as Taylor observed almost 100 years ago, managers must not abandon workers to workers' own devices and inventions. Cooperation between workers and management is essential. Never has the need for a partnership been so great as it is today. If such partnerships between workers and managers, assisted through the medium of FJA focus groups, are extended into the fundamental business of (re)designing the work done throughout the work-doing system, good will result.

Chapter 18

FJA and the Law —
Meeting the Legal Test

U.S. companies have assumed, either voluntarily or by dint of government legislation, a vital HRM function: to provide equal opportunity for all U.S. citizens to access the rewards provided by paid employment (pay, growth, training, status). The overriding principle is that workers should be hired, promoted, and rewarded in a nondiscriminatory way based on individual merit. Their employment suitability should not be prejudged by stereotypes associated with race, gender, handicap, or other group characteristics.

During the past 35 years, a substantial body of federal law has been passed to prohibit employment discrimination. The University of Texas at Austin, Equal Employment Opportunity Office (1997), provides an excellent summary of the major legislation and regulations on its Website:

Title VII of the Civil Rights Act of 1964, as amended in 1972, 1978, and the Civil Rights Act of 1991—The most prominent source of anti-bias employment rules is Title VII of the Civil Rights Act of 1964. It forbids discrimination in all areas of the employer-employee relationship, from advertisement for new employees through termination or retirement, on the basis of race, color, sex (including pregnancy, childbirth, or abortion), religion, or national origin. The Civil Rights Act of 1991 included additional provisions to Title VII reversing or reinforcing certain U.S. Supreme Court decisions, damages for intentional discrimination and removal of exemptions for previously exempted employees of elected officials.

Executive Order 11246—The Executive Order 11246, as amended prohibits job discrimination on the basis of race, color, religion, sex, or national origin and requires affirmative action to ensure quality of opportunity in all aspects of employment.

Age Discrimination in Employment Act of 1967—The Age Discrimination in Employment Act of 1967, as amended, protects applicants and employees

40 years of age or older from discrimination on the basis of age in hiring, promotion, discharge, compensation, terms, conditions or privileges of employment.

Americans With Disabilities Act of 1991—The Americans With Disabilities Act of 1990, as amended protects qualified applicants and employees with disabilities from discrimination in hiring, promotion, discharge, pay, job training, fringe benefits, classification, referral, and other aspects of employment on the basis of disability. The law also requires that covered entities [employers] provide qualified applicants and employees with disabilities with reasonable accommodations that do not impose undue hardship.

Rehabilitation Act of 1973—Section 503 of the Rehabilitation Act of 1973, as amended prohibits job discrimination because of handicap and requires affirmative action to employ and advance in employment qualified individuals with handicaps who, with reasonable accommodation, can perform the essential functions of a job.

Vietnam Era and Special Disabled Veterans—38 U.S.C. 4212 of the Vietnam Era Veterans Readjustment Assistance Act of 1974 prohibits job discrimination and requires affirmative action to employ and advance in employment qualified Vietnam era veterans and qualified special disabled veterans.

Equal Pay Act of 1963—In addition to sex discrimination prohibited by Title VII of the Civil Rights Act, the Equal Pay Act of 1963, as amended, prohibits sex discrimination in payment of wages to women and men performing substantially equal work in the same establishment.

The central tenet of antidiscrimination legislation is that discrimination occurs because people prejudge others based on stereotypes they hold about the other's group. For example, some managers may be less willing to hire women for leadership positions because they hold a stereotype of women as being soft and emotional. Further, they hold a stereotype that effective leadership is synonymous with male-stereotyped characteristics of toughness or taking charge. In the mind of some managers, women as a group do not have what it takes for leadership positions and are not taken seriously and given a chance to compete equally with men on the basis of merit (i.e., their ability to do the job). A second area of stereotyping occurs in pay. Comparable worth advocates have complained for many years that jobs held predominantly by women have been systematically undervalued in comparison to those jobs held by men. They have lobbied for, and in many jurisdictions gotten, equal pay for jobs of equal worth. The tricky part in all of this comes in sorting out stereotypic belief from merit when promoting leaders or the equal worth of jobs when setting compensation rates. Objectivity and impartiality are required to sort the wheat of bona fide occupational requirements from the chaff of stereotypic assumptions. This chapter shows how FJA is used to provide the objective information required for nondiscriminatory and legally defensible employment practices.

PARALLELS BETWEEN FJA THEMES AND
ANTIDISCRIMINATION LEGISLATION

One of the most destructive ways to partialize others is to view and treat them as stereotypes rather than as individuals with talents and capabilities. Our everyday language unconsciously promotes a simplified view of others through numerous stereotyping categories—Black versus White, women versus men, old versus young, disabled versus able-bodied. This stereotyping overwhelms our field of vision so that our perception of that person becomes synonymous with the stereotype. Our relationship with that person becomes one-dimensional and the trust that develops from recognizing the other as a multifaceted and integrated human being cannot develop.

FJA asserts that the worker must be viewed holistically in a job–worker situation: job content and job context. The stereotype-breaking power of this statement can be illustrated by answering the following questions while reading the information contained in an FJA task bank:

Is it possible that any member of the stereotyped group:

- Cannot learn the specific content of the job?
- Does not possess the required functional skills?
- Cannot meet the performance standards laid out by management (lacks the ability)?
- Is neither willing nor able to expend the effort and assume the responsibility required of the job?
- Is neither willing nor able to function within the work conditions offered by management?

In FJA task analyses of hundreds of jobs, we have not yet found a job where these questions could not be answered in the affirmative for group membership based on race, national origin, color, or gender. Members of some religious denominations are occasionally at odds with standards set by management for work attendance on certain religious days, but frequently management makes suitable scheduling accommodations for this. Disabled persons comprise an extremely heterogeneous group that must be dealt with on a case-by-case basis. Provided that management offers reasonable accommodation for disabled individuals, the answers to the previous questions are in the affirmative (that is, an individual can learn the specific content of the job, and possesses the required functional skills, and so on).

Antidiscrimination legislation has prompted many organizations to overhaul their HR principles, policies, and procedures to ensure equality of treatment to all potential employees. Whether their efforts are voluntary or involuntary, antidiscrimination becomes a maintenance goal—the mission of the organization remains to manufacture and to sell a product, deliver a service, or the like. Therefore, senior management adopts the goal of antidiscrimination with varying degrees of enthusiasm: the principle of EEO or affirmative action (AA) may be pursued with vigor, or it may be given lip service and left to the initiative of individual managers. When using FJA to assist in putting antidiscrimination policies and procedures in place, the HR practitioner has to assess the depth of support for these initiatives and sometimes work with fewer resources than desirable. FJA task banks have to be used as a data resource so that HR can squeeze as much value as possible out of them in these resource-lean situations.

A core FJA concept must be kept in mind when integrating underrepresented or nontraditional workers into an organization. Performance is always a matter of the interaction of the three kinds of skills: functional, specific content and adaptive. For example, appreciation of this core concept will lead a mining company in Alaska, which is expanding representation of the native population in its workforce, to develop very different policies and procedures than a social service agency in Milwaukee seeking to increase the number of physically disabled individuals in its offices. The adaptive skills brought to the workplace by the Alaskan native population are far different from the adaptive skills of people with European ancestry. In particular, people raised in traditional Inuit or Indian ways schedule their time according to the rhythm of the seasons and the hunt. The mining manager who expects workers to be available for work 52 weeks a year with 3 weeks vacation during the summer will find these workers conscientious and functionally capable when on the job. However, he or she will also find they expect to be absent for a month or more during the spring hunt causing severe strains for the organization. Both workers and management have to come some distance to resolve these differences. On the other hand, the social service agency in Milwaukee will probably find physically disabled persons have adaptive skills consistent with the general population, but there will be specific impairments in the functional skill of relating to Things. Based on the different constellation of skills that each group brings to the workplace, the two organizations have to implement very different policies and procedures in order to integrate these respective groups into their workforces.

The detailed discussion of legislation here shows that the concept of reasonable accommodation is a central pillar of antidiscrimination efforts. Simply said, reasonable accommodation is a restatement of the FJA theme of management meeting worker concerns halfway. If a listening stance and shared interpretation of experience can be developed between workers and management, then reasonable accommodation of worker needs becomes routine, whether or not these workers are protected by antidis-crimination legislation. The stage is set for a relatively painless and natural segue into becoming an organization that lives and breathes EEO.

USING FJA IN TITLE VII COMPLIANCE

The backbone of antidiscrimination law in the United States is the Civil Rights Act (CRA) of 1866 with its amendments including Title VII of the CRA of 1964 and the CRA of 1991. This legislation has teeth and is enforced by the Equal Employment Opportunity Commission (EEOC; the commis-sion has also taken responsibility for enforcing other federal antidiscrimi-nation legislation, including the ADA). Over the years, the CRA has been applied by courts in deciding numerous discrimination cases, including key decisions such as *Griggs vs. Duke Power* in 1971. (In the *Griggs* decision, the U.S. Supreme Court ruled that it was a discriminatory practice for an organization to use an unvalidated employment test having adverse im-pact against Blacks.) The CRA in its various forms, along with interpreta-tions and precedents set by courts, established core principles that should be kept in mind when developing and implementing all types of employ-ment systems, including the ones described in the applications section of this book. Of special interest here is that court decisions frequently stress the need for job analysis as the basic grounding for employment systems if they are to be defensible under the CRA.

One key EEO concept is *adverse impact*. Adverse impact happens when an employment practice disproportionately excludes protected group members from employment opportunities. The classic case of adverse im-pact occurs where standardized tests of cognitive ability are used to select among applicants for police departments. On average Black individuals score lower than majority group members on these tests, resulting in ad-verse impact: fewer Blacks (as a proportion of those applying for the job) are selected than individuals from the majority group. When this happens, the employer is obligated to prove that the employment practice (here, an employment test) is *job-related* for the position in question and consistent with *business necessity*. The employer must also show there is no alternative employment practice available with less adverse impact. Typically, when it comes to validation, the employer demonstrates the job-relatedness of an employment test by having it professionally validated. Problems posed by selection practices in employment are significant enough that in 1978 the EEOC (along with two other government agencies) published the *Uniform guidelines on employee selection procedures* (Equal Employment Opportunity Commission, 1978) to provide technical guidance, including advice on job analysis, to employers.

Where an employment practice treats groups differently (*disparate treatment*), a prima facie case of discrimination can also be established. The requirement that women applying for a job as a steelworker must take a strength test whereas male applicants are exempted from this requirement exemplifies disparate treatment. A court would obviously infer from this differential treatment that the employer holds a negative stereotype of women as a class and treats them in a discriminatory manner. Disparate treatment also encompasses the rejection of a qualified woman for the job of steelworker but the company keeps the competition open to seek applications from males with the same qualifications. *Mixed-motive cases* occur when the employer had both lawful (job-related) and discriminatory reasons for an employment practice. A mixed-motive case might occur where a retailing chain refuses to hire men to work at its cosmetics counters. Under the 1991 Amendment to the CRA, mixed motive became an unlawful ground for an employment decision and hereby set a standard that makes it more difficult for the employer to win an antidiscrimination suit.

FJA has an important role to play if an employer's HR decisions must be justified to the EEOC or in court. As the previous chapters have shown, FJA provides the basic grounding needed to establish job-relatedness for a wide range of HR interventions. FJA has advantages over standardized job analysis methods in that it uses plain language to establish a commonsense link between the task bank and its applications rather than relying on computer printouts burdened with extensive statistics and technical detail. Because of its directness and simplicity in establishing job-relatedness, FJA can meet the challenges of Title VII.

USING FJA FOR AFFIRMATIVE ACTION (AA)

Many companies and jurisdictions (e.g., cities, municipalities) have set up AA programs over the past 25 years in response to legislation or as a voluntary initiative. These programs have some basic features in common. Employers must:

- determine the present representation of designated group members (e.g., Blacks, handicapped) in their workforces;
- set targets or quotas for hiring and promoting designated group members to increase their numbers in areas where they are presently underrepresented;
- put in place principles, policies, and procedures to remove employment barriers that hinder the advancement of underrepresented groups; and

- monitor their progress toward realizing employment targets or quotas.

AA programs have become controversial with both politicians and the general public arguing the pros and cons of preferential hiring and promotion to address the historical underrepresentation of certain groups in the labor force. These controversies are not addressed here. Instead, we discuss how FJA can assist AA implementation.

FJA contributes to the implementation of AA by

- providing an objective basis for describing what workers do and what gets done which is less susceptible to handicap, race, gender, and other stereotypes than more informal descriptions of work;
- assisting HR managers to identify systematic employment barriers blocking the advancement of designated groups, and
- providing a practical and economical means to eliminate those barriers.

Barriers to designated groups are most often found at several specific points in the employment system. How FJA can help to remove barriers to underepresented groups at these specific points in the employment system follows a brief discussion of these barriers.

Job Design—The operative word in job design for AA purposes is *accommodation*, that is either job content or more often, the job context, has to be changed to allow a member of a designated group an equal chance to perform the job. The best way to accomplish job redesigning for AA purposes is to convene a panel of managers, workers who are members of the designated group, and others who have expert knowledge of the special needs of the group members (e.g., community groups specializing in employment placement for that group). For example, mentally handicapped persons have a low rate of participation in employment. An employer who wishes to include larger numbers of mentally handicapped in a local plant could set up a job redesign panel. This panel could include employment experts identified by the city and state societies for mental disability and workers who are presently operating successfully with the disability (either in the employer's business or a similar business elsewhere in the city) in addition to HR staff and line managers. Much of the job's redesign would focus on functional and adaptive skills—the mentally handicapped worker is likely to need a greater amount of structure in the form of SOPs and WI than other workers in that job. The employer may well find a thorough review of job requirements as part of an AA job design is beneficial for accommodating other workers as well, thereby adding additional value to the AA effort. This is illustrated by the following example.

Nancy Christy runs the Wilson Street Grill, a trendy Madison, Wisconsin, restaurant with an unusual staff—30% of the 30 employees have mental illnesses including major depression, schizophrenia, paranoia, psychosis, and autism. Christy's philosophy and that of co-owner Andrea Craig is "respectful of people's abilities and tolerant of their disabilities." According to the Culinary Arts dean at Madison Area Technical College where Christy helped develop a course on employing mentally impaired individuals, the other 70% of the restaurant staff is on board with Christy's philosophy. Restaurants and the hospitality industry offer many jobs well suited to people with disabilities. However these workers need a lot of structure, which is provided by the steady, repetitive nature of behind-the-scenes restaurant work such as food preparation and washing dishes. They also need to take breaks whenever they feel the need, and Christy and the rest of her staff are committed to accommodating them. One employee's job is to cut bread dough and put it into a machine. Sometimes the loaves look a little goofy, but the variability is something Christy and the others can live with and even find charming. "We take a job and pull it apart and decide how pieces of the job can be done by others. . . . These guys have to perform, and they do," Christy said. One employee, K.K., age 30, landed in a hospital after a major depressive episode and lived and worked part time in sheltered settings with social service agency support. When she started at the restaurant she could handle working only an hour or two a day. After almost a year, she can work 3 to 4 hours a day and sometimes returns at night. She has expanded her job to include backup hostess duty and making sure patrons have refills on water, coffee, and bread. Although she still considers herself mentally disabled and doubts her ability to handle a full-time job, she feels the restaurant "is a wonderful place for me to grow. My mental skills are getting better as I work here" (Marchione, 1998, p. 11).

The area(s) of job content and/or context addressed by job design depends on the designated group. Training that sensitizes supervisors and managers to the cultural differences that put extra stress on workers' adaptive skills may well benefit Black and Hispanic workers. Women benefit from job redesign, which often introduces simple equipment and work aids such as hand trucks and hydraulic lifts to meet heavy lifting requirements. The range of potential accommodations for mentally and physically disabled persons is wide because these disabilities are so numerous and varied. They include spell checkers on word processors for dyslexic persons or ramps to make the workplace more accessible to persons in wheelchairs. Employers cannot possibly anticipate the full range of accommodations possible nor have the entire complement of in-house expertise needed to put these accommodations in place. As noted earlier, the best option is to convene a job design panel using the FJA task bank as a starting point and then rely on expert input and assistance from the larger community. The task bank offers a highly understandable and accessible tool (a shared basis of interpretation about the job content and context) that provides a common language for panel members who come from very different backgrounds and perspectives but who must work together to design a job with necessary but practical accommodations.

Recruitment—The AA program, which is intended to increase representation of designated groups, falters badly if, after hiring, large numbers of individuals from these designated groups discover they are poorly suited to the job and then leave the organization. As shown previously, presentation of realistic job information, especially in the area of adaptive skills, allows individuals the chance to self-select before hiring and so reduce the turnover rate. However, this strategy is a two-edged sword. If conditions in the organization are less than accommodating to designated group members, the FJA realistic job preview makes this apparent and potential applicants will self-select out. The organization must first create a worker-friendly environment responsive to the diversity of its workers. A job is then more attractive to potential applicants who self-select for the right reasons and stay with the organization in the long term, thus furthering AA goals.

Selection—Stereotyping can be a serious problem in selection. The concern is that the manager doing the stereotyping will make snap negative judgments about a person's capabilities and potential for the job in the absence of sufficient objective data to justify that judgment. In so doing, the manager will unfairly disadvantage the designated group member. Stereotypes can operate in many ways, but two examples should suffice. In hiring an individual for a leadership position, a senior manager may assume that traditional masculine traits of toughness and decisiveness are required for the job and screen out all female applicants. Their rationale is that females will not be able to make the hard decisions. An FJA task analysis of the job might show that effective leaders must be good listeners, be able to mobilize consensus in the unit, and be able to gain the trust of subordinates through participative management. Here FJA provides the hard objective data that the senior manager's off-the-cuff judgment cannot. Or an interviewer might view an applicant with a speech impediment as someone who is unintelligent or likely to represent the organization in a bad light. The FJA-based interview would require the interviewer to judge this applicant strictly on the bona fide criteria set out for hiring people for this job and in so doing dispel the negative stereotype. Stated plainly, the best antidote to stereotyping in employment is to provide decision makers with valid information based on objective job requirements and to insist that they stick with these data when making judgments about the suitability of people seeking work.

Performance Appraisal—Workers and managers sometimes legitimately disagree when assessing and discussing performance. As cultural backgrounds and expectations become more diverse through the introduction of AA, the number of disagreements over performance assessments likely increases. A manager's best stance is to focus on the results and performance standards the worker is responsible for, and if performance is at or beyond expectations, avoid wide-ranging forays into how these results were achieved. As FJA shows, some degree of discretion is always required of the worker, and he or she applies this discretion in a unique way drawing on adaptive and functional skills developed through family, educational, and cultural experiences. This is a necessary part of the holistic capabilities that workers bring to the work situation and should not be second-guessed. AA goals are better served if the manager and worker together focus on the ends to be achieved—the performance standards—and enter into dialogue about means only if performance does not meet management expectations.

Promotion—Promotion usually assumes that performance appraisals have been previously conducted and the results found at least satisfactory. The question then is: Should this person be promoted to a position with greater responsibility? Promotion usually moves a worker to a job of higher WI and more complex Data and People requirements. FJA can be used to identify the bona fide requirements of the higher position. Then an interview or other assessment(s) can be developed from the task bank to evaluate promotion candidates for their capabilities and qualifications for the higher-level position. Given the aim of AA to balance representation of designated and majority groups at all organizational levels, promotion becomes a crucial HRM process. By making this process more objective and less susceptible to stereotyping on the basis of group characteristics (e.g., the erroneous belief minority groups cannot accept higher levels of responsibility), FJA can help an organization to achieve AA targets.

Layoff, Transfer, and Termination—As applied to designated groups, layoff and termination usually have the reverse effect of promotion by reducing their overall representation in the workforce. Where layoffs occur in order of the best performing to poorest performing workers, FJA has a role in reducing discriminatory practices. Managers of employees affected by the layoff have to meet and make the case for retention or layoff based on the discussion and comparison of results their workers have achieved. Movement of workers up or down the layoff list should be made with reference to the data taken from the job task bank and previous performance appraisals for each worker. If a worker's reasons for previous low performance ratings differ from the supervisor's or peers', they should be taken into consideration as they are part of the record. The rationale for layoff decisions must be documented and laid-off workers should have access to their individual records stating the detailed reason for layoff and their ranking in the layoff list.

Fine was a consultant to the U.S. Department of Labor in a case where a large scientific laboratory had a 10% reduction in force. The laboratory claimed the discharged workers were failing in performance. An FJA analysis of a sample of the incumbents indicated they met their performance standards consistently over period of years. However, the fact they were all 55 years of age or older suggested the true reason for their termination. The outcome was reinstatement.

Worker transfers occur for a number of reasons as when they are a part of a job rotation program meant to expand the range and depth of worker skills. The concern here is with a negative reason for transfer, for example, a manager wants a worker out of his or her unit due to poor performance, personality conflicts, or other reasons. AA purposes are best served if the manager is held responsible for documenting valid, job-related reasons for the transfer and presenting those reasons to higher management for review and approval (again FJA can help pinpoint this type of information). If a satisfactory rationale based on job performance is not presented (and this rationale might be double-checked by the manager responsible for AA or EEO), higher management should reject the transfer request and set in motion a process to investigate and mediate problems within the unit.

Termination is always difficult for both managers and workers, but as unpleasant as this might be, terminations are sometimes necessary. If a worker is grossly negligent in his or her duties or is threatening or abusing managers and other workers, termination may well be called for and must be carried out with due dispatch. By and large, a terminated worker's difficulties will find their source in a failure of adaptive skills on and sometimes off the job. If a termination decision is to be made fairly, these adaptive skills must be thoroughly understood along with their impact on job performance. FJA provides the tools needed for this purpose and in the hands of a psychologist can be very useful for uncovering the sources of difficulty and how they might be dealt with. The investigation may in fact indicate that a leave of absence, combined with counseling or coaching by a skilled professional, is a viable and humane alternative to termination. Termination may be especially problematic with designated groups, where cultural or gender differences, or disability, raise questions of whether the worker was terminated for the right reasons and whether reasonable accommodations were made to forestall the termination. Wrongly terminating workers from designated groups, in addition to the individual injustice involved, makes it more difficult for employers to meet AA targets.

USING FJA TO COMPLY WITH DISABILITIES LEGISLATION

FJA can provide assistance to employers in implementing the ADA of 1991 and the Rehabilitation Act of 1973, which has similar wording. The ADA requires employers to provide "equal employment opportunities for qualified individuals with disabilities." As with any legislation, the specific definitions offered become pivotal to properly implementing the ADA. These definitions are now presented and related to core FJA concepts. FJA provides a powerful methodology for translating key ADA concepts to practical employment principles, policies, procedures, and practices.

Disability—The ADA defines the term *disability* as "a[n] [individual] physical or mental impairment that substantially limits one or more of the major life activities of such individual." One of these major life activities is work. The act further defines *physical or mental impairment* as "any physiological disorder, or condition, cosmetic disfigurement, or anatomical loss" affecting one or more of several body systems or "any mental or psychological disorder, such as mental retardation, organic brain syndrome, emotional or mental illness, and specific learning disabilities." The existence of an impairment is defined without reference to mitigating measures such as hearing aids, prosthetics, medicines, and the like. Understood in the light of FJA, an impairment sets limits on the physical, mental, and interpersonal potentials that a worker can bring to bear in meeting employer performance standards (note that some emotional or mental illnesses such as autism have their impact in the interpersonal as well as physical and mental spheres of activity). Depending on the disability, the job requirements, and the environment the job is performed in, these limitations may be quite broad or very specific in their impact on job performance.

Substantially Limit—The ADA states that a disability must "substantially limit" one or more major life activities. In other words, the determination of whether a worker has a disability depends on the limiting effect the disability has in an individual's life including work, rather than being based only on the "name or diagnosis" of the impairment.

For an impairment to substantially limit a worker, the limitations must apply to a class or family of jobs having similar requirements (training, KSAs) in a given geographical area. The FJA task bank and its associated ratings provide a basis for defining a class or family of jobs having similar requirements. For this purpose the following informational sources can also be used because they draw on concepts and language similar to that of the FJA task bank: The *Dictionary of occupational titles* of the U.S. Department of Labor, the *Canadian classification and dictionary of occupations,* and the *National occupational classification of Canada.* Use of the FJA task bank helps to establish whether given disabilities, identified on a case-by-case basis, do indeed substantially limit a worker and place him or her under the protection of the ADA or similar legislation.

Essential Functions—According to the ADA, the decision of whether an individual with a disability is qualified for a job hinges on two factors: (a) he or she must satisfy the prerequisites of the position in terms of education, experience, skills, and so on; and (b) he or she must be able to perform the essential functions (as opposed to marginal functions) of the position, with or without reasonable accommodation. The determination of what comprises essential functions of the job becomes crucial to the proper implementation of the ADA. FJA provides considerable guidance in this matter and use of FJA to sort out essential from marginal functions is illustrated in the example of the Policy Service Representative (PSR) presented later.

Reasonable Accommodation—The ADA states that a person is a "qualified individual with a disability" if he or she can perform the essential functions of the job with or without reasonable *accommodation.* An accommodation is defined as "any change in the work environment or the way things are customarily done that enables an individual with a disability to enjoy equal employment opportunities." Accommodations can be achieved in various ways, including modifying existing facilities, job restructuring, changes in work schedules, acquiring or modifying equipment, and so on. The act stresses that to determine the appropriate accommodation the employer and worker (or job applicant) may have to "initiate an informal, interactive process with the qualified individual with a disability in need of the accommodation." At this point the FJA task bank becomes especially useful for reviewing the job in a thorough yet efficient manner. Its usefulness derives from the language in which tasks are written. This language is immediately convertible to the training and KSAs called for in order for a worker to perform the job. In addition the results expected are clearly delineated. The supervisor and disabled worker, with the aid of the task bank, are quickly able to pinpoint the necessary accommodation(s) by reading through the task bank together. If the disabled person is a job applicant, the task bank offers a convenient and readily understandable tool that the company recruiter and applicant can review together in deciding whether posthire accommodations can be made to the job.

Closely linked with the concept of reasonable accommodation is that of *undue hardship*. Under this provision, the employer is not obligated to provide an accommodation imposing an undue hardship too costly, extensive, substantial, or disruptive to the employer. In addition, if no accommodation can be found that either eliminates or reduces a direct threat to the health or safety of the disabled person or others, that individual can be discharged or refused employment. This direct threat must pose a significant risk of substantial harm to relieve employers of their duty for reasonable accommodation under the ADA.

Ways to use job analysis—more specifically, FJA—in implementing ADA, have been suggested. However, the EEOC, which administers the ADA, goes further than *suggesting* job analysis in its interpretive guidelines. These guidelines state that unless the accommodation is obvious to both the employer and qualified individual with a disability (e.g., the need for wheelchair ramps up to the front door of a building), the employer *should* use "a problem-solving approach" that involves "analyzing actual job duties and determining the true purpose or object of the job." Only then can the employer and qualified individual with a disability together assess the effects of the disability on performance of the job's essential functions and determine the accommodation needed. In other words, job analysis is a basic and indispensable tool for providing reasonable accommodation in all but simple cases.

An example will help to clarify how FJA can be used to accommodate a man being considered for hire by an insurance company as a Policy Service Representative (PSR). The man is confined to a wheelchair and has no use of his legs due to a spinal cord injury. PSRs with this company work out of individual workstations located within a cubicle and equipped with a desk, computer, printer, and telephone. The first question is whether the man is qualified for the job within the meaning of the ADA. Through the use of work sample tests and a structured interview, it is established that the man has the necessary skills, training, education, and experience for the position. Next it must be determined whether he can perform the essential functions of the position. At this point, the FJA task bank for the PSR is brought out and reviewed (there is probably no need to collect additional data—all the required information is likely to be contained in the task bank). Essential functions in the ADA are analogous to primary outputs in FJA, therefore outputs in the PSR task bank provide the basic information for qualifying individuals under the ADA for this job. The outputs from the PSR task bank are as follows (along with a brief synopsis of the tasks covered under each):

1.0   Starting work (3 tasks: logging on to computer; planning the day's activities; and retrieving necessary documents and other materials).

2.0   Handling policy listings (2 tasks: reading and reviewing customer policies; sorting and distributing computer listing of policies requiring further action).

3.0   Filing policy materials (2 tasks: sorting and distributing materials into bins at central work station; sorting and placing processed change forms into garbage or shredder).

4.0   Handling correspondence (2 tasks: writing letters to policyholders; printing related documents).

5.0   Issuing reinstatements (3 tasks: reviewing and approving policy reinstatement requests; routing policy reinstatement letters to work processing department).

6.0   Making policy changes (5 tasks: reviewing, entering, changing and verifying policy information using computer system; computing client premiums; setting up payment plans).

7.0   Contacting others (3 tasks: responding to customer inquiries and complaints; providing and requesting policy and other information).

The determination of which outputs are essential functions and which are marginal is assisted in this instance by ratings of task importance collected from incumbents by the job analyst. These ratings show the tasks under output 3.0 (filing policy materials) are rated as being of lower importance than the tasks of the other six outputs. Furthermore, filing is an output that serves the maintenance goals rather than the mission/purpose goals of the organization, and leads to the conclusion that this output is a marginal function for ADA purposes. The remaining outputs are essential functions. They are relatively high in importance and closely related to the mission/purpose goals of the PSR. They are all directly involved in or required for servicing customer accounts. Because output 3.0 also requires the worker to frequently move from the work station to a central area elsewhere in the building (and all other outputs are performed within the individual work station), management decides this disabled worker can be accommodated by moving the marginal task out of this position. After hire, the worker will receive a filing basket at the workstation for all materials needing to be filed and those requiring shredding. These latter can be marked with a red tag. Another worker will take the materials on a regular trip to the central workstation and either deposit them in a bin or place them in the shredder. The disabled applicant must be able to perform the remaining outputs deemed to be essential functions with these reasonable accommodations. The disabled applicant and a manager review the PSR task bank and together visit one of the individualized workstations. They decide that several relatively inexpensive accommodations (e.g., a special chair for the workstation, setting supply bins and manuals within the workstation to a reachable level), will enable the applicant to perform the essential functions of the job and he is subsequently hired.

One question must be continuously asked when reviewing the FJA task bank with reasonable accommodation in mind: Can the result for the task(s) be achieved through a different means (other than the one used by a typical nondisabled worker)? A good example of using a different means comes from a task for the job of switchboard, office supply, mail and files personnel taken from *Benchmark tasks for job analysis* (Fine & Getkate, 1995).

> Pick up newspapers at newsstand and mail at U.S. Postal Station in building, carry or drag (if very heavy) to mail room, relying on physical strength and following SOP in order to have mail available for sorting and papers ready for delivery to persons designated.

Assume the just-mentioned task is part of an essential function for the job. One of the workers who is disabled with a back impairment requests reasonable accommodation, and this is one of the tasks singled out for attention. The required result is to have the mail/newspapers available in the mailroom for sorting and delivery (the ADA emphasizes that both disabled and nondisabled workers are subject to the same performance standards as long as reasonable accommodation is provided). What is up for negotiation is the means by which this task will be performed (action), equipment and tools used, and training or instruction provided. It may not be necessary for the worker to carry or drag mail bags to the mail room if he or she is provided with a hand truck. Further, the disabled worker can receive the training needed to safely lift the mailbags on and off the hand truck with minimal back strain. The task can now be rewritten as follows to reflect the accommodation:

> Pick up newspapers at newsstand and mail at U.S. Postal Station in building, carry or drag (if very heavy) or deliver by hand truck, to mail room, relying on physical strength, knowledge of heavy lifting techniques and following SOP in order to have mail available for sorting and papers ready for delivery to persons designated.

The disabled worker can now perform the task to obtain exactly the same result as before despite a back injury. Some nondisabled workers may also opt for the hand truck rather than carry or drag heavy bags resulting (coincidentally) in greater efficiency in moving the mail and fewer strain injuries on the job. In this case, a straightforward accommodation for

the disabled individual resulted in work improvements for the nondisabled, lower workers' compensation claims, and greater efficiency in the
work-doing system. Note that such accommodations are not limited to the
ADA. They could also provide equal employment opportunity for women
under Title VII of the Civil Rights Act or for disabled veterans under the
Vietnam Era Veterans Readjustment Assistance Act.

USING FJA FOR PAY EQUITY

An earlier reference in this chapter cited people's tendency to stereotype
other people based on their race, gender, age, and so on. Research shows
this same tendency occurs with respect to jobs: Historically, jobs have become associated as being suited to males or females. For example, shop
jobs such as welder or pipefitter are male stereotyped (held mostly by, and
believed best suited for, men) and office jobs such as clerk or secretary are
female stereotyped (held mostly by, and believed best suited for, women).
The concern addressed by the Equal Pay Act of 1963, and by comparable
worth legislation in a number of states, is that these job stereotypes cause
organization decision makers to systematically underpay women's jobs
compared to men's jobs of either equal or comparable value. This legislation, by requiring organizations to modify their existing job evaluation
procedures to eliminate any gender bias in their pay systems, contributes
to reducing the overall gap in wages between men and women. A question
addressed in this part of the chapter is whether FJA can help in identifying
and eliminating gender bias in job evaluation.

The FJA approach to job evaluation is described in chapter 16. FJA provides the only job evaluation system based on an explicitly stated theory of
work. All other systems, whether ranking, point method, factor-compari-
son method, job analysis questionnaire-based, or other are based on a
methodology, and not a theory, of job evaluation. The theory-based nature
of FJA becomes a notable advantage when used in pay equity. A central
concern of pay equity is to remove gender bias from the job evaluation
process to make the pay structure equitable and fair.

Cronshaw's (1991) *Industrial Psychology in Canada* described four stages
in the job evaluation process where gender bias is most likely to occur. A
brief summary of these stages as they occur in FJA job evaluation follows
along with a means to reduce or eliminate gender bias at each stage.

Stage 1

Gender bias can make major inroads in job evaluation when the job analysis is conducted and the results written into a job description for subse-

quent rating by a job evaluation committee. In their book, Pay equity: Issues, options and experience, Weiner and Gunderson (1990) stated that bias in collecting job information is minimized by:

- having a number of knowledgeable people (preferably job incumbents) provide the job information,
- using a standard job analysis, and
- employing only properly trained job analysts

FJA is particularly strong on all of these criteria.

Stage 2

Gender bias can enter when subfactors are selected for inclusion in the job evaluation system. The concern here is that subfactors for female aspects of the job (such as fine motor skill, responsibility for people, and amount of interruption on the job) will be excluded. The major advantage of FJA in this regard is that it is based on a theoretical understanding of work that reflects *all* aspects of a worker's involvement (chap. 16). The four components and their particular factors are comprehensive of both female and male job aspects across the range of jobs in an organization. This should work to minimize the opportunity for gender bias by exclusion.

Stage 3

Gender bias can enter with the weighting and assignment of point values to subfactors. For example, a job evaluation system might assign maximum scale scores on subfactors representing female aspects that are too low compared to maximum scores assigned to subfactors representing male aspects. In FJA this bias would tend to show up on the relative values that an organization assigns to TDP in carrying out its overall mission. At this point the bias represented by the assigned values can be questioned and corrected. This approach contrasts starkly with many other job evaluation systems (for example, the Hay system), which weight Data and, sometimes Things, to the exclusion of People. Given the frequent complaint by pay equity advocates that working with people (a female job aspect) is given short shrift in job evaluation, the balance among the three functional areas—Things, Data, and People—achieved by FJA is a good beginning to a nongender-biased pay system. One example of an adaptive subfactor commonly overlooked in female-dominated jobs is the stress that results from frequent interruptions and multiple demands. These adaptive skills (willingness to work under difficult or exceptional environmental conditions) are brought out during the FJA focus group for the job, but it is up to

the job evaluator to recognize them as Premium factors and give them appropriate weighting in the job evaluation system.

Stage 4

Gender bias can enter when a job evaluation committee rates job descriptions and assigns job evaluation points. In keeping with the theme of
openness and trust stressed throughout this book, care should be taken to
ensure that a cross-section of management and workers make up the membership of the job evaluation committee. Acceptance of the final results of
the job evaluation (in the form of posted pay rates) are enhanced if workers and management have been involved in all aspects of the design and
administration of the pay system. Note that FJA requires worker participation at the beginning of the process—the job analysis focus group—and
much is gained by enlisting this worker involvement throughout the job
evaluation and pay-setting process. Of course the job evaluation committee should include both women and men, particularly women from the
underpaid positions most impacted by pay equity in order to reduce the
possibility of gender bias at this stage of job evaluation.

FJA job evaluation results in a flatter, more egalitarian pay structure
than most other job evaluation methods. That is, the difference between the
lowest- and highest-paid jobs in the organization will be narrower than
most managers are accustomed to. For a company, the point spread between the highest rated job of executive director and the lowest rated job of
food service aide can be three to one. If in fact FJA works to correct gender
bias, it is to be expected that application of FJA will reduce pay differences
between the top and bottom of the organization given that women in large
organizations tend to cluster in low-paying jobs. Managers using FJA for
job evaluation should be prepared to have time-worn assumptions about
pay challenged, especially the belief that job evaluation points should revolve around Data functions with a minor contribution of working conditions thrown in. This traditional approach, which incidentally favors sen-
ior- and middle-level managers with a larger spread in pay relative to the
lower ranks, must be discarded if pay equity is to be fully approached. The
resulting pay system achieves greater balance in financial rewards between workers and managers and should in turn help to solidify the basic
trust between workers and management on which organizations so heavily depend.

SUMMARY OF FJA AND THE LAW

As this chapter has attempted to show, job analysis is an indispensable tool
for properly implementing a wide range of antidiscrimination legislation.

In a job analysis world dominated by structured questionnaires with limited sensitivity to local conditions, FJA offers a means to economically and effectively implement important provisions of this legislation on a case-by-case basis. The most eloquent statement of this need is in the interpretive guidelines of the ADA, "[we] must rely on objective, factual evidence—not on subjective perceptions, irrational fears, patronizing attitudes, or stereotypes." Employers need to not only apply this principle in enacting all types of antidiscrimination legislation but extend it to all aspects of the employment relationship. Many years of experience with FJA have convinced us that FJA can play a significant role in promoting more trusting and respectful employment relationships by grounding workers' and managers' everyday experience through a shared understanding of the objective and factual bedrock underlying all work. The applications presented in the last section of this book help them work together to develop less discriminatory organizations and healthier work relationships as the world of work undergoes organizational and societal transitions into the third millennium.

Appendix **A**

FJA Scales

THINGS FUNCTIONS SCALE

Working with Things literally means the physical interaction with tangibles, including taken-for-granted items such as desktop equipment (pencils, paper clips, telephone, handstamps, etc.), blackboards and chalk, and cars. Physical involvement with tangibles such as desktop equipment, etc., may not seem very important in tasks primarily concerned with Data or People, but their importance is quickly apparent when handicap or ineptness occurs. An involvement with Things can be manifested in requirements for neatness, arrangements, and/or security of the workplace. Workers who make decisions or take actions concerning the disposition of Things (tools, materials, or machines) are considered to be working mainly with Data, although they physically handle Things (e.g., records, telephone, and catalogs).

> The Things Functions Scale includes: physical interaction with and response to tangibles—touched, felt, observed, and related to in space; images visualized spatially.

The Arabic number assigned to definitions represents the successive levels of this ordinal scale. The A, B, C, and D definitions are variations on the same level.

Level 1A: Handling

Works (cuts, shapes, assembles, etc.), digs, moves, or carries objects or materials where objects, materials, tools, etc., are one or few in number and are the primary involvement of the worker. Precision requirements are relatively gross. Includes the use of dollies, handtrucks, and the like; writing tools, telephones, and other desktop equipment; and the casual or optional use of tools and other tangibles.

Level 1B: Feeding-Offbearing

Inserts, throws, dumps, or places materials into, or removes them from, machines, equipment, or measuring devices that are automatic or tended/operated by other workers. Precision requirements are built-in, largely out of control of worker.

Level 2A: Machine Tending I—
Material Products and Processing

Starts, stops, and monitors the functioning of machines and equipment set up by other workers, where the precision of output depends on keeping one to several controls in adjustment in response to automatic signals according to specifications. Includes all machine situations where there is no significant setup or change of setup, where cycles are very short, alternatives to nonstandard performance are few, and adjustments are highly prescribed.

Level 2B: Machine Tending II—
Data Processing and Duplication

Starts, stops, monitors the functioning of machines and equipment that are preprogrammed to perform the basic functions involved in data processing, document copying, and printing. Machines/equipment are activated at keyboard terminals or touch control panels and can accomplish special effects for particular activities through the input of special codes. Nonproductive use of calculators, typewriters, and similar office equipment is included here.

Level 3A: Manipulating

Works (cuts, shapes, assembles, etc.), digs, moves, guides, or places objects or materials where objects, tools, controls, etc., are several in number. Precision requirements range from gross to fine. Includes waiting on tables and the use of ordinary portable power tools with interchangeable parts and ordinary tools around the home such as kitchen and garden tools used for food preparation, installation, and minor repairs.

Level 3B: Operating-Controlling I

Starts, stops, controls, and adjusts a machine or equipment designed to fabricate and/or process TDP. The worker may be involved in activating the machine, as in word processing or turning wood, or the involvement may occur primarily at startup and stop as with a semi-automatic machine. Operating a machine involves readying and adjusting the machine and/or material as work progresses. Controlling equipment involves monitoring gauges, dials, and so on, and turning valves and other devices to control such items as temperature, pressure, flow of liquids, speed of pumps, and reaction of materials. (This rating is applied only to operators of one machine or one unit of equipment.)

Level 3C: Driving-Controlling

Starts, stops, and controls (steers, guides) the actions of machines in two-dimensional space for which a course must be followed to move things or people. Actions regulating controls require continuous attention and readiness of response to surface traffic conditions.

Level 3D: Starting Up

Readies powered mobile equipment for operation, typically following standard procedures. Manipulates controls to start up engines, allows for warmup and pressure buildup as necessary, checks mobility where movement is involved, and working parts (as in construction equipment), brakes, gauges indicating serviceability (fuel, pressure, temperature, battery output, etc.) and visually checks for leaks and other unusual conditions. Includes reverse shut-down procedures.

Level 4A: Precision Working

Works, moves, guides, or places objects or materials according to standard practical procedures where the number of objects, materials, tools, and so on embraces an entire craft and accuracy expected is within final finished tolerances established for the craft. (Use this rating where work primarily involves manual or power hand tools.)

Level 4B: Setting Up

Installs machines or equipment; inserts tools, alters jigs, fixtures, and attachments and/or repairs machines or equipment to ready and/or restore them to their proper functioning according to job order or blueprint specifications. Involves primary responsibility for accuracy. May involve one or a number of machines for other workers or worker's own operations.

Level 4C: Operating-Controlling II

Starts, stops, controls, and continuously modifies setup of equipment designed to hoist and move materials or transport persons and/or materials in multidimensional space; includes the operation of heavy equipment to reshape and/or pave the earth's surface. Manipulation of controls requires continuous attention to changing conditions, and readiness of response to activate the equipment in lateral, vertical, and/or angular operations.

DATA FUNCTIONS SCALE

Data should be understood to mean information, ideas, facts, and statistics. Involvement with Data is inherent in the simplest job instruction in the form of recognizing the relationship of a tool to its function or the significance of a pointing instruction. Data are always present in a task, although the major emphasis of the task might be dealing with Things and/or People. Where Things are primarily involved, Data tend to show up as specifications. Where People are primarily involved, Data tend to show up as information about objective events or conditions, information about feelings, or ideas that could be tinged with objective information and/or feeling. The Data Scale measures the degree to which workers might be expected to become involved with Data in the tasks they are asked to perform, from simple recognition through degrees of arranging, executing, and modifying to reconceptualizing Data

The data functions in work and learning are the same, but there is an important difference. In work situations the functions tend to be demarcated and allocated to specific assignments reflecting organization structure and production flow. In the learning situation, functions know no bounds. Every new learning can be a challenge involving aspects of creativity (synthesizing), and hence involve all subsidiary functions in the Data Scale— either slowly or quickly. Thus, the Data scale basically reflects the cognitive development that occurs in human learning.

Data are information, ideas, facts, statistics, specification of output, knowledge of conditions, techniques; mental operations.

The Arabic number assigned to definitions represents the successive levels of this ordinal scale. The A, B, C, and D definitions are variations on the same level.

Level 1: Comparing

Selects, sorts, or arranges TDP, judging whether their readily observable functional, structural, or compositional characteristics are similar to or different from prescribed standards. Examples: checks oil level, tire pressure, worn cables; observes and responds to hand signal of worker indicating movement of load; sizes, sorts, and culls tangibles being conveyed to workers; compares lists of names and numbers for similarity.

Level 2: Copying

Transcribes, enters, and/or posts data, following a schema or plan to assemble or make things, using a variety of work aids. Transfers information mentally from plans, diagrams, instructions to workpiece or work site. Examples: attends to stakes showing a grade line to be followed while operating equipment.

Level 3A: Computing

Performs arithmetic operations and makes reports and/or carries out a prescribed action in relation to them. Interprets mathematical data on plans, specifications, diagrams, or blueprints, transferring them to workpiece; for example, reads and follows specifications on stakes.

Level 3B: Compiling

Gathers, collates, or classifies information about TDP, following schema or system but using discretion in application. Examples: considers wind, weather (rain or shine), shape, weight and type of load, height, and capacity of boom in making lift using a crane; converts information in a book (title, author, subject, etc., into a standard library code).

Level 4: Analyzing

Examines and evaluates data (about TDP) with reference to the criteria, standards, and/or requirements of a particular discipline, art, technique, or craft to determine interaction effects (consequences) and to consider alternatives. Examples: considers/evaluates instructions, site and climatic conditions, nature of load, capacity of equipment, other crafts engaged with in order to situate (spot) a crane to best advantage; researches a problem in a particular subject matter area to consider and enumerate the options available in dealing with it.

Level 5A: Innovating

Modifies, alters, and/or adapts existing designs, procedures, or methods to meet unique specifications, unusual conditions, or specific standards of effectiveness within the overall framework of operating theories, principles, and/or organizational contexts; for example, improvises, using existing attachments, or modifies customary equipment to meet unusual conditions and fulfill specifications.

Level 5B: Coordinating

Decides times, place, and sequence of operations of a process, system, or organization, and/or the need for revision of goals, policies (boundary conditions), or procedures on the basis of analysis of data and of performance review of pertinent objectives and requirements. Includes overseeing and/or executing decisions and/or reporting on events; for example, selects/proposes equipment best suited to achieve an output considering resources (equipment, costs, personnel) available to get the job done.

Level 6: Synthesizing

Takes off in new directions on the basis of personal intuitions, feelings, and ideas (with or without regard for tradition, experience, and existing parameters) to conceive new approaches to or statements of problems and the development of system, operational, or aesthetic solutions or resolutions of them typically outside of existing theoretical, stylistic, or organizational context.

PEOPLE FUNCTIONS SCALE

The substance of the live interaction between people (and animals) is communication. In the broadest sense, the communication can be verbal or nonverbal. What makes communication complex is the heavy load that messages carry; for example, Data in their objective and subjective forms— the way in which they are delivered (volume, tone, accompanying gesture, and the formal rules and informal customs that govern the context of the communication). Because there is a large subjective element on the part of both the sender and the receiver of a communication, it is very difficult to measure or to assign absolute values or primary importance to one or another type of information in the interaction.

What further complicates pinning down the nature of specific interpersonal behavior is that *affect* can serve as a tool for managing oneself in the interaction as well as the informational substance of the interaction. Affect, as information and as tool, can occur in the simplest as well as the most complex interaction. For example, affect expressed as a sulky manner, perhaps to gain attention or perhaps to express resentment on the part of a worker, can quickly become the informational substance of the interaction when the supervisor asks nonreactively, "Don't you feel well?" and gets the answer, "No, I don't. My child is ill. I should be home."

The functions in the People scale deal with these complex questions only indirectly. The assumption of ordinality is more tenuous than in the

Things and Data Scales and depends more heavily on role, status, and authority, which are often associated with, but not necessarily a part of, skill. In effect, the functions try to capture the variety of interpersonal behavior assigned in various work situations and are more or less arranged, as in the other scales, according to the need, in general, to deal with increasing numbers of variables and with greater degrees of discretion. (The function least likely to fit this pattern is Supervising, which probably could have a scale of its own.)

Skill in dealing with people is undoubtedly as much an art as a methodology. Although measurement in this area is in a primitive state, it is essential to delineate descriptive and numerical standards by which a function can be appraised in the task in which it occurs. One should especially note cultural boundary conditions in matters of courtesy, diplomatic protocol, and "rule" of behavior in patient–doctor relationships.

The people scale measures live interaction between people, and people and animals.

Level 1A: Taking Instructions—Helping

Attends to the work assignment, instructions, or orders of supervisor. No immediate response or verbal exchange is required unless clarification of instruction is needed.

Level 1B: Serving

Attends to the needs or requests of people or animals or to the expressed or implicit wishes of people. Immediate response is involved.

Level 2: Exchanging Information

Talks to, converses with, and/or signals people to convey or obtain information, or to clarify and work out details of an assignment, within the framework of well-established procedure; for example, requests clarification of a verbal signal (in person or on radio) or hand signal.

Level 3A: Sourcing Information

Serves as a primary and central source to external public or internal workforce of system information that is crucial in directing/routing people or workers to their destination or areas of concern, which makes it possible for system/organization to function. Examples: information personnel in stores and terminals; reception/routing person in large office; inventory and/or stock clerk.

Level 3B: Persuading

Influences others in favor of a product, service, or point of view by talks or demonstration. Examples: demonstrates safety procedures required on a piece of equipment for compliance with new regulations; sales personnel in hardware and furniture stores or boutiques.

Level 3C: Coaching

Befriends and encourages individuals on a personal, caring basis by approximating a peer- or family-type relationship either in a one-on-one or small group situation; gives instruction, advice, and personal assistance concerning activities of daily living, the use of various institutional services, and participation in groups. Examples: gives support or encouragement to apprentice or journeyperson on unfamiliar piece of equipment, coaches students on school athletic team, sponsors new employees in a training situation.

Level 3D: Diverting

Amuses/performs to entertain or distract individuals and/or audience or to lighten a situation. Examples: day care teaching; story telling; street entertaining.

Level 4A: Consulting

Serves as a source of technical knowledge and provides such knowledge as well as related ideas to define, clarify, enlarge upon, or sharpen procedures, capabilities, or product specifications. Examples: informs project managers of effective and appropriate use of equipment to achieve output within constraints (time, money, etc.); presents options to solve particular problems.

Level 4B: Instructing

Teaches subject matter to others or trains others, including animals, through explanation, demonstration, and test, bringing them to a desired level of performance.

Level 4C: Treating

Acts on or interacts with individuals or small groups of people or animals who need help (as in sickness) to carry out specialized therapeutic or adjustment procedures. Systematically observes results of treatment within the framework of total personal behavior since unique individual reactions to prescriptions (chemical, physical, or behavioral) may not fall within the range of expectation/prediction. Motivates, supports, and instructs individuals to accept or cooperate with therapeutic adjustment procedures when necessary.

Level 5: Supervising

Determines and/or interprets work procedure for a group of workers, assigns specific duties to them delineating prescribed and discretionary content; maintains harmonious relations among them, evaluates performance (both prescribed and discretionary), and promotes efficiency and other organizational values; makes decisions on procedural and technical levels.

Level 6: Negotiating

Bargains and discusses on a formal basis, as a representative of one side of a transaction, for advantages in resources, rights, privileges, and/or contractual obligations, giving and taking within the limits provided by authority or within the framework of the perceived requirements and integrity of a problem.

Level 7: Mentoring

Works with individuals having problems affecting their life adjustment in order to advise, counsel, and/or guide them according to legal, scientific, clinical, spiritual, and/or other professional principles. Advises clients on implications of analyses or diagnoses made of problems, courses of action open to deal with them, and merits of one strategy over another.

Level 8: Leading

Sets forth/asserts a vision that has an impact upon and defines the mission, culture, and values of an organization; sets direction, time perspective, and organizational structure for achievement of goals and objectives; models behavior that inspires and motivates achievement (distinct from management).

WI SCALE

Level 1

Inputs, outputs, tools, and equipment, and procedures are all specified. Almost everything the worker needs to know is contained in the assignment.

The worker usually turns out a specified amount of work or a standard number of units per hour or day.

Level 2

Inputs, outputs, tools, and equipment are all specified, but the worker has some leeway in the procedures and methods used to get the job done. Almost all the information needed is in the assignment instructions. Production is measured on a daily or weekly basis.

Level 3

Inputs and outputs are specified, but the worker has considerable freedom as to procedure and timing, including the use of tools and/or equipment. The worker may have to refer to several standard sources for information (handbooks, catalogs, wall charts). Time to complete a particular product or service is specified, but this varies up to several hours.

Level 4

Output (product or service) is specified in the assignment, which may be in the form of a memorandum or of a schematic (sketch or blueprint). The worker must work out own way of getting the job done, including selection and use of tools and/or equipment, sequence of operations (tasks), and obtaining important information (handbooks, etc.). Worker may either do the work or set up standards and procedures for others to do it.

Level 5

Same as Level 4, but in addition the workers are expected to know and employ theory so that they understand the "whys" and "wherefores" of the various options that are available for dealing with a problem and can independently select from among them. Workers may have to do some reading in the professional and/or trade literature in order to gain this understanding and/or seek assistance from a technical "expert."

Level 6

Various possible outputs are described that can meet stated technical or administrative needs. The worker must investigate the various possible outputs and evaluate them in regard to performance characteristics and input demands. This usually requires creative use of theory well beyond referring to standard sources. There is no specification of inputs, methods, sequences, sources, or the like.

Level 7

There is some question as to what the need or problem really is or what directions should be pursued in dealing with it. In order to define the problem, to control and explore the behavior of the variables, and to formulate possible outputs and their performance characteristics, the worker must consult largely unspecified sources of information and devise investigations, surveys, or data analysis studies (strategies).

Level 8

Information and/or direction comes to the worker in terms of needs (tactical, organizational, strategic, financial). Worker must call for staff reports and recommendations concerning methods of dealing with them. He or she coordinates both organizational and technical data in order to make decisions and determinations regarding courses of action (outputs) for major sections (divisions, groups) of the organization.

REASONING DEVELOPMENT SCALE

The Reasoning Development Scale is concerned with knowledge and ability to deal with theory versus practice, abstract versus concrete, and many versus few variables.

Level 1

Have the commonsense understanding to carry out simple one- or two-step instructions in the context of highly standardized situations.

Recognize unacceptable variations from the standard and take emergency action to reject inputs or stop operations.

Level 2

Have the commonsense understanding to carry out detailed but uninvolved instructions where the work involves a few concrete/specific variables in or from standard/typical situations.

Level 3

Have the commonsense understanding to carry out instruction where the work involves several concrete/specific variables in or from standard/typical situations.

Level 4

Have knowledge of a system of interrelated procedures, such as bookkeeping, internal combustion engines, electric wiring systems, nursing, farm management, ship sailing, or machining, and the ability to access optional solutions to ordinary problems.

Apply principles to solve practical everyday problems and deal with a variety of concrete variables in situations where only limited standardization exists.

Interpret a variety of instructions furnished in written, oral, diagrammatic, or schedule form.

Level 5

Have knowledge of a field of study (engineering, literature, history, business administration) having immediate applicability to the affairs of the world.

Define problems, collect data, establish facts, and draw valid conclusions in controlled situations.

Interpret an extensive variety of technical material in books, manuals, texts, and so on.

Deal with some abstract but mostly concrete variables.

Level 6

Have knowledge of a field of study of the highest abstractive order (e.g., mathematics, physics, chemistry, logic, philosophy, art criticism).

Deal with nonverbal symbols in formulas, equations, or graphs.

Understand the most difficult classes of concepts.

Deal with a large number of variables and determine a specific course of action (e.g., research, production) on the basis of need.

MATHEMATICAL DEVELOPMENT SCALE

The Mathematical Development Scale is concerned with knowledge and ability to deal with mathematical problems and operations from counting and simple addition to higher mathematics.

Level 1

Counting to simple addition and subtraction; reading; copying, and/or recording of figures.

Level 2

Use arithmetic to add, subtract, multiply, and divide whole numbers.

Reading scales and gauges as in powered equipment where reading and signals are indicative of conditions and actions to be taken.

Level 3

Make arithmetic calculations involving fractions, decimals, and percentages. Mentally acts upon dimensional specifications marked on material or stakes.

Level 4

Performs arithmetic, and algebraic and/or geometric procedures in standard practical applications.

Level 5

Have knowledge of advanced mathematical and statistical techniques such as differential and integral calculus, factor analysis, and probability determination.

Work with a wide variety of theoretical mathematical concepts.

Make original applications of mathematical procedures, as in empirical and differential equations.

LANGUAGE DEVELOPMENT SCALE

The Language Development Scale is concerned with knowledge and ability to speak, read, or write language materials from simple verbal instructions to complex sources of written information and ideas.

Level 1

Cannot read or write but can follow simple oral, pointing-out instructions.

Sign name and understand ordinary, routine agreements when explained, such as those relevant to leasing a house; employment (hours, wages, etc.); procuring a driver's license.

Read lists, addresses, traffic signs, safety warnings.

Level 2

Read material containing short sentences, simple concrete vocabulary, words that avoid complex Latin derivatives (comic books, popular tabloids, "westerns").

Converse with service personnel (waitpersons, ushers, cashiers).

Copy ordinary, everyday written records or business letter precisely without error. Keep taxi driver's trip record or service maintenance record.

Level 3

Comprehend orally expressed trade terminology (jargon) of a specific technical nature.

Read material on level of the *Reader's Digest* and straight news reporting in popular mass newspapers.

Comprehend ordinary newscasting (uninvolved sentences and vocabulary with focus on events rather than on their analysis).

Copy written material from one record to another, catching gross errors in grammar.

Fill in report forms, such as Medicare forms, employment applications, and card form for income tax.

Conduct house-to-house surveys to obtain common census-type information or market data, such as preferences for commercial products in everyday life.

Level 4

Write routine business correspondence reflecting standard procedures.

Interview job applicants to determine work best suited for their abilities and experience; contact employers to interest them in services of agency.

Read and comprehend technical manuals and written instructions as well as drawings associated with practising a craft.

Conduct opinion research surveys involving stratified samples of the population.

Guide people on tours through historical or public buildings and relate relevant anecdotes and historical material.

Level 5

Write instructions for assembly of prefabricated parts into units.

Write instructions and specifications concerning proper use of machinery.

Write copy for advertising.

Report news for the newspapers, radio, or television.

Prepare and deliver lectures for audiences that seek information about the arts, sciences, and humanities in an informal way.

Level 6

Report, write, edit article for technical and scientific journal (e.g., *Journal of Educational Sociology, Science, Physical Review, Daedalus*) or journals specializing in advanced literary criticism, (e.g., *The New Yorker, New York Review of Books*).

Prepare and draw up deeds, leases, wills, mortgages, and contracts.

Prepare and deliver lectures on politics, economics, education, or science to specialized students and/or professional societies.

Comprehend and apply technical engineering data for designing buildings and bridges.

Comprehend and discuss works of a highly symbolic nature, such as works in logic and philosophy (e.g., Kant, Whitehead, Russell).

Appendix **B**

Selecting Functional Job Analysts

Facilitating FJA job analysis sessions requires professional skills akin to counseling and interviewing skills. These skills are based on advanced training and experience in personnel psychology. Individuals who most profit from FJA job analyst training are persons who wish to build on such a background and take the additional specific content training. This specific content, listed in Appendix C of *Benchmark Task for Job Analysis* (Fine & Getkate, 1995), includes:

- FJA model/method
- FJA scales
- Group dynamics
- Job analysis: purpose and applications in HRM, for example, selection, training, job design
- Role of job analyst/consultant
- EEO legislation
- Relevant professional/ethical guidelines

In addition, the training involves a practicum that is required for certification as an FJA facilitator.

As background selection requirements, a potential FJA facilitator must possess the following essential skills:

- Verbal ability—the facilitator must be able to understand rapid oral communications from several sources where this information may be of a highly technical nature, organize and sort through this verbal information mentally, and write down grammatically complex sentences to form an

FJA task bank. Above average verbal ability is required—just how far above average is not known, a lot depends on the other requisite skills.

- Listening skills.
- Facilitation skills—engages focus group participants in a creative endeavor; develops rapport, communicates support and sense of participants' self-worth, shows sensitivity to individual feelings.
- Initiative, flexibility, adaptability.

Taken together, these skills have much in common with the Theory Y management style discussed in Part I of this book. When facilitating an FJA focus group the individual with a Theory Y orientation could be expected to engage in a number of behaviors essential for a successful functional job analyst:

- Listen carefully to participant suggestions.
- Avoid imposing own wording on task formulations.
- Avoid any criticism of participant input.
- Provide participants with considerable discretion in organizing the focus group information (while staying with theory and methodology framework provided by FJA).
- Reinforce participant ownership of task bank.
- Be sensitive to participant discomfort with the FJA process.
- Avoid pressuring focus group participants.
- Ask questions as necessary to obtain clarification.
- Respect individual differences in how participants get their jobs done.
- Reassure participants they will finish on time.
- Recognize and show sensitivity to different personalities in the focus group.
- Encourage all participants to speak up when they have a contribution to make.
- Support the right of all participants to contribute to the task bank and express differences with what is being developed.
- Maintain an attitude of openness and candor always.

All of these facilitator behaviors show *trust of* and *respect for* the participants, as well as *considerate behavior* directed to them as individuals. The participants are the preeminent authorities on what they do. This is recognized throughout the 2-day focus group in facilitator word and deed. In its major features then, FJA has a great deal in common with what McGregor would ask of the Theory Y manager. These are demanding standards to ask a facilitator to meet and not every person being considered as an FJA trainee is comfortable with these expectations. If the prospective facilitator prefers a Theory X style with its emphasis on control of, and administration over, the minutiae of the worker's activities, it can be expected that the same Theory X style carries over into the conduct of the focus group. In that case, FJA facilitation is definitely not recommended because the focus group, instead of being an entirely new and different experience, is more of what participants are accustomed to and have no faith in.

The suggested approach to recruiting and selecting suitable functional job analysts parallels the approach recommended to organizations in recruiting, selecting, and interviewing workers in Chapters 10, 11, and 12 of this book. The three steps in this suggested approach are:

- Prospective analysts are given a realistic FJA preview similar to the realistic job preview recommended in chapter 10 and allowed to select themselves out if they are uncomfortable with the FJA philosophy and approach.
- A managerial style questionnaire can be administered; for example, the Managerial Philosophies Scale developed by Jacoby and Terborg (1995). Individuals whose results indicate a Theory Y style would be directed toward FJA facilitation.
- The prospective FJA analyst can be interviewed for suitability. The performance standards provided for FJA facilitation in Appendix C should help in designing and scoring interview questions of this type.

The previous three suggestions could be augmented with observations from coworkers and subordinates regarding an individual's preference for a Theory X or Theory Y style.

The obvious way to assess whether a prospective facilitator is suited to FJA work is to train an individual and then observe him or her conducting a focus group during the certification process. Although this approach certainly gives the desired information, unnecessary costs to the organization ensue if the facilitator does not have the required skills and orientation for FJA facilitation. Along with the costs of training the facilitator, the organization has to contend with the problem of a poorly written task bank (possibly resulting in the need to redo the focus group), disgruntled participants, and bad publicity for the FJA process. In the long run it is cheaper and more efficient to recruit and select the right FJA facilitators than to assume that any staff member is up to the job.

Appendix **C**

Training and Accrediting Functional Job Analysts

FJA is complex in theory, methodology, and application. Fine has certified functional job analysts on satisfactory completion of at least three requirements.

- Attendance at a 5-day FJA training workshop consisting of lectures, demonstrations, and practical exercises covering FJA theory, conduct of the FJA focus group, rating of tasks on the functional scales, and typical applications of FJA to HRM. This requirement provides adequate knowledge and insight necessary to understand the purpose of FJA, the role of the analyst in facilitating the FJA focus group, and the dynamics of the FJA focus group itself.
- Attendance at, and observation of, a 2-day FJA focus group facilitated by a certified functional job analyst. The observer and analyst need to set aside adequate time at the end of each day to discuss the facilitation process and deal with any questions that arise. This requirement gives the FJA trainee an appreciation of the flow and rhythm of a well-conducted FJA focus group.
- The FJA trainee then conducts a 2-day focus group under the supervision of a certified functional job analyst. Adequate time during coffee and lunch breaks as well as in the evening must be allowed for the certified analyst to give detailed constructive feedback on all aspects of the facilitation (the performance checklist included here has been found useful as a means for giving targeted feedback to FJA trainees). This supervision should continue through the editing and revalidation of the task bank. Together the certified analyst and the trainee should rate at least a subset of the tasks when the focus group participants return the task bank after revalidation.

In individual cases, more training and experience may be required before the trainee is competent to facilitate an FJA focus group. Cronshaw can be contacted to arrange for FJA training workshops, focus groups, or supervision.

Performance Checklist for Certification of FJA Facilitators

Instructions to Rater

1. Be sure to read *"Generating Task Data With Workers: The FJA Focus Group,"* which is chapter 7 of this book.
2. Rate every item.
3. Check *Yes* or *No* in *Performs Task* column.
4. If candidate performs task and is in *Meets Requirements* range, check this column.
5. If candidate's performance *Needs Help* or is *Outstanding*, check appropriate columns and keep notes. *A back-up critical incident is required for each one of these checks.*
6. A candidate qualifies when he or she *Meets Requirements* and/or is *Outstanding* in a majority of items in each category. In addition, the candidate should demonstrate responsiveness to the observer's evaluation and suggestions made on the basis of ratings. These suggestions could be shared during the breaks.

Preliminaries	Performs Task		Meets Req'ts	Needs Help	Out- standing
	Yes	No			
Has FJA Facilitator arranged for and checked on the following:					
• Organization sends letter to SMEs indicating its purpose for the workshop.					
• Personal letter to SMEs using model letter provided and adapted as necessary.					
• An organization person to be responsible for arrangements: a) two flip charts and markers, b) a quiet room with seminar seating, c) refreshments for two breaks.					
• Someone to type the material produced by SMEs and written on flip charts.					
• Flip charts prepared in advance: own name and title of workshop, the five questions, and the FJA paradigm for a task statement.					

| Performs Task | | Meets | Needs | Out- |
Yes	No	Req'ts	Help	standing

Introduction

- Greets group with enthusiasm; is informal in manner. It helps to tell a little about oneself—job, education, family. After all, the SMEs are suspicious, and it is not likely that they have ever been approached in this way.
- Asks SMEs to print names on name cards and then to introduce themselves.
- Asks SMEs if they have any questions about the letters they received and answers their questions frankly and directly. If does not know, says so.
- Explains that information they generate will be used as a basis for various personnel operations such as training and selection or, if part of a program of activity, explain the program.
- Explains that the workshop will take two days with morning, and afternoon breaks (10–15 minutes) and lunch break (60–75 minutes). Closure will be at 4:30 p.m. (if workshop has started at 8:30 a.m.).
- States that workshop will focus on the five questions listed on the flip chart and briefly reviews them.
- Explains that task statements will be written according to the FJA paradigm also illustrated on the flip chart.
- Asks SMEs if they have any further questions on material presented.
- Explains that everything SMEs say will be written on the flip charts and posted on the walls so they can check, correct, or change whatever they see fit.
- Writes as large and clearly as possible so that SMEs can read their input from wherever they are sitting.
- Makes corrections requested by SMEs as neatly as possible so input can still be read.

	Performs Task		Meets	Needs	Out-
	Yes	No	Req'ts	Help	standing
• Explains that all the posted material will be typed and given to them for correction and editing which they will then return to the facilitator for a final integration of comments.					
• Notes that the Task Bank can serve as a permanent record in SME's personnel file (if this is the organization's plan) or it can be kept in their personal file.					

Note: The above items are especially important for insuring credibility of the assertions that this is the SMEs' task bank and their creation.

Outputs

- Asks the first Question in straightforward, matter-of-fact way. Can elaborate as follows if necessary: "What are you expected to produce? What services are you expected to deliver? What are the outcomes of your work?" Elaborates only if group is slow in getting started.
- Avoids use of terms like "activities, duties, tasks," noting, if brought up by SMEs, that they will be discussed later.
- Listens carefully and writes down what is said without being critical.
- Seeks clarification when it appears obvious that certain outputs overlap.
- Points out in noncritical manner, when tasks are proposed for outputs, that these will be gathered later for Question 4. Uses this type of offering to ask: "What output does that task contribute to?"
- Waits a couple of moments when SMEs seem to have run out of ideas, and says: "Let us post what we have. You can always add to this list when you think of something."

	Performs Task		Meets	Needs	Out-
Knowledges and Skills/Abilities KSAs)	**Yes**	**No**	**Req'ts**	**Help**	**standing**

Knowledges and Skills/Abilities KSAs)

- Uses two flip charts, one headed Knowledge and the other Skills/ Abilities
- Explains that SMEs can provide the information in any order they choose. The question they are answering is: "What KSAs are they drawing on to produce the Outputs?"
- Responds to questions from SMEs concerning difference between K and S/A, and S and A by noting that Ks are nouns and Ss are verbs. The difference between S and A is mainly a manner of speaking. Avoids getting technical.
- Follows up categorical statements of K and S/A by asking for particulars or specifications or "How do you mean it?"
- Asks for clarification of acronyms, jargon, and other mystifying language, noting meaning in plain words.
- Avoids making any suggestions with possible exception of reading, writing, and arithmetic, which can appear in both listings.
- Posts each sheet on wall as it is completed or enlists help of SMEs.
- Concludes this part of workshop when SMEs have reached a lull, noting again that the lists can be added to any time.
- Suggests additions to lists with approval of group, when additional items come up during the development of tasks.

The answers to the first three questions are likely to be attained by the time of the first break or shortly thereafter. By this time it should be noticeable that the facilitator has attained credibility with regard to using the SMEs' language at all times. It is possible that by this time they will also have noted the importance of specificity. Also the first signs of inter-

	Performs Task		Meets	Needs	Out-
	Yes	No	Req'ts	Help	standing

action among the SMEs may also have
been evidenced.

Tasks

- Effects an easy transition to the production of tasks, e.g., announcing that
  the list of Outputs will serve as an
  agenda for task development.
- Reminds the SMEs of the structure
  and content of a task statement by referring to the chart used at the start,
  indicating how the information they
  provide will be organized.
- Reinforces SME ownership of data developed by asking them to select
  which Output they wish to work on.
- Listens closely and carefully for consensus and when it appears to have
  been reached, feeds it back to group:
  "Sounds like you want to start with
  . . . Do I have it right?" If the group
  agrees, launches right into it.
- Lists the Output and assigns a number
  as follows: Assuming the Output
  selected is the first on the list then the
  number for this Output will be 1.0 and
  the tasks developed for it will be numbered in sequence 1.1, 1.2, etc. A similar numbering pattern will be used for
  all other Outputs and tasks.
- May need to make the following types
  of remarks to get group started, depending on manifested hesitancy:
  "How does work on this Output get
  started? What is the first task? Don't
  be troubled about getting it just right?
  You could even start in the middle
  and work back if you choose. Things
  usually come full circle." The facilitator needs to be sensitive to the fact
  that the SMEs have never done anything like this, and it is difficult at
  first.
- Another device for obtaining task information for an output is to ask the
  SMEs to briefly outline what gets

	Performs Task		Meets	Needs	Out-
	Yes	No	Req'ts	Help	standing

done in the output (the various results) and what they do to produce
the results (their behaviors). The facilitator can draw a line down the middle
of a chart and note what the SMEs
say—behaviors on the left and results
on the right. (This sheet serves as a
sort of scribble sheet and is not to be
posted.) At this point the facilitator
can say, "It looks like we have (# of)
tasks" and then proceed to outline
what he or she sees as possible tasks.
Don't ask for or expect absolute agreement. Simply say: "Let's get started
with this first one and see where it
takes us." An approach such as this
keeps the momentum of the workshop
going.

Note: Momentum, a productive flow of
input from the SMEs, is important. However, it is not something to be produced
by "pulling teeth," urging on, or in any
way pressuring the SMEs. It is best
achieved by questions built on the data
at hand. The facilitator can always fall
back on something like the following:
"Actually your job is more or less a continuous flow, like everyday living. What
we are trying to do here is to stop the
action at some significant points in order
to get a series of pictures (tasks) in focus
and described in depth."

• Listens actively, and where necessary,
asks appropriate questions to distinguish worker behaviors from results.
Is aware of the difficulty all workers
have in making this distinction, since
the tendency is for all workers to focus
on results. May start writing what appears to be a behavior but as the task
gets described will discover it is a result. (The language of results is much
richer than the language of behaviors).
The facilitator does not hesitate to ask:
"But what do you do to get (such or
such) work done?" For example, when
an SME says, "I recommend" or "I determine" these are usually the results
of particular behaviors.

	Performs Task		Meets	Needs	Out-
	Yes	No	Req'ts	Help	standing

- Is alert to the danger of capturing tasks that are too narrow (more like time and motion study) or too general (subsume an entire activity). This is a common tendency for SMEs. The former are expressed as physical, the latter tend to be introduced by such verbs as "conducts, performs, prepares," which obscure specific behaviors. Aware of this problem, gently presses group to be specific but not minute.

- Uses several verbs as necessary to capture a behavior. The criterion for knowing when the right behavior has been captured is to mentally translate it to a function in the Worker Function Scales.

- Does not start writing a task until he or she has a clear idea of behavior and result or, if the input from the SMEs tends to focus on end result, writes this down at bottom of flip chart and then says, "O.K. Now what do you do to achieve this result?"

- Is sensitive to the need for a behavior that pertains primarily to Things, to have a result that is primarily Things oriented. The same for Data and People whose results must be primarily Data and People oriented.

- Does not insist that tasks follow a definite sequence. Picks up on the fact that different SMEs may follow different sequences.

- Is alert to the fact that certain activities such as a production process, processing a contract or loan, and diagnosing or repairing a mechanical device frequently do have a definite sequence although there may be more than one. Picks up on this by asking SMEs, "Then what do you do?"

- For each task, generates the necessary data relating to instructional level and the KSAs drawn on. Checks that the KSAs are appropriate to the behavior and result. Uses the phrase "drawing

Performs Task		Meets	Needs	Out-
Yes	No	Req'ts	Help	standing

on" preceding the knowledges, and "relying on" preceding the skills.

- After each task is written, reads it slowly to the SMEs so they are satisfied that it is OK, can see their wording and phrasing in it, and also the FJA structure. This reading back also helps reinforce the facilitator's leadership and credibility.

- As appropriate, reinforces the SMEs in the likelihood they don't all perform their jobs in exactly the same way, acknowledges there is room for differences which will emerge when the SMEs get the task banks back for editing and are asked to check off the tasks they as individuals do to get the work done.

- Becomes aware, when writing a great deal for a task, that the task needs further breakdown—inadvertently the facilitator has been caught in what is likely to be an activity, or even a technology, and that further questioning is necessary to determine what is involved. (An exception to this situation can occur for highly skilled jobs of occupational or professional status where the incumbent is indeed engaged in the details of a whole series of activities).

- Note: It is confusing to use "result" and "why" interchangeably. It is best to stick to "result" or "what gets done." The "result" of a task is not the same as "why."

- Asks for examples of specific content—the objects of behavior. Such examples are essential for validating the behavior and later to edit the task.

- Probes to establish the instructional level of a task. Are there specifications for the result? Are there specific instructions in a manual or obtained directly from the supervisor? Is the SME working from guidelines that give him or her leeway, initiative, etc.?

	Performs Task		Meets	Needs	Out-
	Yes	No	Req'ts	Help	standing

Is the instruction built into the training? Does the SME instruct him or herself according to self-imposed standards? What is the role of standing operating procedures (SOP)? How specific are they?

Performance Standards

- Indicates the questions to be addressed in this category: "What do you attend to, watch out for, in getting a job done? What do you see, feel when you can say 'a job well done?' Are the standards you expect of yourself as demanding as those of management? What do you do to put quality into your work?"

- Lists the standards as they are expressed always looking for the adverb or adjective that indicates quality. As necessary, asks SMEs to expand on those standards not immediately apparent.

- Asks SMEs if there are tasks they have listed that especially exemplify particular standards. This can be tricky as they may well truthfully say that any or many of the standards apply to all of the tasks. Abandons this line of questioning if it leads to generalities.

- Is receptive to standards taken from official appraisal forms but still encourages expression of personal standards.

- Takes note of all standards that seem to involve stress, whether negative or positive, since such standards reflect the need for Adaptive Skills.

- Asks if there are any numerical standards that have to be met and what they are.

General

- Reassures SMEs who express doubt they will finish describing all their tasks, that the work will go faster as

	Performs Task		Meets	Needs	Out-
	---	---	---	---	---
	Yes	No	Req'ts	Help	standing

they get the drift, several of the Outputs will not have as many tasks, and
some of the Outputs may collapse into
others. In any case the work is usually
finished in two days. If it isn't finished, the SMEs will be able to add
tasks when they get their task bank for
editing.

- Listens with the "third ear" to the
  group dynamics, the interactions
  among the SMEs, the kinds of things
  they joke about that frequently are
  obstacles in their work and which represent the challenge to their adaptive
  skills. The facilitator needs to make
  mental notes about the challenges and
  the adaptive skills since they have an
  enormous impact on the quality of
  work performed.

- Has been careful to not intervene with
  knowledge or wording that suggests
  greater sophistication with the work
  than that of SMEs.

- From time to time has taken off on a
  personal anecdote or humorous
  incident to cement bond with group
  and introduce an element of lightness
  to workshop.

- Shows sensitivity to different personalities by noting the way they express
  themselves and where possible giving
  each one an opportunity to speak up.
  For example, after completing the
  writing of a task focuses on a quiet
  SME and ask if this corresponds to the
  way he or she does it.

- Avoids put downs, particularly
  against those SMEs who are very ex-
  pressive and tend to be dominant.
  Uses eye contact to invite others to
  participate in such instances.

- From time to time thanks individuals
  for their particular contributions but
  makes sure everyone is a recipient of
  these thanks.

- On rare occasions interrupts long contributions or discussions to indicate

	Performs Task		Meets	Needs	Out-
	Yes	No	Req'ts	Help	standing
that time is of the essence and that the group must move on.					
• Makes certain to thank the SMEs at the conclusion of the workshop for their cooperation, reminding them that they will receive the material for final editing and return to the facilitator.					

Note: The conclusion of the workshop is usually a very positive, even happy, occasion with the SMEs expressing wonder and satisfaction about all they do to get their work done, and thanking the facilitator for the opportunity to discover it.

Appendix D

FJA Task Bank Editing Manual

INTRODUCTION

This appendix is an adaptation of *Functional Job Analysis: How to Standardize Task Statements,* an editing manual for use with the National Task Bank by Sidney A. Fine, Ann M. Holt, Maret F. Hutchinson, and Wretha W. Wiley. This manual is an attempt at definitive, illustrative guidelines for editing task statements, written according to the principles and techniques of FJA. Therefore, this manual is intended for use by persons trained and competent in FJA task analysis. It is not intended as introductory material to the technique

The manual was developed in 1974 as one of a series of publications of the W. E. Upjohn Institute for Employment Research associated with the fulfillment of a contract with the Department of Health, Education, and Welfare (DHEW), which is now the Department of Health and Human Welfare. That contract involved completing FJAs of hundreds of jobs in the human welfare field and accounts for the manual's example tasks being from that field. There is no doubt, however, that the same issues and procedures are relevant across the entire spectrum of jobs.

In addition to serving the very practical purpose of demonstrating how to write and edit tasks to achieve reliability, validity, and uniformity, this manual has historic value. It contains within it the seeds of the FJA of today —in short, it has withstood the test of time. It is especially interesting to note that as a result of the use of this manual in training sessions over the years, the writing of task statements has improved. For example, task statements are now written with knowledge and abilities more explicitly introduced by the phrases, "drawing on," for knowledge and, "relying on," for skills and abilities. (See *Benchmark tasks for job analysis,* Fine & Getkate, 1995.) Thus the test questions lead to answers with more explicit content.

With the exception of editing for gender bias and terminology (e.g., "manpower planning" becomes "HR planning"), no changes have been made from the text in the original manual.

The next section reviews some of the concepts and assumptions dealt with in greater depth in the main body of this book, which are involved in the formulation of task statements and some of the inferences made from them. It also outlines a procedure for standardizing task statements through a group editing process.

A word about the group editing. The project for the government was huge and spread over several years. Employees of the Social and Rehabilitation Administration of DHEW who were trained in the FJA technique wrote many hundreds of tasks in the field. The resulting tasks, written on the Task Analysis form shown in this manual, were sent to the Upjohn Institute in Washington, DC, for editing and inclusion in a National Task Bank of tasks in social welfare. A team of editors from Upjohn and the Social and Rehabilitation Administration worked for many months editing the tasks received from the field. The procedure followed by those editors is the one outlined in the following section.

The concluding section explains how to test the reliability and validity of task statements by using the Checklist for Task Analysis. This section was partially developed in fulfillment of the contract with DHEW. Wiley, a former staff member of the Upjohn Institute, was initially involved in the preparation of the report for that agency.

In no case is it intended to suggest that the techniques are so far advanced that only one answer is possible. The important thing to recognize is that there is a technique and rationale that, when used as described herein, can produce reliable and valid task statements, useful in HR operations.

THE PROCESS OF TASK ANALYSIS

The chances are that you are in the process of task analysis because you are trying to answer questions like the following in a way that provides you with concrete information.

- Can my organization offer jobs at a livable wage and provide opportunities for advancement?
- Are my organization's personnel policies flexible enough to accommodate people with limited work experience and different lifestyles?
- How do I design (restructure) jobs and upgrade people to make room at the bottom of my opportunity system and keep my productivity high?

- How do I make the most of my training resources?
- How can our training people organize effective in-house training courses, particularly for entry workers?
- Do some of our job titles that seem to represent different work and salary levels actually hide the fact that the tasks performed are substantially the same?
- Is our organization using only a fraction of the potential of our work force and looking for talent outside that is already inside?

In trying to answer these questions, you tried to use the information (job descriptions, job evaluation data, etc.) available in your organization and found it inadequate. You therefore looked over job analysis methods that would give you substantial, precise, and controlled information. This is likely to have been one of the reasons you decided to use FJA in the first place. Let us quickly review some of the concepts and assumptions of FJA that were involved in your producing the task statements you are now ready to refine and edit, and that are the basis for their substantive nature.

Conceptualization and Definition of Tasks

In FJA a basic distinction is made between what workers do and what gets done—between behavior and end results. This distinction is carried into the methods of analysis (data gathering) and the formulation of the task statements. The distinction has been essential because historically, most job descriptions dwelt primarily on what got done. Another key concept or assumption of FJA is that task statements, although certainly not the reality of work activity, are as close to that reality as you can get to carry out personnel operations. *Task statements* are verbal formulations of activities that make it possible to describe what workers do *and* what gets done so that recruitment, selection, assignment, training, performance evaluation, and payment can be efficiently and equitably carried out. Therefore, the focus of our attention must be on the formulation—the words and the organization of words in the task statement used to express the task. The formulation must simulate reality; that is, those performing the task must agree that, insofar as the task can be communicated, the task statement does so. Furthermore, because a task is part of a context; namely, a work situation,[1] it is essential that the language of the one task statement be compatible with that of other task statements in that context and that together they can describe the technology of a work situation. For practical

---

[1]During the period of original research, 1948–1953, this was referred to as a job–worker situation.

reasons, then, the *task statement* is the *task*, and in the remainder of this document the two terms are used more or less interchangeably.[2]

In FJA a task is defined in terms of a controlled language, a controlled method of formulation, and in relation to a systems context. The definition is as follows:

> A task is an action or action sequence grouped through time designed to contribute a specified end result to the accomplishment of an objective and for which functional levels and orientation can be reliably assigned. The task action or action sequence may be primarily *physical,* such as *operating* an electric typewriter; or primarily *mental,* such as *analyzing* data; and/or primarily *interpersonal,* such as *consulting* with another person. (Fine & Wiley, 1971, pp. 9–10)

Tasks conceived and formulated according to this definition have permanence that jobs and assignments of everyday parlance to do not have. Although mutable, tasks can become building blocks in personnel practice and HR planning. Hence, it is important to formulate and edit task statements carefully.

A task formulated according to FJA methodology becomes the most fundamental unit of a work-doing system. From it, it is possible to make reliable and valid inferences about the worker, the work organization, and the work.

The worker. The worker's functional level and orientation are indicative of experience, education, and capability to perform the task.

The work organization. The methodology provided for and the output of the Worker Actions must contribute to the Objectives of the organization.

The work. The action, object of the action, equipment provided, and output are indicative of the Performance Standards and Training Content (both functional and specific), as well as the basic skills in reasoning, math, and language required.

The interaction of these three elements can result in both productivity and worker growth (see Figure D.1).

Reliability and Validity of Task Statements

Reliable and valid task statements are essential for efficient and equitable personnel operations. Supervisors and personnel officers must agree on

---

[2]Nevertheless, we must never forget that "the map is not the territory" and therefore the task statement is not the task—it is a simulation, and we must continuously check back with what it is actually doing.

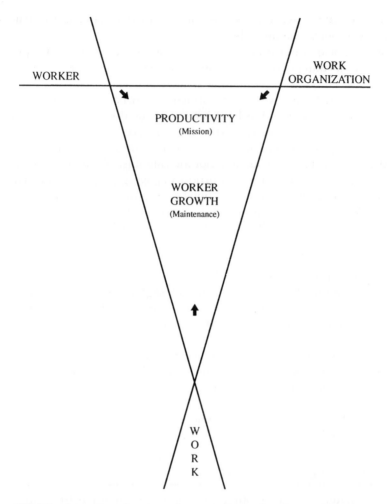

FIG. D.1.   Interaction of work, work organization, and worker to achieve productivity and worker growth.

what must get done, and on the qualifications of workers to get it done. Supervisors and workers must agree on the standards for output and on appropriate procedures to be used. Engineers, supervisors, and workers must have the same or similar expectations about the technology being used to achieve the output. Where disagreements occur about the level of complexity of the work activity or behavioral input, there must be a way to resolve disagreements on the basis of a common frame of reference. There must be no doubt that all those making decisions about work activity, worker behavior, work objectives, and work standards and instructions are talking about the same thing.

In spite of all the effort made by those most concerned with the problem of communicating about work, little progress has been made toward control of the language. Formulating reliable and valid task statements and using them with relative ease in a practical way have remained an elusive pursuit. One reason for this has been the notion that, because tasks are definable as units, they really exist in the world of work activity as discrete phenomena, like rocks or birds, and their attributes can be readily observed and classified. This, of course, is not the way it is. We define tasks and ascribe attributes to them for the purpose of coping with problems. The task statements reflecting our observations are creations of our way of perceiving. If the instrument for articulating our perception is the imperfect tool of everyday language, it is no wonder that formulating reliable and valid task statements has been so difficult.

The technique for writing task statements according to FJA methodology described in Fine and Wiley (1971), and taught in the [Upjohn] Institute's multimedia training course in task analysis (Fine & Bernotavicz, 1973), results in reliable task statements. Persons trained in this method attain high degrees of agreement concerning the meaning of the statements and the inferences that can be made about the worker, the work organization, and the work. Evidently task statements also approximate reality because it is possible to organize them into effective job assignments and career ladders from the standpoints of productivity and worker growth. The organization of task statements into assignments and the decisions made on the basis of such assignments have resulted in predictable outputs. This is the ultimate payoff. This is validity.

Why Undertake Task Analysis?

Organizations are undertaking task analysis for many reasons, including wage and salary programs, development of career ladders, job restructuring for productivity and/or enrichment, improvement of safety, HR utilization studies, and development of affirmative action programs. No matter what the specific objective, the analysis inevitably deals with the organization's mission (production or service) Goals and its maintenance (facility and worker) Goals. Every task has to be responsive to the question, "Why?" *Why* is it being done, and *why* were the standards prescribed? In other words, what is the task contributing to the organization's objectives and ultimately its purpose?

This is a very sensitive and challenging question. It is especially sensitive for the individuals concerned. Workers are likely to consider FJA interviews quite presumptuous unless the organization makes known its commitment to the job analysis and its willingness to take a searching look at itself at the same time that it asks workers to look searchingly at their activities. Only through the cooperative effort of the workers and the organization in this undertaking can clearcut Objectives, which provide the major measurable performance criteria, be established.

The process of determining Objectives helps the organization to clarify its Purpose and Goals and to establish the interconnectedness of all three. In the language of the systems approach, used in conjunction with FJA, Purpose, Goals, and Objectives are intimately related and represent a phasing of activities from ends to means over time.

The phase most removed in time, the Purpose, is the most general statement of an organization's long-run aspiration—its ends. The emphasis of Purpose is on needs and values being served. The intermediate phases of an organization's activity are represented by its Goals. Goals attempt to operationalize the organization's ends by emphasizing the ways and means inherent in the state of the arts to be used in achieving its ends, usually within 1 to 5 years. Objectives are the result of confronting Goals with the reality of the immediate available resources and existing constraints. Objectives emphasize specific means, such as money, human resources, number to be produced or served, and market area. The end results of tasks must contribute to these Objectives because such a contribution provides the basis for objective evaluation of the results of task performance. The end results of tasks are also important for feedback to the worker because they indicate whether or not a good job is being done.

Task analysis is usually undertaken with the maintenance Goals concerned with selection, training, assignment, and promotion of workers. Maintenance Goals rarely receive the same respect and commitment as the more purpose-related mission Goals, and tend to be tolerated rather than embraced. Thus, it is especially necessary to clarify and emphasize the contribution of the task analysis endeavor to the organization's mission Goals and to obtain top-level commitment to its specific Objectives. Without top-level commitment, the time, money, and human resources necessary to achieve Objectives may not be available, and the endeavor is in a vulnerable position, in terms of the respect and cooperation accorded it as well as the resources allotted to it.

How To Produce Effective Task Statements

Following the organization's delineation of its Purpose, Goals, and Objectives, analysts trained in FJA techniques proceed to gather information about the activities of the organization and formulate them into task statements. In this process, they use the FJA scales and task analysis forms.

Although the FJA scales and method go a long way toward controlling an analyst's unique perceptions, personal viewpoint naturally influences observations, analysis, and formulation of task statements. It is therefore important to clarify as many of the analyst's perceptions as possible, identify and correct gaps in task information, and provide feedback to the analyst about how well the technique is being used.

Skill in the technique is not achieved without considerable practice in editing task statements. It is naturally quite difficult to edit one's own work. It is much easier and more of a learning experience to edit other people's work. That is the reason for this manual. It assumes that persons have already had the training, have already been productive, and are now readying their work for final use. In a sense, then, one finally learns to write task statements by editing them.

The Editing Group

The Upjohn Institute's experience suggests that the most effective way of testing whether or not task statements communicate is for a group of analysts to compare their understandings of the tasks and to reach an agreement on their meaning. The broader the range of experience represented by the editing group, the more likely the task statements are to be complete, accurate, and clearly stated, and the less likely the information in them is to be dismissed as merely a matter of opinion. Group editing can increase the objectivity of task analysis and, therefore, the reliability of task statements. Because the tasks are to be used in operations, wherever possible selected program people, clerical workers, supervisors, and managers should be trained in FJA and included in the group. This is particularly appropriate if a separate unit of analysts prepares the tasks from material provided by workers and supervisors at the operating level. Editing provides an opportunity for a group of analysts to bring the operations people back into the process and to obtain the feedback needed from them to check the reliability and validity of the task statements.

The optimal size for a group of editors from the standpoint of productivity, organizational flexibility, and input is three to five persons. Two persons may not agree on anything, or they may agree on everything. More than five persons creates a situation of diminishing returns because too many points of view tend to block progress. A group of five is good because it provides for the inevitable absences of members. When one or two cannot meet with the group, a sufficient number remain to go forward with the work.

The Editing Process

We refer to the process of reaching consensus in the group as *task editing*. Unlike literary editing, which has aesthetic objectives, task editing has operational and strategic objectives. The questions addressed are: Do the task statements work? Do they communicate? Does everyone concerned agree that they approximate reality?

The goal of the editing process is to produce an inventory of effective task statements for use in the organization's activities. The achievement of this goal divides itself into two phases: (a) preediting by individuals to prepare the "rough tasks" for group editing and (b) group editing to achieve consensus.

Preediting. The objective of preediting is basically to introduce editors to the work aids and guidelines that are used in the editing process so that the editors may cull the task statements for unusable material, for repeated gross errors on the part of task writers, and for the good material that checks out well against the criteria.

The word aids include task analysis blanks (see Fig. D.2), model sentence worksheets for task statements (Fig. D.3), and an editing form (Fig. D.4) to minimize the need for constant rewriting because of the same critical components. The questions discussed in the last section are called the Checklist for Task Analysis. They serve as the basic criteria for individual review as well as for group editing, On a form containing the nine questions, analysts check each question against the information in each task statement to make sure that all parts are consistent and that the performance of the task contributes to the desired result—the achievement of an Objective.

It is desirable that the preediting by individuals be started in a group situation so that questions and problems about the work aids and guidelines can be resolved on a more or less common basis. This also has the advantage of initiating group feeling and group process. However, after one or two such sessions, it may be preferable for individuals to work alone and then come together at an appointed time for group editing.

Group Editing. As soon as the tasks have been preedited, the group can begin its work of achieving consensus. In its meetings the group should go over each rough task, using the same work aids and guidelines that were used individually. During group discussions details that did not occur to anyone when a task was preedited come up, and the group may need more detailed guidance than is provided by the Checklist for Task Analysis. The examples and expanded guidelines in the last section provide the group with a starting point from which to work in resolving differences, identifying confusion, and keeping the tasks technically reliable.

To achieve consensus, the members of the group also draw on their experience in different organizational operations. This expertise enables them to add, subtract, or modify the information so that the task statements describe the way work is actually done in the organization. In some

Things	Data	People	Things	Data	People	Worker Instruc-tion	Reason	Math	Lang	
W.F. - LEVEL			W.F. - ORIENTATION				G.E.D.			TASK NO.

GOAL:	OBJECTIVE:

TASK:

PERFORMANCE STANDARDS	TRAINING CONTENT

FIG. D.2. Task analysis blank.

Analyst _____

Who?	Performs what action?	To whom or what?	Upon what instructions? (Source? How Specific?	Using what tools, equipment, work aids?	To produce/achieve what? (expected output)
Subject	Action verbs	Object of verb	Phrase	Phrase	In order to...
the worker					

Task statement:

FIG. D.3.   Model sentence worksheet for task statement.

Task No.	Result only	Worker action only	Verb unclear	Result unclear	Tool, equipment, work aids unclear	Instructions (source, nature) unclear	Other comments

FIG. D.4.   Editing form.

cases, the group may be sharply divided about the way a particular task is performed. This can be resolved by writing task statements that reflect the differing opinions. The group editing process is completed when the group agrees that the task statements communicate and are reliable.

Feedback

After the editing group has achieved consensus on tasks, the tasks need to be validated. Workers should be able to identify the tasks with which they are concerned and should be able to relate to the approaches proposed by the editing group for evaluating performance and the Functional and Specific Training Content. Long-term employees familiar with many of the organization's interrelated operations, SOPs, manuals, guidelines, and the legal or regulatory environment of the organization's operations should also be consulted. Finally, feedback should be obtained from those persons, such as personnel and training staff, who will use the task data.

When feedback starts to come in, the editing group may need to reedit the tasks to ensure that their technical reliability (i.e., the controls represented by the ratings) has not been compromised by changes in task data that were made to enhance validity. The chief problem is likely to be relating to preferred ways of stating a task—a "yes, but" reaction on the part of the worker. In general, if such restating does not change the ratings—in effect, does not change the task—then the altered wording should be used.

At this second stage of the group editing, the group should check itself carefully against the dangers of boredom resulting from the nit-picking aspects of the editing process. It is helpful at this stage for each editor to assume the roles of supervisor, recruiter, and trainer and check out how the task communicates and functions in operation.

Maintaining a Task Bank

A task bank—a collection of tasks produced as described—is a relatively permanent personnel tool. While assignments and job classification change, these changes are fundamentally changes in the task mix or the frequency with which tasks are performed.[3] Most of the changes in a task bank are

---

[3]A good example is the task mix of a typist. In making copies the typist occasionally inserts carbon paper between the sheets, but more frequently he or she inserts sheets with carbons attached or uses a copying machine. Similarly, he or she may erase errors with a rubber eraser, but more likely he or she covers up errors with corrective fluid or tape.

likely to be additions of new tasks or deletions of old tasks. However, changes can occur in existing tasks because of changes made in Performance Standards to meet revised Objectives. This may require some change in Specific Training Content. An example could be a change in the number of units to be produced in a specified unit of time. These changes need to be tracked and incorporated into the inventory of tasks along with additions of new tasks. How can this be done without making it an onerous paperwork job?

The fundamental answer is that it should be done in the normal course of essential operations. For example, when a supervisor calls for a new employee to fill a vacancy, the tasks constituting the old job should be briefly reviewed and a determination made whether there are any new tasks, changes in old tasks, and/or changes in frequency of specified tasks. Similarly, at the time of annual performance review, each worker should have the opportunity to review his or her individual task mix to determine the changes that have occurred. These changes and others developing from other personnel operations should be forwarded to some agency that records them in the task bank. The logical agency for this purpose is the editing team. The editing team can meet periodically or according to need, revise the changes, submit them to the editing process, and issue them to all users.

Conclusion

It was stated in the beginning that FJA is a part of an ongoing systems process. Task editing is a part of FJA. Although the original task inventory may remain useful for the life of the organization, its content will have to be altered constantly—added to, deleted from, and reorganized to meet the needs of changing organizational structure, Goals, and Objectives.

Any organization undertaking FJA task writing should be absolutely certain that it wants to commit the necessary resources in terms of time, money, people, and facilities to the development and maintenance of the tasks before the project is begun. Otherwise, when the tasks have been written, the inventory will become, like so many organizational guidelines, manuals, and other good ideas, another thing that no one uses. It is poor economics to commit the resources required to enter the FJA process without the intention of carrying it through.

As the process gets built into the organization, many members of the organization begin to understand how the process works and how it affects the operations of the organization. Workers begin to understand their effect on the work and the work organization and how they can grow and develop within the structure, both in terms of where they want to go and where the organization wants them to go.

HOW TO TEST RELIABILITY AND VALIDITY
OF TASK STATEMENTS

In an attempt to provide a practical how-to manual, the material that follows is organized around nine questions. These questions, which editors should ask about each task, are each explained through brief narrative and examples. The nine questions are summarized here for quick reference.

1. Does the end Result of the task make a contribution to the output of which it is a part?
2. Does the language describing the Worker Action phrase of the task statement support the Worker Function levels?
3. Are the Worker Action phrase and the Result phrase of the task statement in reasonable relation to one another?
4. Is the Result identified in the task a verifiable Result?
5. Can performance standards, either numerical or descriptive for the action and result, be inferred and specified?
6. Are the inferred Performance Standards reasonable and useful to a supervisor and to a worker?
7. Does the Training Content reflect the knowledges and abilities required to perform the task?
8. Is there more than a one-level spread among Data, WI, and Reasoning Scale ratings?
9. Do the verbs used in the Worker Action phrase of the task statement adequately express the context of the task?

Question 1. Does the End Result of the Task Make a Contribution to the Output of Which It Is a Part?

Can an independent reader see the task result as a contribution to the output of which it is part?

The relationship of a task to an objective is evident in the definition of a task:

> A task is an action or action sequence, grouped through time, designed to contribute a specified end result to the accomplishment of an objective, and for which functional levels and orientation can be reliably assigned. The task action, or action sequence, may be primarily *physical,* such as operating an electric typewriter; or primarily *mental,* such as analyzing data; and/or primarily *interpersonal,* such as consulting with another person. (Fine & Wiley, 1971, p. 9)

A task is not "make-work" or "busy-work," but is an activity designed to contribute to an output. This is confirmed when the worker action provides clear-cut criteria for the achievement of the task Result. These criteria are implied or explicit performance standards.

Question 2: Does the Language Describing the Worker Action Phase of the Task Statement Support the Worker Function Levels?

Are the ratings of Worker Function levels by two independent raters in substantial agreement?

If not,

A. *Reexamine:* Are the Action verbs explicit and concrete, or do they describe work to be done on the level of objectives, but not specific actions of a worker?

B. *Rewrite task:* Add or subtract material until independent readers get the same picture of what the worker is expected to do.

C. *Remember,* however: That the original intent of the task should not be sacrificed in the consensus process. The edited task must be clear to the original writer, to resource people, to other editors, and to you.

Examples: Guides/escorts clients from reception/intake area of the agency to a specific office in agency on request of supervisor, in order to enable client to reach a particular office.

Rater "A"

Worker Function and Orientation						WI	GED		
Things	%	Data	%	People	%		Reasoning	Math	Language
1A	10	2	65	1B	25	1	1	1	1

Rater "B"

Worker Function and Orientation						WI	GED		
Things	%	Data	%	People	%		Reasoning	Math	Language
1A	5	2	50	2	45	1	1	1	1

Independent raters "A" and "B" disagreed on the level of the People function involved in guiding and escorting clients. As written, the task does not involve more than physically leading the client to an office. However, Rater B thought that the worker would be talking with the client, putting him/her at ease. Rater A conceded this possibility, but felt it had not been made explicit enough to justify Level 2.

Question 3: Are the Worker Action Phrase and the Result Phrase in the Task Statement in Reasonable Relation to One Another?

Is the Worker Action described likely to produce the stated Result?

Example: Sets up projector, lectern, blackboard, and other equipment, adjusts lighting and ventilation, in order that community meeting to interpret agency policy and procedures on income maintenance can be carried out.

Setting up the equipment in a meeting room does not result in a meeting's being held. A more reasonable Result would be, *"to prepare equipment and room conditions for community meeting."* Setting up the needed equipment and readying the room can produce the Result of preparing the room for the meeting.

Question 4: Is the Result Identified in the Task a Verifiable Result?

Does the worker know what he or she is expected to produce? Does the supervisor know what he or she should evaluate?

Examples: (a) *in order to make record of scheduled appointments,* (b) *to prepare equipment and room conditions for community meeting,* or (c) *to prepare letter for signature.*

All of the above Results or outputs are relatively concrete and tangible. In each case, the expected output is clear, both to the supervisor and to the worker. Data and Things oriented tasks tend to produce tangible Results.

The Result phrases in People oriented tasks, however, tend to be less tangible, and less easily observed. For example, (d) *to persuade families to apply for a foster child* or (e) *to inform client of agency's policies and procedures.*

When the Result phrase does not describe a tangible, easily observed output (as in the previous example), the Results have to be inferred from the more generalized output represented by the objective and included in a Performance Standard:

A Performance Standard derived from an objective that clarifies (d) might be: *X% of families contacted submit applications for foster child.* A standard of this nature usually is interpreted in relation to an estimated result on the basis of some previous related experience or test. It is necessary to remember that the Standard indicated probably depends on the inputs of a number of tasks, and not just the one indicated.

A Performance Standard derived from an objective that clarifies (e) might be: *less than X # of complaints from clients that they did not understand how to obtain services, due to incomplete or inaccurate explanation of policies and procedures by worker.*

Question 5: Can Performance Standards, Either Numerical or Descriptive for the Action and Result, Be Inferred and Specified?

EXAMPLE: Drives own/agency car, on request of supervisor, in order to transport clients to agency, neighborhood center, doctor's office, etc.

Independent raters assigned the following percentages to this task:

	Rater A	
Things	*Data*	*People*
W.F. - ORIENTATION		
50%	10%	40%

	Rater B	
Things	*Data*	*People*
W.F. - ORIENTATION		
55%	40%	5%

Both raters' emphasis on Things (driving to transport to a specific place) is obviously correct, but without further detail, both can justify their secondary emphasis on Data or People by making appropriate inferences. Such inferences should be made explicit.

Rater A: The rater emphasizing Data may have inferred knowledge of traffic patterns, routings, signs, regulations, forms to be filled out, and so on. However, in order for other editors/readers to agree with this rating, the inferences must be made explicit:

Drives own/agency car, on request of supervisor, selecting routes on basis of knowledge of city and schedule, in order to transport client to agency, neighborhood center, doctor's office, etc.

Rater B: The rater emphasizing People may have inferred interaction between client and driver. Such inference should be made explicit, in order for other editors/readers to agree with the rating:

Drives own/agency car, upon request of supervisor, greeting/talking with clients, in order to transport clients to agency, neighborhood center, doctor's office, etc.

A third possibility could involve a higher Things rating, and equally low People/Data ratings. This possibility would exclude either of the previous inferences and emphasize the fact that the driver followed predetermined routes.

EXAMPLE: Evaluates accepted applications, considers nature of case, current workload, and competence of staff, in order to decide on assignment of new cases for foster home study.

Independent raters assigned the following percentages to this task:

Rater A		
Things	*Data*	*People*
W.F. - ORIENTATION		
5%	40%	55%

Rater B		
Things	*Data*	*People*
W.F. - ORIENTATION		
5%	90%	5%

There is no direct involvement with People in this task as written. *"Evaluating accepted applications"* is primarily a Data-oriented task, as it has been analyzed by Rater B. Rater A may have inferred that the worker was also verbally assigning cases to staff members. However, this is not stated in the task as it was written. A task statement that would include this inference, and would reflect Rater A's orientation assignments, is:

Verbally assigns tasks/gives directions to the staff members, explaining and answering questions about prescribed and discretionary elements of procedures and performance requirements, based on prior assessment of operation flow, workload, and worker's capabilities, in order to ensure that the worker understands his/her duties and responsibilities.

Question 6: Are the Inferred Performance Standards Reasonable and Useful to a Supervisor and to a Worker?

Do they tell a supervisor what to look for and how to assess performance? Do they tell a worker the quality and quantity of work expected, and how to judge when/whether that quality and quantity has been reached?

A. Have performance standards been generated to evaluate both the worker action (behavior) and the result (output)?

EXAMPLE: Asks client questions/listens to/transcribes/writes answers to specified items on application form, in order to complete application form for client.

Performance Standards		What is being evaluated?
Descriptive	*Numerical*	
Form is accurate, complete, and legible.	All (100%) of specified items are filled out on form.	Result: completed form. A portion of Worker Action: transcribes/writes.
Asks questions clearly.	Less than X% of clients complain of lack of clarity in questioning. . .	One phase of Worker Action: asks questions.
Manner is pleasant and courteous.	. . . or of worker's manner.	Worker's behavior/Action toward the client. Process of Actions: asks . . . /listens. . . that Result in: completed form.

B. Performance standards should be consistent with orientation percentage/result.

Data emphasis yields Data Standards.
People emphasis yields People Standards.
Things emphasis yields Things Standards.

EXAMPLE: Visually inspects applicants' files, noting missing information, and indicates omissions on form letter, in order to complete form letter to applicant requesting the missing information by return mail.

Things	*Data*	*People*
W.F. - ORIENTATION		
15%	80%	5%

Performance Standards

Descriptive	Numerical
Checks files carefully and thoroughly. Missing information is recorded accurately and completely on form letter. Files are inspected and omissions noted with reasonable speed.	No more than X# of applicants complain about being requested to send in data previously submitted. No more than X# of complaints of incomplete information in files due to omissions from form letters.

These Standards reflect the orientation of the task toward Data, with a minimal mention of Things (handling of files, paper, etc.). There are no People Standards, as there is no significant interpersonal interaction involved in this task. The 5% assigned reflects the FJA rule never to assign 0% on the assumption that, although not apparent, some relation to People may exist.

C. Performance standards must be feasible.

Be prepared for the fact that Numerical Standards usually require that an organization develop mechanisms and controls for generating and monitoring them. The statement of these Standards may point to ways in which the organization must be innovative and they may also highlight its dependence on the *discretion* of workers, and the limitations of what it can expect from supervisory control.

EXAMPLE: Visually inspects applicant's files, noting missing information, and indicates omissions on form letter, in order to complete form letter to applicant requesting the missing information by return mail.

Performance Standards

Descriptive	Numerical
Manner is pleasant and courteous	No more than X# of complaints from clients about worker's manner.

Is there a process/ procedure for complaints?

Are the clients aware of it?

How reliable is the data?

    Do you hear good as well as bad?

    Can you tell if the client is unhappy with the *system* or with the *worker?*

Note on performance standards:

Because the Worker Action is a *verb*, it tends to be described by an *adverb:*

Asks questions *clearly.*
verb   adverb

Because the Output/Result is a *noun*, it tends to be described by an *adjective:*

Plan is *thorough.*
noun   adjective

Question 7: Does the Training Content Reflect the Knowledges and Abilities Required to Perform the Task?

Does the Functional Training Content reflect (a) the required *knowledges* of processes and (b) the required *abilities* to function/perform actions or behaviors? Does Specific Training Content reflect (a) the required *knowledges* of the plant or organization (procedures, and how they determine the application of Functional abilities) and (b) the required *abilities* to perform under local conditions and specifications (according to knowledge of specific organization or plant)?

Example: Calculates/performs statistical analysis on population movements within state's correctional facilities, using a desk calculator, in order to compute data to be used in report requested by the Bureau Director.

Worker Function and Orientation						*WI*	*GED*		
Things	*%*	*Data*	*%*	*People*	*%*		*Reasoning*	*Math*	*Language*
1C	35	4	60	1A	5	3	3	3	3

Training Content

Functional	*Specific*
How to operate a calculator.	*How to operate X type of calculator.*
How to perform basic statistical analysis (formulae for computing measures of central tendency, deviations, correlations, etc.	*Knowledge of general limitations of particular data: how collected, what type of sample, etc.*
	Knowledge of agency format for presenting statistical data.

Question 8: Is There More Than a One-Level Spread Among Data, WI, and Reasoning Scale Ratings?

If so, can you defend the difference?

Each of these Scales looks at *cognitive functioning* from a somewhat different point of view. There is not an equivalence among levels in these three Scales, but they do closely parallel each other. If there is more than a one-level spread, the difference must be justifiable with evidence available in one or another of the columns.

> *EXAMPLE: Guides parents in selection of resources to help their exceptional child, exploring with them the needs and behavior of the child and their preferences, and advising them regarding the use of available evaluation, training, treatment, and placement resources, in order to help parents to decide on and utilize treatment/placement resources.*

One analyst rated this task:

Worker Function and Orientation						WI	GED		
Things	%	Data	%	People	%		Reasoning	Math	Language
1A	5	4	40	4A	55	6	5	3	5

There is more than a one-level spread between the Data Level 4 and the WI Level 6. Is this difference justifiable, using the information in the task statement? The spread in the ratings for Data, WI, and Reasoning (4, 6, 5, respectively) should raise the question of whether one or another of the ratings is too high or too low. The task of guiding parents in the selection of resources for their exceptional child involves more than *"examining, evaluating data with reference to criteria, standards, and requirements of a particular discipline"* (Data Scale, Level 4, Analyzing).

In order to guide the parents as indicated, it is necessary that the worker *"modify, alter, and/or adapt existing designs, procedures, or methods to meet unique specifications, unusual conditions, or specific standards of effectiveness within the overall framework of operating theories, principles."* We can alter the Analyzing rating to Data Level 5, Innovating, making it more consistent with the other ratings and the task statement.

Worker Function and Orientation						WI	GED		
Things	%	Data	%	People	%		Reasoning	Math	Language
1A	5	5A	40	4A	55	5	5	3	5

On the other hand, if Innovating is not necessary, and the task involves no more than Analyzing, then it has been written in a way that exaggerates the performance expectations with regard to discretion (level of instructions) and the Level 6 rating should be reconsidered and possibly lowered to Level 5.

Question 9: Do the Verbs Used in the Worker Action Phrase of the Task Statement Adequately Express the Context of the Task?

In the process of clarifying and making the action verbs explicit, the context of the task may be lost or at least obscured. This is particularly true if the task is completed over an extended period of time and the action is complex.

A task written and analyzed according to the principles and techniques of FJA provides a structured description of what a worker does and what gets done. However, it is only a description and not reality itself. A worker doing the same task may say, "It's not quite what I do" without being able to pin down the problem.

This communication problem can be resolved to some degree by using a combination of broad process verbs that establish the context for the task and verbal phrases that describe the continuity of the worker's action in that process. Together they tend to connote the dynamics as well as the structure of the action.

> EXAMPLE: *Advises/counsels mother on emotional and legal consequences of decision to place her child in adoptive home, listening to mother, asking questions, and reflecting her feelings and suggesting ways of coping with problems, guilt, and anxieties arising from separation, in order to help mother adjust to permanent separation from child.*

Advises/counsels are process verbs. They express the context of a sequence of actions. However, they are unclear when used alone. The process is clarified by *listening, asking, reflecting,* and *suggesting.* Here the actions are suggested by verbal phrases emphasizing continuity and interaction rather than arbitrary linkage; at the same time the process is clarified.

This task could also have been written as follows:

> *Advises/counsels mother on emotional and legal consequences of decision to place her child in adoptive home, listens to mother, asks questions, and reflects her feelings; and suggests ways of coping with problems, guilt, and anxieties arising from separation, in order to help mother adjust to permanent separation from child.*

In this example it is easier to identify and break down the action verbs. However, in reading the task, some of the sense of process and dynamics may be lost—and the nature of the task may be less clear.

Addendum

In reviewing the material submitted by participants in the Reliability-Validity Study for inclusion here, considerable variation was found in the ratings for the task dealing with "translation," which follows:

> Translate from one language to another questions on the application form and client's request for assistance, in order to enable the client to complete the form.

Independent raters assigned the following levels:

Rater A

Worker Function and Orientation						WI	GED		
Things	%	Data	%	People	%		Reasoning	Math	Language
1	5	4	70	2	35	3/4	3	1	4

Rater B

Worker Function and Orientation						WI	GED		
Things	%	Data	%	People	%		Reasoning	Math	Language
1A	5	3B	30	2	65	3	4	1	4

Rater C

Worker Function and Orientation						WI	GED		
Things	%	Data	%	People	%		Reasoning	Math	Language
1A	5	4	40	2	55	4	4	1	4

Rater D

Worker Function and Orientation						WI	GED		
Things	%	Data	%	People	%		Reasoning	Math	Language
1A	5	2	65	2	30	3	3	1	3

Rater E

Worker Function and Orientation						WI	GED		
Things	%	Data	%	People	%		Reasoning	Math	Language
1A	10	1	30	2	60	2	3	1	3

Rater F

Worker Function and Orientation						WI	GED		
Things	%	Data	%	People	%		Reasoning	Math	Language
1A	5	5B	25	2	70	3	3	1	4

This type of task is often misunderstood in terms of its functional level, because language is typically taken for granted. It should be noted that we are not referring here to the casual, imprecise, word-for-word, potluck translations experienced by tourists or by resorting to a friend or acquaintance with, "You know a little Spanish; please tell me what this client is saying." Obviously, in these situations the translator is not responsible for the accuracy of the translation made.

Although the worker in this task is converting the material from the words (symbols) used by speakers of one language into the words (symbols) used by speakers of another, the basic task—that is, the one for which primary performance standards are applied—is not the translation itself, but the exchange of information that the translation enables the worker and the client to achieve. Thus, the translation is viewed as a catalyst (tool) to get the essential job done.

The task was edited as follows:

Talks about/discusses (in X language) items on English language application form with client (speaker of X language), answering client's questions and explaining meaning and purpose of items on form, elicits answers to items, and records answers in English on form, using own speaking, reading, and writing knowledge of English and X language, in order to complete form for client.

Worker Function and Orientation						WI	GED		
Things	%	Data	%	People	%		Reasoning	Math	Language
1A	5	4	45	2	50	3	3	1	4

Rather than attempt to cover the degree of skill that the worker must have to complete the task as part of the Scale ratings, it should be dealt with in Performance Standards, in which the editor can describe such things as degree of fluency, or correctness of pronunciation and clarity of speech.

Investigation indicates that it is practically impossible for a translator to function at any Data level lower than Analyzing. The translator has to decide whether to make a word-for-word translation, or to translate idiomatically. In word-for-word translation, a large part of the meaning of the original statement may be lost, because words have not only dictionary meanings (denotative meanings), which are standard for all users of the language, but also connotative meanings, or the emotional weight of the words governed by each user's experience.

This involves the worker with a wide range of variables, and a great deal of data. He or she must comply with the rules of structure, syntax, and semantics of both languages. He or she must also understand the content of the statement in the original language, and its equivalent in the second language, in order to give a full translation. Thus, the translator must Analyze.

In *Analyzing,* he/she must:

Examine and evaluate data for
  language equivalents and
  statement content.
Consider with reference to criteria, requirements, and standards
  the content of the statement in the original language,
  the use for which translation is intended,
  the desires of the originator of the statement, and
  the structures, syntax, and semantics of both languages.
Consider interaction effects and alternatives
  to determine which of several possible renderings of the original
  statement into the second language is preferable.

In certain situations, the translator may have to *Innovate.* For instance, in translating a piece of literature he or she may:

Modify, alter, or adapt existing language without departing too far from standard criteria of structure, syntax, or semantics of the two languages and without eliminating the original meaning of the language rendition in order to
  achieve the denotative meaning of the original statement and
  include the connotative meaning of such things as rhyme, rhythm, and meter.

Because the translator must interpret, evaluate, and make choices among alternatives, his or her own style, or personal method of using both languages makes itself felt. This makes it necessary that the rating on the Language Scale (GED) be no lower than Level 4, the first level at which the user's style comes into play. The language level will range through Levels 4, 5, and 6, depending on the content and technicality (relative abstruseness) of the message, as delineated by the scale examples.

This point applies only to truly bilingual tasks, and not to those in which the worker, although bilingual, is using only one language, both in receipt and transmission of signals. The English ability of the worker has nothing to do with his functioning in a situation demanding only Spanish, and vice versa.

Although Analyzing appears to be the minimum Data function when truly bilingual translation tasks are involved, the functional relation to people can range from Exchanging Information (which occurs even in Taking Instructions and Serving situations) through Consulting, and, possibly, Negotiating, where inclusion of a slang term or a term from another language other than the primary language of the discussion or contract is at issue.

Additional Note

Although bilingualism is not involved, to some degree the functional job analyst must function in a similar manner in translating the everyday, casual language of job description (often involving the metaphoric use of verbs, nouns, adjectives, and adverbs) to the precise, taxonomic meanings of FJA. The functional job analyst must continually probe to establish the true involvement of the worker in the task so that a reliable communication can be achieved—one replicable on the basis of scales.

Glossary

These are only brief definitions of terms explained through examples here. In order to understand them within the conceptual framework of FJA, please refer to the first six chapters in this book.

Functional Job Analysis (FJA): A conceptual system for defining dimensions of worker activity and a method of measuring levels of worker activity that provides a set of scales for establishing levels of tasks.

Task: An action or action sequence, grouped through time, designed to contribute a specified end result to the accomplishment of an objective, and for which functional levels and orientation can be reliably assigned.

Worker Function Scales: Three hierarchies of worker functions that define the simplest to the most complex worker behaviors in relation to TDP.

Orientation: A measure that indicates the relative involvement of the worker with TDP in the performance of a given task.

Scale of WI: A scale for measuring the proportions of prescription and discretion in the performance of a given task.

Scales of GED: Three scales—Reasoning, Math, and Language—for determining the basic educational skill requirements necessary to perform a job at specified TDP levels.

Performance Standards: The criteria against which the results of a worker's tasks are assessed. There are two types: descriptive and numerical.

Training Content: The skills and knowledges required to perform a given task. There are two types: functional and specific.

References

Airline chief learned to lead by example. (1995, June 25). *Milwaukee Journal/Sentinel*, p. 15D.

Balaban, S., Keita, C., Lunger, D., Lutz, T.. & Wachiralapphaithoon, M. (n.d.). *Starbucks Coffee Company*. Report for Reginald Bruce, Management 600, filed on the Internet [Online]. Available at: http://www.cbpa.louisville. edu/bruce/cases/starbucks/starbucks.htm

Briscoe, D. R. (1995). *International human resource management*. Englewood Cliffs, NJ: Prentice-Hall.

By way of Canarsie, one large cup of business strategy: Coffee talk with Howard Schultz. (1994, December 14). *The New York Times*, Living Section, p. C1.

Cardy, R. L., & Dobbins, G. H. (1996). Human resource management in a total quality organizational environment: Shifting from a traditional to a TQHRM approach. *Journal of Quality Management, 1*, 5–20.

Choi, T. Y., Rungtusanatham, M. & Kim, J-S. (1997). Continuous improvement on the shop floor: lessons from small to midsize firms. *Business Horizons, 40*(6), 45–50.

Churchman, C. W. (1968). *The systems approach*. New York: Belacorte Press.

Committee for Economic Development, Research and Policy Committee. (1985). *Investing in our children: Business and the public schools (A statement by the Research and Policy Committee of the Committee for Economic Development)*. New York: Committee for Economic Development.

Cronshaw, S. F. (1991). *Industrial psychology in Canada*. Waterloo, ON: North Waterloo Academic Press.

Csikszentmihalyi, M. (1975). *Beyond boredom and anxiety: The experience of play in work and games*. San Francisco: Jossey-Bass.

Csikszentmihalyi, M. (1997). *Finding flow: The psychology of engagement with everyday life*. New York: Basic Books.

Deming, W. E. (1986). *Out of the crisis*. Cambridge, MA: MIT Press.

Dictionary of occupational titles. (1990). (2nd ed.). U.S. Department of Labor.

Equal Employment Opportunity Commission. (1978). Uniform guidelines on employee selection procedures. *Federal Register, 43*, 38290–38315.

Erikson, E. H. (1980). *Identity and the life cycle*. New York: Norton.

Fields, D. (1998). At Harley, workers are boss: Plant's innovations give builders stake, role in management. *The Detroit News*. Issue PSA-2116, Business Section.

Fine, S. A., & Bernotavicz, F. D. (1973). *Task analysis: How to use the national task bank*. Kalamazoo, MI: W.E. Upjohn Institute for Employment Research.

Fine, S. A., & Getkate, M. (1995). *Benchmark tasks for job analysis: A guide to functional job analysis (FJA) scales*. Mahwah, NJ: Lawrence Erlbaum Associates.

Fine, S. A., Holt, A. M., Hutchinson, M. F., & Wiley, W. W. (1974). *Functional job analysis: How to standardize task statements.* Kalamazoo, MI: W. E. Upjohn Institute for Employment Research.

Fine, S. A., & Wiley, W. W. (1971). *An introduction to functional job analysis: A scaling of selected tasks from the social welfare field.* Kalamazoo, MI: W.E. Upjohn Institute for Employment Research.

Fleishman, E. A., & Quaintance, M. K. (1984). *Taxonomies of human performance: The description of human tasks.* New York: Academic Press.

Fleishman, E. A., & Reilly, M. E. (1992). *Handbook of human abilities: Definitions, measurements, and job task requirements.* Palo Alto, CA: Consulting Psychologists Press.

Glastris, P. (1994, August 15). The thin white line. *U.S. News & World Report,* 53–54.

Goldratt, E. M., & Cox, J. (1984). *The goal: A process of ongoing improvement (Rev. Ed.).* Croton-on-Hudson, NY: North River Press.

Hammer, M., & Champy, J. (1993). *Reengineering the corporation: A manifesto for business revolution.* New York: HarperBusiness.

Heckscher, C. C. (1995). *White collar blues: Management loyalties in an age of corporate restructuring.* New York: Basic Books.

Hofstede, G. (1984). *Culture's consequences: International differences in work-related values.* Beverly Hills, CA: Sage.

Huffcutt, A. I., & Arthur, W., Jr. (1994). Hunter and Hunter (1984) revisited: Interview validity for entry-level jobs. *Journal of Applied Psychology, 79,* 184–190.

Imai, M. (1997). *Gemba kaizen: A commonsense, low-cost approach to management.* New York: McGraw-Hill.

Jacoby, J., & Terborg, J. R. (1995). *Managerial Philosophies Scale (MPS).* The Woodlands, TX: Teleometrics International.

Jacques, E. (1956). *Measurement of responsibility.* Falls Church, VA: Cason Hall.

Janz, T., Hellervik, L., & Gilmore, D. C. (1986). *Behavior description interviewing: New, accurate, cost effective.* Boston: Allyn & Bacon.

Kamarck, E., Goddard, T., & Riback, C. (1988). Has the White House delivered on promises to reinvent government? *Insight on the News, 14*(22), 24–27.

Latham, G. P., Saari, L. M., Pursell, E. D., & Campion, M. A. (1980). The situational interview. *Journal of Applied Psychology, 69,* 422–427.

Lawler, E. E., III (1990). *Strategic pay: Aligning organizational strategies and pay systems.* San Francisco: Jossey-Bass.

Lawler, E. E., III (1986). *High-involvement management.* San Francisco: Jossey-Bass.

Levering, R. (1988). *A great place to work.* New York: Random House.

Locke, E. A., & Latham, G. P. (1990). *A theory of goal setting & task performance.* Englewood Cliffs, NJ: Prentice-Hall.

MacLachlan, R. (1995). The pioneers who put people first. *People Management, 1*(16), 20–23.

Marchione, M. (1998, July 8). Restaurant works to employ the mentally ill. *Milwaukee Journal/Sentinel,* p. 11.

Mayer, R. C., Davis, J. H., & Schoorman, F. D. (1995). An integrative model of organizational trust. *Academy of Management Review, 20,* 709–734.

McGregor, D. (1960). *The human side of enterprise.* New York: McGraw-Hill.

Melohn, T. (1994). *The new partnership: Profit by bringing out the best in your people, customers, and yourself.* New York: Wiley.

Miller, K. I., & Monge, P. R. (1986). Participation, satisfaction, and productivity: A meta-analytic review. *Academy of Management Journal, 29,* 727–753.

Morfopoulos, R., & Roth, W. (1996). Job analysis and the Americans with Disabilities Act. *Business Horizons, 39*(6), 68–72.

Morin, W. J. (1990). *Trust me.* New York: Harcourt, Brace & Co.

Mowday, R. T., Porter, L. W., & Steers, R. M. (1982). *Employee- organization linkages: The psychology of commitment, absenteeism, and turnover.* New York: Academic Press.

Myers, D., & Fine, S. A. (1985). Development of a methodology to obtain and assess applicant experiences for employment. *Public Personnel Management, 14*(1), 51–64.

Nolan, R. L., & Croson, D. C. (1995). *Creative destruction: A six-stage process for transforming the organization.* Boston: Harvard Business School Press.

O'Herron, P., & Simonsen, P. (1995). Career development gets a change at Sears Credit. *Personnel Journal, 74*(5), 103–106.

Olson, H. C., Fine, S. A., Myers, D. C., & Jennings, M. (1981). The use of functional job analysis in establishing performance performance standards for heavy equipment operators. *Personnel Psychology, 34,* 351–364.

Partlow, C. G. (1996). Human-resources practices of TQM hotels. *Cornell Hotel & Restaurant Administration Quarterly, 37*(5), 67–77.

Patten, T. H. (1981). *Organizational development through teambuilding.* New York: Wiley.

Petersen, D. E., & Hillkirk, J. (1991). *A better idea: Redefining the way Americans work.* Boston: Houghton Mifflin.

Polanyi, M. (1983). *The tacit dimension.* Gloucester, MA: Peter Smith.

Polanyi, M., & Prosch, H. (1975). *Meaning.* Chicago: The University of Chicago Press.

Porter, L. W., Lawler, E. E., & Hackman, J. R. (1975). *Behavior in organizations.* New York: McGraw-Hill.

Pritchett, P. (1994). *The employee handbook of new work habits for a radically changing world: 13 ground rules for job success in the information age.* Dallas, TX: Pritchett & Associates, Inc.

Quinones, M. A., Ford, J. K., & Teachout, M. S. (1995). The relationship between work experience and job performance: A conceptual and meta-analytic review. *Personnel Psychology, 48,* 887–910.

Renfrew, C. (1997). *Critical incident reporting in an anaesthetic department* [Online]. Available at: http://reddwarf.qub.ac.uk/lists/hci-discussion-list/0028.html

Rush, H. M. F. (1971). *Job design for motivation: Experiments in job enlargement and job enrichment* (Report 515). New York: The Conference Board.

Shapiro, E. R., & Carr, A. W. (1991). *Lost in familiar places: Creating new connections between individual and society.* New Haven, CT: Yale University Press.

Sharma-Jensen, G. (1997, October 29). Prizing employees. *Milwaukee Journal Sentinel,* Business Section, p. 1.

Spreitzer, G. M. (1996). Social structural characteristics of psychological empowerment. *Academy of Management Journal, 39,* 483–504.

Stamatis, D. H. (1996). *Total quality service: Principles, practices, and implementation.* Delray Beach, FL: St. Lucie Press.

Stewart, T. (1996). Taking on the last bureaucracy. *Fortune, 133*(1), 105–108..

Stanley, G. (1995, June 26). Airline chief learned to lead by example. *Milwaukee Journal/Sentinel.*

Stokes, G. S., Mumford, M. D., & Owens, W. A. (1994). *Biodata handbook: Theory, research, and use of biographical information in selection and performance prediction.* Palo Alto, CA: Consulting Psychologists Press.

Taylor, F. W. (1911). *The principles of scientific management.* New York: W. W. Norton.

University of Texas at Austin, The Equal Employment Opportunity Office. (1997). *Major laws prohibiting employment discrimination* [Online]. Available at: http://www.utexas.edu/admin/ohr/eeo/the_law.html

Villanova, P., Bernardin, H. J., Johnson, D. L., & Dahmus, S. A. (1994). The validity of a measure of job compatibility in the prediction of job performance and turnover of motion picture theater personnel. *Personnel Psychology, 47,* 73–90.

Walker, C. R., & Guest, R. H. (1952). *The man on the assembly line.* Cambridge, MA: Harvard University Press.

Walster, E., Walster, G. W., & Berscheid, E. (1978). *Equity: Theory and research.* Boston: Allyn & Bacon.

Weiner, N., & Gunderson, M. (1990). *Pay equity: Issues, options and experiences.* Toronto: Butterworths.

Wernimont, P. F., & Campbell, J. P. (1968). Signs, samples, and criteria. *Journal of Applied Psychology, 52,* 372–376.

Wiesner, W. H., & Cronshaw, S. F. (1988). A meta-analytic investigation of the impact of interview format and degree of structure on the validity of the employment interview. *Journal of Occupational Psychology, 61,* 275–290.

Zuckerman, L. (1998, June 9). Vote of no confidence in Northwest Strike. *The New York Times,* National Report.

Author Index

A

Arthur, W., Jr., 129, 300

B

Balaban, S., 29, 143, 299
Bernardin, H. J., 122, 126, 301
Bernotavicz, F. D., 275, 299
Berscheid, E., 190, 302
Briscoe, D. R., 116, 299

C

Campbell, J. P., 120, 302
Campion, M. A., 132, 300
Cardy, R. L., 95, 96, 97, 299
Carr, A. W., 61, 62, 63, 71, 74, 81, 210, 301
Champy, J., 28, 103, 211, 300
Choi, T. Y., 213, 299
Churchman, C. W., 18, 299
Cox, J., 28, 300
Cronshaw, S. F., 129, 236, 299, 302
Croson, D. C., 64, 301
Csikszentmihalyi, M., 140, 141, 149, 158, 159, 168, 209, 299

D

Dahmus, S. A., 122, 126, 301
Davis, J. H., 56, 300
Deming, W. E., 156, 299

D

Dobbins, G. H., 95, 96, 97, 299

E

Erikson, E. H., 180, 299

F

Fields, D., 207, 299
Fine, S. A., 94, 111, 125, 235, 255, 270, 273, 275, 283, 299, 300, 301
Fleishman, E. A., 43, 300
Ford, J. K., 122, 301

G

Getkate, M., 94, 235, 255, 270, 299
Gilmore, D. C., 131, 300
Glastris, P., 121, 300
Goddard, T., 58, 300
Goldratt, E. M., 28, 300
Guest, R. H., 215, 301
Gunderson, M., 237, 302

H

Hackman, J. R., 59, 301
Hammer, M., 28, 103, 211, 300
Heckscher, C. C., 65, 300
Hellervik, L., 131, 300
Hillkirk, J., 60, 301
Hofstede, G., 211, 300

303

Holt, A. M., 270, 299
Huffcult, A. I., 129, 300
Hutchinson, M. F., 270, 299

I

Imai, M., 210, 212, 300

J

Jacoby, J., 257, 300
Jacques, E., 53, 300
Janz, T., 131, 300
Jennings, M., 125, 301
Johnson, D. L., 122, 126, 301

K

Kamarck, E., 58, 300
Keita, C., 29, 143, 299
Kim, J-S., 213, 299

L

Latham, G. P., 132, 140, 157, 300
Lawler, E. E., 59, 190, 192, 216, 300, 301
Levering, R., 103, 300
Locke, E. A., 140, 157, 300
Lunger, D., 29, 143, 299
Lutz, T., 29, 143, 299

M

MacLachlan, R., 104, 300
Marchione, M., 227, 300
Mayer, R. C., 56, 300
McGregor, D., 58, 59, 300
Melohn, T., 115, 119,130, 300
Miller, K. I., 60, 300
Monge, P. R., 60, 300
Morfopoulos, R., 105, 300
Morin, W. J., 56, 57, 60, 66, 300
Mowday, R. T., 117, 301
Mumford, M. D., 111, 122, 301
Myers, D. 111, 125, 301

N

Nolan, R. L., 64, 301

O

O'Herron, P., 178, 301
Olson, H. C., 125, 301
Owens, W. A., 111, 122, 301

P

Partlow, C. G., 92, 156, 301

Patten, T. H., 25, 42, 43, 61, 301
Petersen, D. E., 60, 301
Polanyi, M., 35, 301
Porter, L. W., 59, 117, 301
Pritchett, P., 219, 301
Pursell, E. D., 132, 300

Q

Quaintance, M. K., 43, 300
Quinones, M. A., 122, 301

R

Reilly, M. E., 43, 300
Renfrew, C., 173, 301
Riback, C., 58, 300
Roth, W., 105, 300
Rungtusanatham, M. 213, 299
Rush, H. M. F., 57, 301

S

Saari, L. M., 132, 300
Schoorman, F. D., 56, 300
Shapiro, E. R., 61, 62, 63, 71, 74, 81, 210, 301
Simonsen, P., 178, 301
Spreitzer, G. M., 66, 301
Stamatis, D. H., 92, 95, 301
Steers, R. M., 117, 301
Stewart, T., 1, 301
Stokes, G. S., 111, 122, 301

T

Taylor, F. W., 208, 301
Teachout, M. S., 122, 301
Terborg, J. R., 257, 300

V

Villanova, P., 122, 126, 301

W

Wachiralapphaithoon, M., 29, 143, 299
Walker, C. R., 215, 301
Walster, E., 190, 302
Walster, G. W., 190, 302
Weiner, N., 237, 302
Wernimont, P. F., 120, 302
Wiesner, W. H., 129, 302
Wiley, W. W., 270, 273, 275, 283, 299, 300

Z

Zuckerman, L., 165, 302

Subject Index

A

Ability, 37
Americans with Disabilities Act, 221, 231

C

Career development, 177, 179–180
  career counseling, 178
    influences of FJA, 180
  professional counselor, 186

D

Dictionary of Occupational Titles, 46, 49, 215

E

Employer accommodation, 108, 119, 218

F

FJ Analysts, 255
  selecting, 255–257
  training, 258–269
FJA employment interview, 129–130
  assessing skills, 130–133
    adaptive, 130
    functional, 133
  behavior description questions, 131–132
  closing interview, 136
  hiring applicant, 136

  hypothetical scenario questions, 132
  training interviewers, 136
  instructional interviews, 128–129
FJA focus groups, 71, 77–80, 86
  environment, 81
  KSA, 76
  momentum, 80
  outputs, 74–75
  performance standards, 82
  presentation, 73
  setting, 72
  task generation, 77–80
FJA and law, 220
  affirmative action, 225–230
  antidiscrimination legislation, 222
  disabilities legislation, 231–236
  Title VII compliance, 224
FJA Scales, 240–250
FJA Task Bank Editing Manual, 270–297
Flow, 140, 149, 158, 209

G

Goal-setting, 25, 140

H

HRM, 1–4, 99–100

I

Introducing FJA, 84
  editing task banks, 87

management, 85
reinventing work, 88

J

Job design, 207–208
    synergy, 208
    worker and manager, 208–210
Job evaluation, 195–205

K

Knowledge, 36

L

Language development, 252–254
Language of worker behavior, 46
    TDP vocabulary, 46–47

M

Mathematical development, 251

O

Outputs, 74

P

Pay, 190
    pay equity, 236–238
    ways of paying workers, 191
Performance appraisal, 156
    evaluator training, 171
    FJA themes, 165–169
    FJA suggested procedures, 169
    interview, 173–176
    job analysis, 169
    ratings, 170, 196
    records, 172
    requirements, 157–158
    use of task bank in, 159–163
Performance standards, 150, 163
    descriptive, 151–152, 164–165
    numerical, 164–165
    quantifiable, 151–152
Pre-employment questionnaire, 109–113

Q

Quality, 90
    continuous improvement, 211
    how FJA helps, 91
    managers' role, 94–97

standardization, 93–94

R

Reasoning development, 250
Recruitment, 101
    functional level of work, 104
    growth opportunities, 107
    recruitment, traditional, 109
    vision and mission, 103
    working conditions, 105

S

Shared interpretation of experience, 63, 210
Skill, 37, 40
    adaptive, 39, 80–81, 148, 162
    functional, 39, 146, 152, 162, 195
    evaluation in pay, 192–195
    specific content, 39, 148, 153, 162

T

Tasks, 49–52
    generating tasks, 77–80
    structure, 75
    system module, 49
TDP concept, 181, 198
    job preferences, 182
    personal growth, 183
    RIASEC, 183
    worker function chart, 38
Testing applicants, 115
    degree of selectivity, 116
    measurement issues, 126
    performance testing, 123–126
    psychological testing, 120
    screening process, 115
Theory X–Y, 58–60, 97
Training, 139
    building relationships, 140
    experience, 149–150
    needs analysis, 146–147
    orientation, 142
    skills, 152–154
Trust, 56
    assumptions, 57
    building, 62
    community of purpose, 66
    nondependent, 67
    obstacles, 61

V

Validation, 126
    content, 126

construct-oriented, 127
criterion-related, 126
Validity, 126
face, 127

W

Work, 45 *see also* Work doing system; Work
  organization
  content, 35, 119, 167, 216
  context, 35, 119, 167, 216
Work doing system, 13, 55 *see also* Work;
  Work organization; Worker
  advantages, 14, 17–18
  characteristics, 14–17
  components, 19–23
  example, 13
  limitations, 18–19
Work organization, 24 *see also* Work; Work
  doing system; Worker
  constraints, 15, 24

feedback, 16, 27, 158, 166
goals, 25–26
  maintenance, 26
  mission, 26
  objectives, 25
  policies, 29
  principles, 28
  problems, 31
  procedures, 30
  purpose, 25
  resources, 15, 24
Worker, 34 *see also* Work; Work doing system; Work organization
  functions, 38, 48
  growth, 34, 107
  holistic viewpoint, 34–35, 199–203
  job design, 42–44
  needs, 108–109
  tacit knowledge, 35
  whole person concept, 34, 119, 166, 179,
    215
Worker instructions, 52–54